Modern British Drama

compiled by

Charles A. Carpenter
State University of New York at Binghamton

AHM Publishing Corporation
Arlington Heights, Illinois 60004

ISBN: 0-88295-559-4, paper
ISBN: 0-88295-568-3, cloth

Library of Congress Card Number: 76-4654

PRINTED IN THE UNITED STATES OF AMERICA
729

Contents

       Under each dramatist, editions and nondramatic writings of significance are listed first, then bibliographic and reference material (if any), then scholarly, critical, and expository works.

CONTENTS

Preface

THE FOLLOWING BIBLIOGRAPHY is intended for graduate and advanced undergraduate students in courses with a major focus on modern English and Irish drama. Designed as a convenient guide to scholarship and criticism in the field, the listing is deliberately selective. However, every effort has been made to provide ample coverage of significant topics and dramatists, from the well-made play to post-absurdism and from T. W. Robertson to Edward Bond, David Storey, and Peter Shaffer. The bibliography is updated, in effect, by the compiler's annual checklists of modern drama studies in the journal *Modern Drama* (see item 7).

In order to keep this bibliography to a practical size, certain types of references have been omitted: bibliographies of bibliography, unpublished dissertations, all but the most noteworthy reviews of performances, short notes and explications (unless they contain important material), and the great majority of foreign-language studies. The emphasis has been placed on literary rather than theatrical aspects of the field. In general, the compiler has tried to steer a middle course between the comprehensive bibliographies of a limited subject (those of E. H. Mikhail, for example) and the highly selective lists included in such scholarly textbooks as the Block-Shedd *Masters of Modern Drama*. This bibliography should materially assist the student of modern British drama to survey and study a topic independently in preparation for class reports or examinations, and to lay the groundwork for writing extended research papers.

Attention is called to certain features intended to enhance the utility of this volume:

(1) All items are numbered consecutively throughout the book. Thus each title can be readily identified by its number, both in cross references and in the index.

(2) Wide margins on each page provide space for listing the call numbers of frequently used references.

(3) Extra space at the bottom of each page can be used for additional references and pertinent notes.

(4) More space is provided for personal annotations and com-

ments on the blank pages, headed "Notes," following the index.

(5) Works of special importance are designated by an asterisk (*), and those available in paperback editions in the United States or Great Britain are followed by a dagger (†).

Following is a list of symbols for journals frequently cited. These have been taken, with a few exceptions, from the Table of Symbols at the beginning of recent MLA bibliographies. Several other abbreviations have been used to save space. Besides the obvious (such as ed., repr., lit., bibl., mag., univ. and the like), these include:

NY (New York), *Bos* (Boston), *Lon* (London), *Dub* (Dublin), *Bul* (Bulletin), *Eng* (English), *J* (Journal), *Pr* (Press), *Q* (Quarterly), *Rev* (Review), *St* (Studies), *UP* (University Press).

Abbreviations

ArQ	Arizona Quarterly
BB	Bulletin of Bibliography
BNYPL	Bulletin of the New York Public Library
CathW	Catholic World
CE	College English
CentR	Centennial Review
CL	Comparative Literature
CLA J	C.L.A. Journal
CLQ	Colby Library Quarterly
CoD	Comparative Drama
Con L	Contemporary Literature
Cos	Costerus
CritQ	Critical Quarterly
DM	Dublin Magazine
DR	Dalhousie Review
DrS	Drama Survey
E&S	Essays and Studies
EIC	Essays in Criticism
Eire	Éire/Ireland
ELH	ELH: A Journal of English Literary History
ELT	English Literature in Transition (1880–1920)
ETJ	Educational Theatre Journal
FortR	Fortnightly Review
FR	French Review
HudR	Hudson Review
ITA	International Theatre Annual
IUR	Irish University Review
JEGP	Journal of English and Germanic Philology
JIL	Journal of Irish Literature
JJQ	James Joyce Quarterly
JML	Journal of Modern Literature
KanQ	Kansas Quarterly
KR	Kenyon Review
LonM	London Magazine
MD	Modern Drama
MFS	Modern Fiction Studies
MLQ	Modern Language Quarterly
MR	Massachusetts Review
NS	Die Neueren Sprachen
NTM	New Theatre Magazine
PLL	Papers on Language and Literature
PMLA	PMLA: Publications of the Modern Language Association
PoL	Poet Lore
PQ	Philological Quarterly

ABBREVIATIONS

QJS	Quarterly Journal of Speech
QQ	Queen's Quarterly
Ren	Renascence
SAQ	South Atlantic Quarterly
SFQ	Southern Folklore Quarterly
ShR	Shaw Review
SoR	Southern Review
SOR	Sean O'Casey Review
SR	Sewanee Review
Stu	Studies (Dublin)
Sym	Symposium
TA	Theatre Annual
TAM	Theatre Arts Monthly
TC	Twentieth Century
TCL	Twentieth Century Literature
TDR	Tulane Drama Review
ThQ	Theatre Quarterly
TrR	Transatlantic Review
TSLL	Texas Studies in Literature and Language
UKCR	University of Kansas City Review
UTQ	University of Toronto Quarterly
VQR	Virginia Quarterly Review
WSCL	Wisconsin Studies in Contemporary Literature
YeS	Yeats Studies
YFS	Yale French Studies
YR	Yale Review
ZAA	Zeitschrift für Anglistik und Amerikanistik

NOTE: *The publisher and compiler invite suggestions for additions to future editions of the bibliography.*

Bibliographies

1 *Abstracts of English Studies,* 1957–. (Summarizes a wide range of periodical articles and some monographs in series.)

2 ADELMAN, Irving, and Rita DWORKIN. *Modern Drama: A Checklist of Critical Literature on 20th Century Plays.* Metuchen, NJ: Scarecrow, 1967. (Largely but not entirely superseded by **5**.)

3 "Annual Review Number, [1970–]." *JML,* 1971–. (Book reviews, lists of articles and theses, etc.; limited to English-language material.)

4 BAKER, Blanch M. *Theatre and Allied Arts: A Guide to Books Dealing with the History, Criticism, and Technic of the Drama and Theatre and Related Arts and Crafts.* NY: Blom, 1967 [c. 1952]. (Selective, annotated older list.)

5 BREED, Paul F., and Florence M. SNIDERMAN. *Dramatic Criticism Index: A Bibliography of Commentaries on Playwrights from Ibsen to the Avant-Garde.* Detroit: Gale, 1972.*

6 BRITISH DRAMA LEAGUE. *The Player's Library: The Catalogue of the Library of the British Drama League.* NY: Theatre Arts Books, 1950. (Supplements.)

7 CARPENTER, Charles A. "Modern Drama Studies: An Annual Bibliography [for 1972–]." *MD,* 17– (1974–). (Comprehensive multilingual list.)*

8 COLEMAN, Arthur, and Gary R. TYLER. *Drama Criticism. Volume 1: A Checklist of Interpretation Since 1940 of English and American Plays.* Denver: Swallow, 1966. (Largely but not entirely superseded by **5**.)

9 *Cumulated Dramatic Index, 1909–1949. A Cumulation of the F. W. Faxon Company's Dramatic Index.* Bos: Hall, 1965. 2 vols. (Useful for tracing reviews, illustrations, and ephemera.)

10 DUBOIS, William R. *English and American Stage Productions: An Annotated Checklist of Prompt Books, 1800–1900, from the Nisbet-Snyder Drama Collection, Northern Illinois Univ. Libraries.* Bos: Hall, 1973.

11 EAGER, Alan R. *A Guide to Irish Bibliographical Material, Being a Bibliography of Irish Bibliographies and Some Sources of Information.* Lon: Lib. Assn., 1964. (Lists almost 4000 works.)

12 ENGLISH ASSN., LONDON. *The Year's Work in English Studies, 1919/20–.* (Essay-reviews of books and articles.)

12A FINNERAN, Richard J., ed. *Anglo-Irish Literature: A Review of Research.* NY: Modern Language Assn., 1976. (Includes bibliographical essays on modern drama, Shaw, Yeats, Synge, and O'Casey.)

13 FRENCH, Frances-Jane. *The Abbey Theatre Series of Plays: A Bibliography.* Dub: Dolmen, 1969.

14 HAYES, Richard J., ed. *Sources for the History of Irish Civilization: Articles in Irish Periodicals.* Bos: Hall, 1970. 9 vols.

15 INTERNATIONAL ASSN. FOR THE STUDY OF ANGLO-IRISH LITERATURE. "Bibliography Bulletin." *IUR,* 2– (1972–).

16 LEVITT, Paul M. "The Well-Made Problem Play: A Selective Bibliography." *ELT,* 11 (1968), 190–94.

17 LITTO, Fredric M. *American Dissertations on the Drama and Theatre: A Bibliography.* Kent, OH: Kent State UP, 1969.

BIBLIOGRAPHIES

18 LOEWENBERG, Alfred. *The Theatre of the British Isles, Excluding London: A Bibliography*. Lon: Society for Theatrical Research, 1950.

19 McNAMEE, Lawrence F. *Dissertations in English and American Literature: Theses Accepted by American, British, and German Universities 1865–1964*. NY: Bowker, 1968. (Also supplements for 1964–68 and 1969–73.)

20 MIKHAIL, Edward H. *A Bibliography of Modern Irish Drama, 1899–1970*. Seattle: Univ. of Washington Pr., 1972. (Treats general and special topics other than authors.)

21 MIKHAIL, Edward H. *British Drama, 1900–1950: A Bibliographical Guide to Information Sources*. Detroit: Gale, 1977.*

22 MIKHAIL, Edward H. *Contemporary British Drama, 1950–1976: An Annotated Bibliography*. Totowa, NJ: Rowman & Littlefield, 1977.*

23 MIKHAIL, Edward H. *Dissertations on Anglo-Irish Drama: A Bibliography of Studies, 1870–1970*. Totowa, FJ: Rowman & Littlefield, 1973.

24 MODERN HUMANITIES RESEARCH ASSN. *Annual Bibliography of English Language and Literature [for 1920–]*. (The most comprehensive source for material through 1956, and still more complete on British topics than the MLA lists.)*

25 MODERN LANGUAGE ASSN. "MLA International Bibliography of Books and Articles on the Modern Languages and Literatures." *PMLA*, 1957–1969 (May, then June issues annually). (Pre-1957 issues list only the work of American scholars, and are thus negligible.)*

26 MODERN LANGUAGE ASSN. *MLA International Bibliography [for 1969–]*. Vol. 1: General, English, American, etc. NY: MLA, 1970–. (Successor to above item.)*

27 NEW YORK PUBLIC LIBRARY. *Catalog of the Theatre and Drama Collections*. Bos: Hall, 1967. 21 vols.

28 NICOLL, Allardyce. "Hand-List of Plays, 1850–1900." *A History of English Drama*, **192**, 229–850.

29 NICOLL, Allardyce. "Hand-List of Plays, 1900–1930." *English Drama, 1900–1930*, **226**, 451–1053.

30 POWNALL, David E. *Articles on Twentieth Century Literature: An Annotated Bibliography, 1955–1970*. Millwood, NY: Kraus-Thomson, 1973–. 7 vols. (Cumulated from the journal *TCL*, with many additions. Updated continuously in *TCL*.)*

31 *Revue d'Histoire du Théâtre*, 1948–. (The entire fourth issue annually is a bibl. of wide scope.)

32 SCHOOLCRAFT, Ralph N., ed. *Performing Arts Books in Print: An Annotated Bibliography*. NY: Drama Book Specialists, 1973. (New ed. of *Theatre Books in Print*. Updated by the periodical *Annotated Bibliography of New Publications in the Performing Arts*..)

33 SHEDD, Robert G., et al. "Modern Drama: A Selective Bibliography of Works Published in English in [1959–1967]." *MD*, 3–11 (1960–68).

34 STOLL, Karl-Heinz. *The New British Drama: A Bibliography, with Particular Reference to Arden, Bond, Osborne, Pinter, Wesker*. Bern: Lang, 1975. (Perfunctory checklist.)

35 STRATMAN, Carl J. *Britain's Theatrical Periodicals, 1720–1967: A Bibliography*. NY: New York Public Lib., 1972.

36 *Theatre/Drama & Speech Index*, 1974–. Crete, NB: Theatre/Drama & Speech Information Service, 1974–. (Triannual index to 60 journals from 15 countries; only three issues by late 1977.)

2

37 WATSON, George, general ed. *The New Cambridge Bibliography of English Literature.* Vol. 3: 1800–1900; Vol. 4: 1900–1950. Lon: Cambridge UP, 1969, 1972.*

38 WELLS, Stanley, ed. *English Drama (Excluding Shakespeare): Select Bibliographical Guides.* Lon: Oxford UP, 1975, 213–98. (Sections on recent periods of English and Irish drama.)

39 WILSON, Sheila. *The Theatre of the 'Fifties.* Lon: Lib. Assn., 1963. (Classified list of limited scope.)

Modern Drama

40 ARCHER, William. *Play-Making: A Manual of Craftsmanship.* 4th ed. Lon: Chapman & Hall, 1930. (Standard older book on the well-made play, first publ. 1912.)

41 BALMFORTH, Ramsden. *The Problem Play and Its Influence on Modern Thought and Life.* Lon: Allen & Unwin, 1928.

42 BENTLEY, Eric. *The Playwright as Thinker: A Study of Drama in Modern Times.* Amended ed. Cleve.: Meridian, 1955. (Seminal study first publ. 1946.)* †

43 BERMEL, Albert. *Contradictory Characters: An Interpretation of the Modern Theatre.* NY: Dutton, 1973.†

44 BROCKETT, Oscar G., and Robert R. FINDLAY. *Century of Innovation: A History of European and American Theatre and Drama Since 1870.* Englewood Cliffs, NJ: Prentice-Hall, 1973.

45 BRUSTEIN, Robert. *The Theatre of Revolt: An Approach to the Modern Drama.* Bos: Little, Brown, 1964.†

46 CHIARI, Joseph. *Landmarks of Contemporary Drama.* Lon: Jenkins, 1965. (Post–World War II drama.)

47 COHN, Ruby. *Currents in Contemporary Drama.* Bloomington: Indiana UP, 1969. (Post–World War II drama.)†

48 COHN, Ruby. *Modern Shakespeare Offshoots.* Princeton, NJ: Princeton UP, 1976.

49 DAVISON, Peter H. "Contemporary Drama and Popular Dramatic Forms." In *Aspects of Drama and the Theatre* [essays by several authors]. Sydney: Sydney UP, 1965, 143–97.

50 DRIVER, Tom F. *Romantic Quest and Modern Query: A History of the Modern Theatre.* NY: Delacorte, 1970. (Goethe to Brecht and Genet.)†

51 EASTMAN, Fred. *Christ in the Drama: A Study of the Influence of Christ on the Drama of England and America.* NY: Macmillan, 1947.

52 ELSOM, John. *Erotic Theatre.* NY: Taplinger, 1974.

53 ESSLIN, Martin. "From the Avant-garde of the Fifties . . . to the Avant-garde of the Seventies." *Eng Q,* 5 (Spring–Summer 1972), 7–16.

54 ESSLIN, Martin. *The Theatre of the Absurd.* 3rd ed. Lon: Methuen, 1974. (Classic first publ. 1962. See also his later essay, "The Theatre of the Absurd Reconsidered," *Brief Chronicles,* **102,** 219–27.)*†

55 FREEDLEY, George, and John A. REEVES. *A History of the Theatre.* 3rd ed. NY: Crown, 1968.

56 GASCOIGNE, Bamber. *Twentieth-Century Drama*. Lon: Hutchinson, 1963. (Since Pirandello.)†

57 GASKELL, Ronald. *Drama and Reality: The European Theatre Since Ibsen*. Lon: Routledge, 1972.†

58 GASSNER, John. *Directions in Modern Theatre and Drama*. NY: Holt, 1965. (Expanded ed. of *Form and Idea in Modern Theatre*.)

59 GASSNER, John. *Masters of the Drama*. 3rd ed. NY: Dover, 1954.

60 KILLINGER, John. *World in Collapse: The Vision of Absurd Drama*. NY: Dell, 1971.†

61 KRUTCH, Joseph W. *"Modernism" in Modern Drama: A Definition and an Estimate*. Ithaca, NY: Cornell UP, 1953.†

62 LAMM, Martin. *Modern Drama*, tr. Karin Elliott. Oxford: Blackwell, 1952.

63 LEWIS, Allan. *The Contemporary Theatre: The Significant Playwrights of Our Time*. Rev. ed. NY: Crown, 1971.

64 MARRIOTT, James W. *Modern Drama*. Lon: Nelson, 1934.

65 OLIVER, William I. "Between Absurdity and the Playwright." In 93, 3–19.

66 PARKER, R. B. "The Theory and Theatre of the Absurd." *QQ*, 73 (1966), 421–41.

67 PEACOCK, Ronald. *The Poet in the Theatre*, Enl. ed. NY: Hill & Wang, 1960.†

68 SPANOS, William V. "Modern Drama and the Aristotelian Tradition: The Formal Imperatives of Absurd Time." *ConL*, 12 (1971), 345–72. (Theoretical approach to absurd drama.)

69 STANTON, Stephen S. "Introduction: The Well-Made Play and the Modern Theatre." In *Camille and Other Plays*, ed. S.S. Stanton. NY: Hill & Wang, 1957, vii–xxxix.†

70 STYAN, J. L. *The Dark Comedy: The Development of Modern Comic Tragedy*. 2nd ed. Cambridge, Eng.: Univ. Pr., 1968.†

71 STYAN, J. L. *The Elements of Drama*. Cambridge, Eng.: Univ. Pr., 1960.†

72 WILLIAMS, Raymond. *Drama from Ibsen to Brecht*. NY: Oxford UP, 1969. (New version of *Drama from Ibsen to Eliot*. Stresses English drama.)*†

73 WILLIAMS, Raymond. *Modern Tragedy*. Stanford, CA: Stanford UP, 1966.†

Reference Works

74 CHICOREL, Marietta, and Richard SAMUELSON, eds. *Chicorel Theater Index to Plays in Anthologies, Periodicals, Discs, and Tapes*. NY: Chicorel Lib., 1970–71. 2 vols. (Also *Chicorel Theater Index to Plays in Anthologies and Collections, 1970–1976*. 1976.)

75 *Crowell's Handbook of Contemporary Drama: A Critical Handbook of Plays and Playwriting Since the Second World War*. NY: Crowell, 1971. (A collaborative work. Michael Anderson's essays on English topics are valuable.)*

76 *Drama: The Quarterly Theatre Review*, 1919–. (British Drama League journal that systematically reviews performances in Great Britain.)

77 HARTNOLL, Phyllis. *Oxford Companion to the Theatre*. 3rd ed. Lon: Oxford UP, 1967.

78 HOLDEN, David F. *An Analytical Index to Modern Drama, Volumes 1–13*.

Toronto: Hakkert, 1973. (Detailed name and subject index to the most important journal in the field.)

79 *McGraw-Hill Encyclopedia of World Drama.* NY: McGraw-Hill, 1972. 4 vols.

80 MATLAW, Myron. *Modern World Drama: An Encyclopedia.* NY: Dutton, 1972.*

81 OTTEMILLER, John H., John M. and Billie M. CONNOR. *Ottemiller's Index to Plays in Collections: An Author and Title Index to Plays Appearing in Collections Published Between 1900 and Mid-1970.* 5th ed. Metuchen, NJ: Scarecrow, 1971.*

82 SHARP, Harold S., and Marjorie Z. SHARP. *Index to Characters in the Performing Arts. Part I: Non-musical Plays; An Alphabetical Listing of 30,000 Characters.* NY: Scarecrow, 1966. 2 vols.

83 *Stagecast: Irish Stage and Screen Directory.* Dub: Stagecast Publications, 1962–. (Annual.)

84 TEMPLE, Ruth Z., and Martin TUCKER. *Twentieth Century British Literature: A Reference Guide and Bibliography.* NY: Ungar, 1968.

85 *Theatre 71–: Plays, Players, Playwrights, Theatres, Opera, Ballet,* ed. Sheridan Morley. Lon: Hutchinson, 1971–. (Annual.)

86 *Theatre World Annual (London): A Pictorial Review of West End Productions with a Record of Plays and Players,* Nos. 1–16. Lon: Rockliff [and others], 1950–65.

87 *Theatrefacts: International Theatre Reference,* 1974–. (Offshoot of the journal *Theatre Quarterly.*)

88 VINSON, James, ed. *Contemporary Dramatists.* 2nd ed. Lon: St. James, 1977. (Biobibliographical dictionary of English language playwrights.)

89 *Who's Who in the Theatre: A Biographical Record of the Contemporary Stage.* 15th ed. Lon: Pitman, 1972. (Early editions are valuable for data no longer current.)

Collections of Essays, Reviews, and Interviews

90 ARMSTRONG, William A., ed. *Experimental Drama.* Lon: Bell, 1963.*

91 BENTLEY, Eric. *In Search of Theater.* NY: Knopf, 1953.†

92 BENTLEY, Eric. *What Is Theatre? Incorporating The Dramatic Event and Other Reviews, 1944–1967.* NY: Atheneum, 1968.†

93 BOGARD, Travis, and William I. OLIVER, eds. *Modern Drama: Essays in Criticism.* NY: Oxford UP, 1965.†

94 BROWN, John Mason. *Dramatis Personae: A Retrospective Show.* NY: Viking, 1963. (Selections, including the complete text of *The Modern Theatre in Revolt.*)†

95 BRUSTEIN, Robert. *Seasons of Discontent: Dramatic Opinions, 1959–1965.* NY: Simon & Schuster, 1965.

96 CLURMAN, Harold. *The Divine Pastime: Theatre Essays.* NY: Macmillan, 1974.

97 CLURMAN, Harold. *Lies Like Truth: Theatre Reviews and Essays.* NY: Grove, 1958.†

98 CLURMAN, Harold. *The Naked Image: Observations on the Modern Theatre.* NY: Macmillan, 1966.

99 COLE, Toby, ed. *Playwrights on Playwriting: The Meaning and Making of Modern Drama from Ibsen to Ionesco.* NY: Hill & Wang, 1961.†

100 *Contemporary Theatre.* Stratford-upon-Avon Studies, 4. Lon: Arnold, 1962.

101 DENNIS, Nigel. *Dramatic Essays.* Lon: Weidenfeld & Nicolson, 1962.

102 ESSLIN, Martin. *Brief Chronicles: Essays on Modern Theatre.* Lon: T. Smith, 1970. (Abr. ed. is entitled *Reflections.*†)

103 FREEDMAN, Morris, ed. *Essays in the Modern Drama.* Bos: Heath, 1964.†

104 GASSNER, John. *Dramatic Soundings: Evaluations and Retractions Culled from 30 Years of Dramatic Criticism.* NY: Crown, 1968.

105 GASSNER, John. *The Theatre in Our Times.* NY: Crown, 1954.†

106 GILMAN, Richard. *Common and Uncommon Masks: Writings on Theatre 1961–1970.* NY: Random, 1971.

107 GOTTFRIED, Martin. *Opening Nights: Theater Criticism of the Sixties.* NY: Putnam's, 1969.

108 HAYMAN, Ronald. *Playback.* NY: Horizon, 1974. ("Essay-interviews" with recent theatrical figures. Larger collection publ. in England as *Playback* and *Playback 2.*)

109 KAUFFMANN, Stanley. *Persons of the Drama: Theater Criticism and Comment.* NY: Harper & Row, 1976.

110 KOTT, Jan. *Theatre Notebook, 1947–1967,* tr. Boleslaw Taborski. Garden City, NY: Doubleday, 1968.

111 LAHR, John. *Astonish Me: Adventures in Contemporary Theater.* NY: Viking, 1973.†

112 LAHR, John. *Up Against the Fourth Wall: Essays on Modern Theater.* NY: Grove, 1970.†

113 McCARTHY. Mary. *Theatre Chronicles 1937–1962.* NY: Noonday, 1963.†

114 McCRINDLE, Joseph F., ed. *Behind the Scenes: Theater and Film Interviews from The Transatlantic Review.* NY: Holt, 1971.†

115 NATHAN, George Jean. *The Magic Mirror: Selected Writings on the Theatre,* ed. Thomas Q. Curtiss. NY: Knopf, 1960.

116 NATHAN, George Jean. *The World of George Jean Nathan,* ed. Charles Angoff. NY: Knopf, 1952.

117 SCOTT, Nathan A., ed. *Man in the Modern Theatre.* Richmond: John Knox Pr., 1965.†

118 SIMON, John. *Acid Test.* NY: Stein & Day, 1963.

119 SIMON, John. *Singularities: Essays on the Theater, 1964–1973.* NY: Random, 1976.

120 TREWIN, John C., ed. *Theatre Programme.* Lon: Muller, 1954. (English theatrical scene from thirties to fifties.)

121 WAGER, Walter, ed. *The Playwrights Speak.* NY: Dell, 1967. (Interviews with intros.)†

122 WIMSATT, W. K., ed. *English Stage Comedy.* English Institute Essays, 1954. NY: Columbia UP, 1955.

123 YOUNG, Stark. *Immortal Shadows: A Book of Dramatic Criticism.* NY: Hill & Wang, 1948. (Selections from his *New Republic* criticisms, 1921–47. See also the later selection, *The Theatre,* 1958.)

Anthologies of Modern British Plays

124 BARNET, Sylvan, Morton BERMAN, and William BURTO, eds. *The Genius of the Irish Theatre*. NY: New Amer. Lib., 1960. (Seven plays, with notes and selected essays.)†

125 *The Best One-Act Plays*. Lon: Harrap, 1931–. (Annual.)

126 BLOCK, Haskell M., and Robert G. SHEDD, eds. *Masters of Modern Drama*. NY: Random, 1962. (Includes nine plays by major British dramatists up to Osborne.)

127 BOOTH, Michael R., ed. *English Plays of the Nineteenth Century. Volume 2: From 1850 to 1900*. Oxford: Clarendon, 1969.

128 CANFIELD, Curtis, ed. *Plays of Changing Ireland*. NY: Macmillan, 1936. (Plays of the early thirties, with valuable background information.)

129 CANFIELD, Curtis, ed. *Plays of the Irish Renaissance, 1880–1930*. NY: Macmillan, 1929.

130 CORRIGAN, Robert W., ed. *The Modern Theatre*. NY: Macmillan, 1964. (Eight plays by British dramatists, with essays by each.)

131 GASSNER, John, and Bernard F. DUKORE, eds. *A Treasury of the Theatre, Volume II: From Henrik Ibsen to Robert Lowell*. 4th ed. NY: Simon & Schuster, 1970. (Ten plays by major British figures from Wilde to Pinter.)

132 HOGAN, Robert, and James KILROY, eds. *Lost Plays of the Irish Renaissance*. Dixon, CA: Proscenium Pr., 1970. (The Press also issues a "Lost Play" series.)

133 HOGAN, Robert, ed. *Seven Irish Plays, 1946–1964*. Minneapolis: Univ. of Minnesota Pr., 1967. (With intro. and notes.)

134 MOSES, Montrose J., ed. *Representative British Dramas, Victorian and Modern*. Rev. ed. Bos: Brown, 1931.

135 NATHAN, George J., ed. *Five Irish Plays*. NY: Modern Lib., 1941.

136 *New English Dramatists*. Harmondsworth: Penguin, 1959–. (Irregular series; about 15 volumes so far.)†

137 POPKIN, Henry, ed. *The New British Drama*. NY: Grove, 1964. (Includes essays by Arden, Wesker, and Pinter.)†

138 ROWELL, George, ed. *Late Victorian Plays, 1890–1914*. 2nd ed. Lon: Oxford UP, 1972.†

139 SALERNO, Henry F. *English Drama in Transition: 1880–1920*. NY: Pegasus, 1968.†

140 TREWIN, John C., ed. *Plays of the Year, 1948–9–*. Lon: Elek, 1949–.

141 WEALES, Gerald, ed. *Edwardian Plays*. NY: Hill & Wang, 1962.†

Modern English Drama

142 BRADBROOK, Muriel C. *English Dramatic Form: A History of Its Development.* Lon: Chatto & Windus, 1965.

143 CHURCHILL, R. C. "The Comedy of Ideas: Cross-Currents in the Fiction and Drama of the Twentieth Century." In *The Modern Age. Pelican Guide to English Literature, Vol. 7,* ed. Boris Ford. Baltimore, MD: Penguin, 1963, 221–30.†

144 CLARK, Barrett H. "The English Drama." *A Study of the Modern Drama.* New ed. NY: Appleton, 1936 [c. 1928], 219–27.

145 COX, C. B., and A. E. DYSON, eds. *The Twentieth Century Mind: History, Ideas, and Literature in Britain.* Lon: Oxford UP, 1972. 3 vols. (Each volume contains an essay on drama.)

146 CUNLIFFE, John W. *Modern English Playwrights: A Short History of the English Drama from 1825.* NY: Harper, 1927. (Reliable early survey up to Coward and O'Casey.)

147 DAICHES, David. "Drama." *The Present Age in British Literature.* Bloomington: Indiana UP, 1958, 148–67.

148 DICKINSON, Thomas H. *The Contemporary Drama of England.* Rev. ed. Bos: Little, Brown, 1931. (Informed, full account first publ. 1917.)

149 DISHER, M. Willson. *Melodrama: Plots That Thrilled.* Lon: Rockliff, 1954. (Survey of British melodrama, 1850–1950.)

150 DOWNER, Alan S. *The British Drama: A Handbook and Brief Chronicle.* NY: Appleton, 1950.

151 EVANS, B. Ifor. *A Short History of English Drama.* 2nd ed. Bos: Houghton, 1965, 144–208.

152 FREEDLEY, George. "England and Ireland." In *A History of Modern Drama,* ed. Barrett H. Clark and George Freedley. NY: Appleton, 1947, 160–232.

153 GASSNER, John. "Bernard Shaw and the British Compromise." *Masters of the Drama,* **59,** 575–628. (Robertson to Rattigan.)

154 GOETSCH, Paul, ed. *English Dramatic Theories: 20th Century.* Tübingen: Niemeyer, 1972. (Anthology.)

155 HOWE, Percival P. *Dramatic Portraits.* Lon: Seck3r, 913. (Pinero to Galsworthy.)

156 HUDSON, Lynton A. *The Twentieth-Century Drama.* Lon: Harrap, 1946. (Survey of English drama.)

157 HUNTER, G. K. "English Drama 1900–1960." In *The Twentieth Century,* ed. Bernard Bergonzi. Lon: Barrie & Jenkins, 1970, 310–35.

158 KENNEDY, Andrew K. *Six Dramatists in Search of a Language: Studies in Dramatic Language.* Cambridge, Eng.: Univ. Pr., 1975. (Shaw, Eliot, Beckett, Pinter, Osborne, and Arden.)*†

159 KNIGHT, G. Wilson. *The Golden Labyrinth: A Study of British Drama.* NY: Norton, 1962.†

160 KRONENBERGER, Louis. *The Thread of Laughter: Chapters on English Stage Comedy from Jonson to Maugham.* NY: Knopf, 1952.†

161 LUMLEY, Frederick. "The State of Drama: Britain." *New Trends in 20th*

Century Drama: A Survey Since Ibsen and Shaw. 4th ed. NY: Oxford UP, 1972, 256–324. (Superficial survey.)

162 MORGAN, Margery M. "Strindberg and the English Theatre." *MD*, 7 (1964), 161–73.

163 NICOLL, Allardyce. *British Drama.* 5th ed. NY: Barnes & Noble, 1963.

164 NICOLL, Allardyce. *English Drama: A Modern Viewpoint.* NY: Barnes & Noble, 1968.

165 OPPEL, Horst, ed. *Das moderne englische Drama: Interpretationen.* 3rd ed. Berlin: Schmidt, 1976. (Long analyses, all in German, of important plays.)

166 PRIOR, Moody E. "The Present Age [in British Drama])." *The Language of Tragedy.* NY: Columbia UP, 1947, 291–379.†

167 REYNOLDS, Ernest. *Modern English Drama: A Survey of the Theatre from 1900.* 2nd ed. Norman: Univ. of Oklahoma Pr., 1951.

168 ROSTON, Murray. "The Modern Era." *Biblical Drama in England from the Middle Ages to the Present Day.* Evanston, IL: Northwestern UP, 1968, 233–321.

169 SAWYER, Newell W. *The Comedy of Manners from Sheridan to Maugham.* Phila.: Univ. of Pennsylvania Pr., 1931. (Extends to 1914 only.)

170 TAYLOR, John R. *The Rise and Fall of the Well-Made Play.* NY: Hill & Wang, 1967. (Focuses on English drama.)*†

171 TETZELI VON ROSADOR, Kurt. *Das englische Geschichtsdrama seit Shaw.* Heidelberg: Winter, 1976.

172 WEALES, Gerald. *Religion in Modern English Drama.* Phila.: Univ. of Pennsylvania Pr., 1961.

173 WEIAND, Hermann J., ed. *Insight IV: Analyses of Modern British and American Drama.* Frankfurt: Hirschgraben, 1975. (Includes analyses—all in English—of plays by 13 British dramatists.)

174 WORTH, Katharine J. *Revolutions in Modern English Drama.* Lon: Bell, 1973.*

To the 1890s

Under "Dramatists," see especially Gilbert, Jones, Pinero, and Robertson.

175 ARCHER, William. *English Dramatists of To-day.* Lon: Low, Marston, 1882.

176 ARCHER, William. *The Old Drama and the New: An Essay in Re-Valuation.* Lon: Heinemann, 1923. (Lectures X–XIV are relevant.)

177 ARCHER, William. *The Theatrical "World"* [of 1893–1897]. Lon: W. Scott, 1894–98. 5 vols. (Largely reviews from *The World.*)

178 BAYLEN, Joseph O. "Edmund Gosse, William Archer, and Ibsen in Late Victorian Britain." *Tennessee St in Lit,* 20 (1975), 124–37.

179 BOOTH, Michael R. *English Melodrama.* Lon: Jenkins, 1965.

180 BORSA, Mario. *The English Stage of To-Day,* tr. Selwyn Brinton. Lon: Bodley Head, 1908. (Intelligent Italian account.)

181 CUNLIFFE, John W. *Modern English Playwrights,* **146.** (Stresses pre-Shavian drama.)

182 ELLEHAUGE, Martin O. M. "The Initial Stages in the Development of the English Problem Play." *Englische Studien,* 66 (1932), 373–401.

183 FILON, Pierre M. A. *The English Stage: Being an Account of the Victorian Stage,* tr. Frederic Whyte; intro. by Henry Arthur Jones. Lon: Milne, 1897.

184 FRANC, Miriam A. *Ibsen in England.* Bos: Four Seas Co., 1919.

185 GRANVILLE-BARKER, Harley. "The Coming of Ibsen." In *The Eighteen-Eighties: Essays by Fellows of the Royal Society of Literature,* ed. Walter de la Mare. Cambridge, Eng.: Univ. Pr., 1930, 159–96.

186 GRANVILLE-BARKER, Harley. "Exit Planché—Enter Gilbert." In *The Eighteen-Sixties. . .,* ed. John Drinkwater. Cambridge, Eng.: Univ. Pr., 1932, 102–48.

187 GRANVILLE-BARKER, Harley. "Tennyson, Swinburne, Meredith—and the Theatre." In *The Eighteen-Seventies. . .,* ed. Harley Granville-Barker. Cambridge, Eng.: Univ. Pr., 1929, 161–91.

188 JONES, Henry Arthur. *The Renascence of the English Drama,* **1167.***

189 KOSOK, Heinz, ed. *Das englische Drama im 18. und 19. Jahrhundert: Interpretationen.* Berlin: Schmidt, 1976.

190 MEISEL, Martin. *Shaw and the Nineteenth-Century Theater.* Princeton, NJ: Princeton UP, 1963. (Chapters on popular genres.)*†

191 MOORE, George. "Our Dramatists and Their Literature." In *Impressions and Opinions,* **1267,** 139–61. (An 1891 essay.)

192 NICOLL, Allardyce. *A History of English Drama, 1660–1900. Volume V: Late Nineteenth Century Drama, 1850–1900.* 2nd ed. Cambridge, Eng.: Univ. Pr., 1959. (900-page standard survey.)*

193 PINERO, Arthur Wing. "The Theatre in the 'Seventies." In *The Eighteen-Seventies,* **187,** 133–60.

194 PRICE, Cecil J. L. "The Victorian Theatre." In *The Victorians,* ed. Arthur Pollard. Lon: Barrie & Jenkins, 1970, 386–402.

195 RAHILL, Frank. "England." *The World of Melodrama.* Univ. Park: Pennsylvania State UP, 1967, 103–222.

196 ROWELL, George, ed. *Victorian Dramatic Criticism.* Lon: Methuen, 1971. (Anthology.)†

197 ROWELL, George. *The Victorian Theatre: A Survey.* Lon: Oxford UP, 1956.

198 SELLE, Carl M. "Introduction." *The New Drama: The Liars, by Henry Arthur Jones; The Notorious Mrs. Ebbsmith, by Sir Arthur Wing Pinero.* Coral Gables, FL: Univ. of Miami Pr., 1963, 1–60.†

199 SHAW, G. Bernard. *Our Theatres in the Nineties.* Lon: Constable, 1932. 3 vols. (His *Saturday Review* essays, 1895–1898. A good paperback selection is *Shaw's Dramatic Criticism, 1895–1898,* ed. John Matthews [NY: Hill & Wang, 1959].)*

200 WALKLEY, Arthur B. *Playhouse Impressions.* Lon: Unwin, 1892.

201 WEST, E. J. "From a Player's to a Playwright's Theatre: The London Stage, 1870–1890." *QJS,* 28 (1942), 430–36.

1890s to 1930s

Under "Dramatists," see especially Barrie, Coward, Galsworthy, Granville-Barker, Hankin, Jones, Maugham, Pinero, Shaw, and Wilde.

202 AGATE, James. *James Agate, an Anthology,* ed. Herbert Van Thal. NY: Hill & Wang, 1961. (Sunday London *Times* critic, 1923–47.)

203 AGATE, James. *The Selective "Ego": The Diaries of James Agate,* ed. Tim Beaumont. Lon: Harrap, 1976.

1890s TO 1930s

204 AGATE, James. *A Short View of the English Stage, 1900–26*. Lon: Jenkins, 1926.

205 ARCHER, William. *The Old Drama and the New,* **176.**

206 BAKER, Donald. "Thomas Hardy: Prophet of Total Theatre." *CoD,* 7 (1973), 121–34.

207 BARNES, T. R. "Shaw and the London Theatre." In *The Modern Age,* **143,** 209–20.

208 BEERBOHM, Max. *Around Theatres.* NY: Simon & Schuster, 1954 [c. 1924]. (Selected dramatic criticisms. The rest are printed in *More Theatres, 1893– 1903,* and *Last Theatres, 1904–1910* [NY: Taplinger, 1969, 1970].)*

209 BORSA, Mario. *The English Stage of To-Day,* **180.**

210 BRIDGES-ADAMS, William. "Theatre." In *Edwardian England, 1901– 1914.* ed. Simon Nowell-Smith. Lon: Oxford UP, 1964, 367–409.

211 BRIGHOUSE, Harold. "Introduction." In *The Works of Stanley Houghton,* ed. Harold Brighouse. Lon: Constable, 1914, I, ix–lix. (By and about playwrights of the "Manchester school.")

212 CHAPPLE, J. A. V. *Documentary and Imaginative Literature, 1880–1920.* NY: Barnes & Noble, 1970. (Viewpoint of "British studies.")

213 CHEW, Samuel C. "Modern Drama." In *A Literary History of England,* ed. Albert C. Baugh. NY: Appleton, 1948, 1516–31. (Deals only with the period 1890–1930.)

214 DONALDSON, Frances. *Freddy Lonsdale.* Lon: Heinemann, 1957. (On a popular dramatist of the period.)

215 ELLEHAUGE, Martin O. M. *Striking Figures Among Modern English Dramatists.* Copenhagen: Levin & Munksgaard, 1931.

216 ELLIS-FERMOR, Una. "The English Theatre in the Nineties." *The Irish Dramatic Movement,* **420,** 18–32.

217 ERVINE, St. John. *The Theatre in My Time.* Lon: Rich & Cowan, 1933.

218 FECHTER, Paul. "Der Weg ins Helle." *Das europäische Drama.* Mannheim: Bibliographisches Institut, 1957, II, 204–70. (On English drama, with stress on Shaw.)

219 GILLIE, Christopher. "Drama 1900–1940." *Movements in English Literature 1900–1940.* Cambridge, Eng.: Univ. Pr., 1975, 164–82.

220 GLICKSBERG, Charles I. "The Sexual Revolution and the Modern Drama." *The Sexual Revolution in Modern English Literature.* The Hague: Nijhoff, 1973, 43–70. (Stresses Shaw, Maugham, and Coward.)

221 LAUTERBACH, Edward S., and W. Eugene DAVIS. "Drama." *The Transitional Age: British Literature, 1880–1920.* Troy, NY: Whitston, 1973, 45–58. (Survey.)

222 MacCARTHY, Desmond. *The Court Theatre, 1904–1907,* ed. Stanley Weintraub. Coral Gables, FL: Univ. of Miami Pr., 1966. (The 1907 ed. with valuable intro. and appendices.)*

223 MacCARTHY, Desmond. *Drama.* Lon: Putnam, 1940. (Reviews, 1913–35.)

224 McINNES, Edward. "Naturalism and the English Theatre." *Forum for Modern Language St.,* 1 (1965), 197–206. (Describes its critical reception in the 1890s.)

225 MILLER, Anna I. "The Independent Theatres of England." *The Independent Theatre in Europe, 1887 to the Present.* NY: Blom, 1966 [c. 1931], 164–254. (Standard older account.)

226 NICOLL, Allardyce. *English Drama, 1900–1930: The Beginnings of the*

Modern Period. Cambridge, Eng.: Univ. Pr., 1973. (Full account by an eminent drama historian.)*

227 NICOLL, Allardyce. "Wilde and Shaw: Plays of the Nineties." *A History of English Drama,* **192**, 187–214.

228 NORWOOD, Gilbert. "English Drama Between Two Wars." *DR,* 22 (1943), 405–20.

229 NORWOOD, Gilbert. "The Present Renaissance of English Drama." *Euripides and Shaw, with Other Essays.* Bos: Luce, 1921, 49–108.

230 PELLIZZI, Camillo. *English Drama: The Last Great Phase,* tr. Rowan Williams. Lon: Macmillan, 1935. (English and Irish drama, stressing 1895–1915.)

231 PRATT, Tinsley. "The Manchester Dramatists." *Papers of the Manchester Literary Club,* 40 (July 1914), 213–29.

232 ROSS, Robert H. *The Georgian Revolt, 1910–1922: Rise and Fall of a Poetic Ideal.* Carbondale: Southern Illinois UP, 1965. (Treats the poetic drama of Bottomley, Drinkwater, and Abercrombie.)

233 ROY, Emil. *British Drama Since Shaw.* Carbondale: Southern Illinois UP, 1972. (Introductory essays on major figures.)

234 SHAW, G. Bernard. *Our Theatres in the Nineties,* **199**.*

235 SKELTON, Robin. "A Literary Theatre: A Note on English Poetic Drama in the Time of Yeats." In **2313**, 133–40. (Davidson to Bottomley.)

236 *"The Stage" Year Book [for 1907–1924].* Lon: Carson & Comerford, 1908–10; "The Stage" Publishers, 1911–25. (Annual survey, stressing Britain. Useful for factual data.)

237 THOULESS, Priscilla. *Modern Poetic Drama.* Oxford: Blackwell, 1934. (Covers Phillips, Bottomley, etc.)

238 TRESIDDER, Argus. "Arnold Bennett and the Drama." In *Studies in Speech and Drama in Honor of Alexander M. Drummond.* Ithaca, NY: Cornell UP, 1944, 224–43.

239 TREWIN, John C. *The Edwardian Theatre,* **385**.

240 TREWIN, John C. *Theatre Since 1900.* Lon: Dakers, 1951. (Largely reprinted reviews.)

241 WALKLEY, Arthur B. *Drama and Life.* Lon: Methuen, 1907. (Reviews by the London *Times* critic, 1900–1926.)

242 WILSON, Albert E. *Edwardian Theatre.* Lon: Barker, 1951.

243 WOODBRIDGE, Homer E. "William Archer: Prophet of Modern Drama." *SR,* 44 (1936), 207–21.

1930s to 1950s

Under "Dramatists," see especially Coward, Duncan, Eliot, Fry, Priestley, Shaw, Thomas, and Williams.

244 ARMSTRONG, William A. "The Playwright and His Theatre, 1945–62." In **90**, 15–35.

245 BAXTER, Beverley. *First Nights and Footlights.* Lon: Hutchinson, 1955.

246 CABOCHE, Lucien. *Le Théâtre en Grande-Bretagne pendant la seconde guerre mondiale.* Paris: Didier, 1969. (Stresses theatrical conditions.)

247 CHIARI, Joseph. "Poetic Drama." *Landmarks of Contemporary Drama,* **46**, 81–106.

248 COOKMAN, A. V. "The Prose Drama." In **120**, 33–48. (Focuses on the forties.)

249 DARLINGTON, William A. *Six Thousand and One Nights: Forty Years a Critic.* Lon: Harrap, 1960.

250 DOBRÉE, Bonamy. "Poetic Drama in England Today." *SoR,* 4 (1939), 581–99.

251 DONOGHUE, Denis. *The Third Voice: Modern British and American Verse Drama.* Princeton, NJ: Princeton UP, 1959.*†

252 FECHTER, Paul. "England." *Das europäische Drama.* Mannheim: Bibliographisches Institut, 1958, III, 367–403. (Covers Coward and Priestley to Osborne.)

253 FINDLATER, Richard. *The Unholy Trade.* Lon: Gollancz, 1952. (Full background picture of the state of the theatre.)*

254 FRASER, G. S. "The Revival of Poetic Drama." *The Modern Writer and His World.* 2nd ed. Baltimore, MD: Penguin, 1964, 212-26.†

255 GERSTENBERGER, Donna. *The Complex Configuration: Modern Verse Drama.* Salzburg: Institut für Englische Sprache und Literatur, Univ. Salzburg, 1973. (Yeats through Fry.)

255A HINCHLIFFE, Arnold P. *Modern Verse Drama.* Lon: Methuen, 1977.

256 HOBSON, Harold. *The Theatre Now.* Lon: Longmans, 1953.

257 HOSKINS, Katharine B. "On the Left: Drama." *Today the Struggle: Literature and Politics in England During the Spanish Civil War.* Austin: Univ. of Texas Pr., 1969, 143–82.

258 JONES, Leonard A. "The Workers' Theatre Movement in Britain in the Thirties." *ZAA,* 23 (1975), 300–13.

259 JURAK, Mirko. "Commitment and Character Portrayal in the British Politico-Poetic Drama of the 1930s." *ETJ,* 26 (1974), 342–51. (Treats Spender and MacNeice as well as Auden and Isherwood.)

259A JURAK, Mirko. "Dramaturgic Concepts of the English Group Theatre: The Totality of Artistic Involvement." *MD,* 16 (1973), 81-86. (Stresses Auden and Isherwood.)

260 JURAK, Mirko. "English Political Verse Drama of the Thirties: Revision and Alteration." *Acta Neophilologica,* 1 (1968), 67–78.

260A JURAK, Mirko. "The Group Theatre: Its Development and Significance for the Modern English Theatre." *Acta Neophilologica,* 2 (1969), 3–43.

261 KERNODLE, George R. "England's Religious-Drama Movement." *CE,* 1 (1940), 414–26.

262 LAMBERT, J. W. "The Verse Drama." In **120**, 51–72.

263 McLEOD, Stuart R. *Modern Verse Drama.* Salzburg: Institut für Englische Sprache und Literatur, Univ. Salzburg, 1972.

264 MUIR, Kenneth. "Verse and Prose." In **100**, 97–115. (Treats poetic drama, whether in verse or prose.)

265 PRIOR, Moody E. "Poetic Drama: An Analysis and a Suggestion." In *English Institute Essays, 1949,* ed. Alan S. Downer. NY: Columbia UP, 1950, 3–32.

266 RATTIGAN, Terence. "Preface" to each vol. of *The Collected Plays of Terence Rattigan.* Lon: Hamilton, 1953–64. 3 vols. (Continuing defense of the appeal of well-made drama to "Aunt Edna.")

267 ROY, Emil. *British Drama Since Shaw,* **233**.

268 SPANOS, William V. *The Christian Tradition in Modern British Verse Drama: The Poetics of Sacramental Time.* New Brunswick, NJ: Rutgers UP, 1967. (Stresses Eliot and Williams.)*

269 TREWIN, John C. *Dramatists of Today.* Lon: Staples, 1953.

270 TREWIN, John C. *Theatre Since 1900,* **240**.

271 TREWIN, John C., ed. *The Year's Work in the Theatre* [*1948–49 to 1950–51*]. Lon: Longmans, 1949–51. 3 vols.

272 TYNAN, Kenneth. *A View of the English Stage, 1944–63.* Lon: Davis-Poynter, 1975.

273 WELLAND, Dennis. "Some Post-War Experiments in Poetic Drama." In **90**, 36–55.

274 WILSON, Albert E. *Post-War Theatre.* Lon: Home & Van Thal, [1950?]. (Covers 1945–49 review fashion.)

275 WORSLEY, T. C. *The Fugitive Art: Dramatic Commentaries, 1947–1951.* Lon: Lehmann, 1952.

1950s to 1970s

Under "Dramatists," see especially Arden, Beckett, Bolt, Bond, Delaney, Jellicoe, Orton, Osborne, Pinter, Shaffer, Simpson, Stoppard, Storey, Wesker, and Whiting.

276 ANDERSON, Michael. *Anger and Detachment: A Study of Arden, Osborne and Pinter.* Lon: Pitman, 1976. (Introductory study.)

277 ANSORGE, Peter. *Disrupting the Spectacle,* **331**.

278 BARKER, Clive. "Contemporary Shakespearean Parody in British Theatre." *Shakespeare Jahrbuch* (Weimar), 105 (1969), 104–20.

279 [The British Theatre Today.] *TC,* 169 (1961), 99–220. (Symposium of theatre figures.)

280 BROWN, John R., ed. *Modern British Dramatists: A Collection of Critical Essays.* Englewood Cliffs, NJ: Prentice-Hall, 1968. (Reprinted essays on post–World War II drama.)*

281 BROWN, John R. *Theatre Language: A Study of Arden, Osborne, Pinter and Wesker.* NY: Taplinger, 1972.*

282 BRYDEN, Ronald. *The Unfinished Hero, and Other Essays.* Lon: Faber, 1969. (Includes many drama reviews.)

283 CALLEN, Anthony. "Stoppard's Godot: Some French Influences on Post-War English Drama." *NTM,* 10 (Winter 1970), 22–30.

284 CHIARI, Joseph. "Drama in England." *Landmarks of Contemporary Drama,* **46**, 107–34. (Treats Osborne and his successors.)

285 ELSOM, John. *Post-War British Theatre,* **349**.

286 *Encore,* 1954–1965. (London theatrical review that championed the avant garde. Absorbed by *Plays and Players,* a more commercial monthly.)

287 ESSLIN, Martin. "Brecht and the English Theatre." *Brief Chronicles,* **102**, 84–96. (Reprinted from 1966 *TDR.*)

288 ESSLIN, Martin. "Contemporary English Drama and the Mass Media." *Brief Chronicles,* **102**, 272–84. (From 1969 *English.*)

289 "Four Points of View: English Theatre Today." *ITA*, 3 (1958), 140–66. (Contributions by Robert Bolt, John Hall, Bernard Kops, and Derek Monsey.)

290 FRASER, G. S. "The Wind of Change in the 1950s [in English Drama]." *The Modern Writer and His World*, **254**, 227–44.

291 "*Gambit* Discussion: New Gothics, Realists and Phantasists." *Gambit*, 8, No. 29 (1976), 5–29. (Views of twelve playwrights.)

292 GIANNETTI, Louis D. "Henry Livings: A Neglected Voice in the New Drama." *MD*, 12 (1969), 38–48.

293 GILLETT, Eric. "Regional Realism: Shelagh Delaney, Alun Owen, Keith Waterhouse, and Willis Hall." In **90**, 186–203.

294 GILLIATT, Penelope. *Unholy Fools: Wits, Comics, Disturbers of the Peace: Film & Theater*. NY: Viking, 1973. (Reviews.)

295 GRIFFITHS, Gareth. "New Lines—English Theatre in the Sixties and After." *KanQ*, 3 (Spring 1971), 77–88.

296 HAHNLOSER-INGOLD, Margrit. *Das englische Theater und Bert. Brecht: Die Dramen von W. H. Auden, John Osborne, John Arden in ihrer Beziehung zum epischen Theater von Bert. Brecht und den gemeinsamen elisabethanischen Quellen.* Bern: Francke, 1970.

297 HALL, Stuart. "Beyond Naturalism Pure: The First Five Years." In **308**, 212–20. (Trends, 1956–61.)

298 HAMMERSCHMIDT, Hildegard. *Das historische Drama in England (1956–1971): Erscheinungsformen und Entwicklungstendenzen.* Wiesbaden: Humanitas, 1972.

299 HAYS, H. R. "Transcending Naturalism." *MD*, 5 (1962), 27–36. (On the new British drama.)

300 HINCHLIFFE, Arnold P. *British Theatre 1950–70*. Oxford: Blackwell, 1974. (Brief survey of important trends and figures in both drama and theatre.)

301 "Is the Left Going in the Right Direction?" *ITA*, 5 (1961), 170–254. (Symposium on current British drama, with articles by Lindsay Anderson, John Arden, Tom Milne, etc.)

302 KITCHIN, Laurence. "Theatre in the Raw: The New English Drama" and "The Second Wave: Developments in Formal Structure." *Mid-Century Drama*. 2nd ed. Lon: Faber, 1962, 98–122.†

303 KNIGHT, G. Wilson. "The Kitchen Sink: On Recent Developments in Drama." *Encounter*, 21 (Dec. 1963), 48–54.

304 LAHR, John. "Heathcote Williams' *AC/DC:* Flushing the Toilet in the Brain." *Astonish Me*, **111**, 157–81.

305 LAMBERT, Jack W. *Drama in Britain, 1964–1973*, **365**.

306 LANDSTONE, Charles. "From John Osborne to Shelagh Delaney." *World Theatre*, 8 (1959), 203–16.

307 MAROWITZ, Charles. *Confessions of a Counterfeit Critic: A London Theatre Notebook, 1958–1971*. Lon: Eyre Methuen, 1973.†

308 MAROWITZ, Charles, Tom MILNE, and Owen HALE, eds. *The Encore Reader: A Chronicle of the New Drama*. Lon: Methuen, 1965. (Selected essays and reviews, 1957–63; see **286**.)†

309 MAROWITZ, Charles, and Simon TRUSSLER, eds. *Theatre at Work: Playwrights and Productions in the Modern British Theatre*. NY: Hill & Wang, 1967. (Includes interviews with Whiting, Arden, Bolt, Wesker, and Pinter.)†

310 MATLACK, Cynthia S. "Metaphor and Dramatic Structure in [Enid Bagnold's] *The Chalk Garden*." *QJS*, 59 (1973), 304–10.

311 MATTHEWS, Honor. "The Myth of the Warring Brothers in the Contemporary Theatre: The Disappearance of the Image in England and America." *The Primal Curse: The Myth of Cain and Abel in the Theatre*. NY: Schocken, 1967, 187–205.

312 "A New English Theatre?" *LonM*, 7 (July 1960), 7–39. (Symposium of theatre figures.)

313 *New Theatre Magazine: Thrice Yearly Journal of Drama and Theatre Studies*, 1959–1973. (Univ. of Bristol theatrical review.)

314 OPPEL, Horst, ed. *Das englische Drama der Gegenwart: Interpretationen*. Berlin: Schmidt, 1976. (Long analyses, all in German.)

315 SALEM, Daniel. *La Révolution théâtrale actuelle en Angleterre: Essai*. Paris: Denoël, 1969. (French survey of the new theatre since Osborne.)

316 "The State of the Nation's Theatre." *ThQ*, 3 (July–Sept. 1973), 29–69; 3 (Oct.–Dec.), 4–59, 113.

317 STEIN, Karen F. "Metaphysical Silence in Absurd Drama." *MD*, 13 (1971), 423–31. (Stresses Beckett and Pinter.)

318 TAYLOR, John R. *Anger & After: A Guide to the New British Drama* [American title: *The Angry Theatre*]. Rev. ed. Lon: Methuen, 1969. (Standard detailed account.)* †

319 TAYLOR, John R. *The Second Wave: British Drama for the Seventies*. NY: Hill & Wang, 1971. (Sequel to above title.)*

320 THOMPSON, Marjorie. "The Image of Youth in the Contemporary [British] Theater." *MD*, 7 (1965), 433–45.

321 TREWIN, John C. *Drama in Britain, 1951–1964*. Lon: Longmans, 1965. (Brief survey of developments in both drama and theatre.)

322 TRILLING, Ossia. "The New English Realism." *TDR*, 7 (Winter 1962), 184–93.

323 TRILLING, Ossia. "The Young British Drama." *MD*, 3 (1960), 168–77. (An early survey of the regeneration.)

324 TRUSSLER, Simon. "British Neo-naturalism." *TDR*, 13 (Winter 1968), 130–36.

325 TSCHUDIN, Marcus. *A Writer's Theatre*, **389**.

326 TYNAN, Kenneth. "The Angry Young Movement." *Curtains: Selections from the Drama Criticism, and Related Writings*. NY: Atheneum, 1961, 190–98. (A 1958 background picture.)

327 TYNAN, Kenneth. "The British Theatre." *Curtains*, **326**, 3–241.

328 WEISE, Wolf-Dietrich. *Die "Neuen englischen Dramatiker" in ihrem Verhältnis zu Brecht (unter besonderer Berücksichtigung von Wesker, Osborne und Arden)*. Berlin: Gehlen, 1969.

329 WELLWARTH, George E. "The New English Dramatists." *The Theater of Protest and Paradox: Developments in the Avant-Garde Drama*. Rev. ed. NY: New York UP, 1971, 223–317.†

330 WILLIAMS, Raymond. "Recent English Drama." In *The Modern Age*, **143**, 496–508.

Theatre in England
Since the 1860s

331 ANSORGE, Peter. *Disrupting the Spectacle: Five Years of Experimental and Fringe Theatre in Britain.* Lon: Pitman, 1975.

332 ARMSTRONG, William A. "Modern Developments in the British Theatre." *Neuphilologische Mitteilungen,* 51 (Feb. 1950), 19–34. (Describes the postwar theatrical scene.)

333 BABLET, Denis. *Edward Gordon Craig,* tr. Daphne Woodward. NY: Theatre Arts Books, 1966.

334 BARKER, Kathleen. *The Theatre Royal, Bristol, 1766–1966: Two Centuries of Stage History.* Lon: Society for Theatre Research, 1974.

335 BOAS, Frederick S. "The Malvern Theatrical Festival: 1929–1939." *QQ,* 47 (1940), 219–30.

336 BROOK, Peter. *The Empty Space.* NY: Atheneum, 1968.†

337 BROWNE, Terry W. *Playwrights' Theatre: The English Stage Company at the Royal Court Theatre.* Lon: Pitman, 1975.

338 CARTER, Huntly. "England." *The New Spirit in the European Theatre, 1914–1924: A Comparative Study of the Changes Effected by the War and Revolution.* Lon: Benn, 1925, 1–119.

339 CARTER, Huntly. "The New Spirit in London." *The New Spirit in Drama & Art.* NY: Kennerley, 1913, 7–45.

340 CHISHOLM, Cecil. *Repertory: An Outline of the Modern Theatre Movement.* Lon: Davies, 1934.

341 CONOLLY, L. W. "The Abolition of Theatre Censorship in Great Britain: The Theatres Act of 1968." *QQ,* 75 (1968), 569–83.

342 COPPIETERS, Frank. "Arnold Wesker's Centre Fortytwo," **2068**.

343 CRAIG, Edward Gordon. *On the Art of the Theatre.* Lon: Heinemann, 1911.†

344 CRAIG, Edward Gordon. *The Theatre Advancing.* NY: Blom, 1963 [c. 1947].

345 CROYDEN, Margaret. "The Achievement of Peter Brook: From Commercialism to the Avant-Garde." *Lunatics, Lovers and Poets: The Contemporary Experimental Theatre.* NY: McGraw-Hill, 1974, 229–85.

346 DAMISCH, I. "Theatre Workshop: A British People's Theatre." *Recherches Anglaises et Américaines,* No. 5 (1972), 121–43.

347 DONALDSON, Frances L. *The Actor-Managers.* Lon: Weidenfeld & Nicolson, 1970.

348 DOWNER, Alan S. "Harley Granville-Barker." *SR,* 55 (1947), 627–45. (As director and critic.)

349 ELSOM, John. *Post-War British Theatre.* Lon: Routledge & K. Paul, 1976.

350 ELSOM, John. *Theatre Outside London.* Lon: Macmillan, 1971. (Survey of the present situation.)

351 FINDLATER, Richard. *Banned! A Review of Theatrical Censorship in Britain.* Lon: MacGibbon & Kee, 1967.

352 FINDLATER, Richard. *The Unholy Trade,* **253**.

17

353 GLASSTONE, Victor. *Victorian and Edwardian Theatres: An Architectural and Social Survey.* Cambridge, MA: Harvard UP, 1975.

354 GOLDIE, Grace W. *Liverpool Repertory Theatre, 1911–1934.* Liverpool: Univ. of Liverpool Pr., 1935.

355 GREAT BRITAIN. Joint Committee on Censorship of the Theatre. *Report, Together with the Proceedings of the Committee, Minutes of Evidence . . .* Lon: H. M. S. O., 1969.

356 GREAT BRITAIN. Joint Select Committee of the House of Lords and the House of Commons on the Stage Plays (Censorship). *Minutes of Evidence.* Lon: H. M. S. O., 1909.

356A GREAT BRITAIN. Select Committee on Theatres and Places of Entertainment. *Report . . . Together with the Proceedings of the Committee. Minutes of Evidence . . .* Lon: H.M.S.O., 1892.

357 HAMMOND, Jonathan. "A Potted History of the Fringe." *ThQ,* 3 (Oct.– Dec. 1973), 37–46.

358 HAYMAN, Ronald. "The Royal Court 1956–1972." *Drama,* No. 105 (Summer 1972), 45-53.

359 HAYMAN, Ronald. *The Set-up: An Anatomy of the English Theatre Today.* Lon: Eyre Methuen, 1974.* †

360 HUDSON, Lynton A. *The English Stage, 1850–1950.* Lon: Harrap, 1951. (Decade-by-decade account.)

361 HYNES, Samuel. "The Theater and the Lord Chamberlain." *The Edwardian Turn of Mind.* Princeton, NJ: Princeton UP, 1968, 212–53.

362 JACKSON, Anthony. "Harley Granville Barker as Director at the Royal Court Theatre, 1904–1907." *Theatre Research,* 12 (1972), 126–38.

363 JONES, Henry Arthur. "The Censorship." *The Foundations of a National Drama,* **1168,** 269–358.

364 JONES, Leonard A. "The Workers' Theatre Movement in the 'Twenties." *ZAA,* 14 (1966), 259–81.

365 LAMBERT, Jack W. *Drama in Britain, 1964–1973.* Harlow: Longman for the British Council, 1974. (Treats developments in theatre rather than drama.)†

366 LANDSTONE, Charles. *Off-Stage: A Personal Record of the First Twelve Years of State Sponsored Drama in Great Britain.* Lon: Elek, 1953. (Covers 1940–52.)

367 MacCOLL, Ewan. "Grass Roots of Theatre Workshop." *ThQ,* 3 (Jan.– March 1973), 58–68.

368 MacQUEEN-POPE, Walter. *Carriages at Eleven: The Story of Edwardian Theatre.* New ed. Lon: Hale, 1972.

369 MacQUEEN-POPE, Walter. *The Footlights Flickered.* Lon: Jenkins, 1959. (Theatre in the decade after World War I.)

370 MANDER, Raymond, and Joe MITCHENSON. *The Theatres of London.* New ed. Lon: New Eng. Lib., 1975.

371 MAROWITZ, Charles, and Simon TRUSSLER, eds. *Theatre at Work,* **309.**

372 MARSHALL, Norman. *The Other Theatre.* Lon: Lehmann, 1947. (Pioneering non-commercial theatres in Britain.)

373 MAY, Robin. *A Companion to the Theatre: The Anglo-American Stage from 1920.* Guildford: Lutterworth, 1973.

374 MILLER, Anna I. "The Independent Theatres of England," **225.**

375 NOBLE, Peter. *British Theatre*. Lon: British Yearbooks, 1946. (Short articles and factual data concerning theatre during World War II.)

376 PHELPS, William L. *The Twentieth-Century Theatre: Observations on the Contemporary English and American Stage*. NY: Macmillan, 1918.

377 POGSON, Rex. *Miss Horniman and the Gaiety Theatre, Manchester*. Lon: Rockliff, 1952. (Stresses 1908–1914.)

378 RAFFLES, Gerald. "Theatre Workshop." *ITA*, 3 (1958), 167–79.

379 ROWELL, George. *The Victorian Theatre: A Survey*. Lon: Oxford UP, 1956.*

380 SCHEVILL, James. "Joan Littlewood: Towards a Theatre of Ideal Comedians." *Break Out! In Search of New Theatrical Environments*. Chicago: Swallow, 1973, 322–35.†

381 SCHOONDERWOERD, N. *J. T. Grein, Ambassador of the Theatre, 1862–1935: A Study in Anglo-Continental Theatrical Relations*. Assen: Van Gorcum, 1963.

382 "The State of the Nation's Theatre." *ThQ*, 3 (July–Sept. 1973), 29–69; 3 (Oct.–Dec.), 4–59, 113.

383 STOKES, John. "A Literary Theatre: The Lessons of the Independent Theatre." *Resistible Theatres: Enterprise and Experiment in the Late Nineteenth Century*. Lon: Elek, 1972, 111–80.

384 TREWIN, John C. *The Birmingham Repertory Theatre, 1913–1963*. Lon: Barrie & Rockliff, 1963.

385 TREWIN, John C. *The Edwardian Theatre*. Totowa, NJ: Rowman & Littlefield, 1976.

386 TREWIN, John C. *The Gay Twenties: A Decade of the Theatre*. Lon: Macdonald, 1958. (Well illustrated year-by-year account.)

387 TREWIN, John C. *Peter Brook: A Biography*. Lon: Macdonald, 1971.

388 TREWIN, John C. *The Turbulent Thirties: A Further Decade of the Theatre*. Macdonald, 1960.

389 TSCHUDIN, Marcus. *A Writer's Theatre: George Devine and the English Stage Company at the Royal Court 1956–1965*. Bern: Lang, 1972.

390 VERNON, Frank. *The Twentieth-Century Theatre*. Lon: Harrap, 1924. (Describes theatrical conditions before, during, and after World War I in England.)

391 WEARING, J. P. *The London Stage, 1890–1899: A Calendar of Plays and Players*. Metuchen, NJ: Scarecrow, 1976. 2 vols.

392 WHITWORTH, Geoffrey A. *The Making of a National Theatre*. Lon: Faber, 1951.

393 WILSON, Albert E. *Edwardian Theatre*. Lon: Barker, 1951.

394 WILSON, Albert E. *Post-War Theatre, 274*.

Modern Scottish and Welsh Drama and Theatre

Under "Dramatists," see Barrie, Bridie, and Thomas.

395 BANNISTER, Winifred. "The Foundation of the Modern Scottish Theatre." In *International Theatre,* ed. John Andrews and Ossia Trilling. Lon: Low, 1949, 111–21.

396 BELL, H. Idris. "Drama." In *A History of Welsh Literature,* by Thomas Parry, tr. H. I. Bell. Oxford: Clarendon, 1955, 484–97. (Focuses on twentieth-century drama.)

397 BROWN, Ivor. "The Modern Scottish Theatre." In **120**, 93–110.

398 BROWN, Ivor. "Wales and Scotland: The Tributary Theatre." *TAM,* 23 (1939), 469–74.

399 CRAWFORD, Iain. "Scottish Renaissance." *TAM,* 34 (1950), 32–37.

400 FINDLATER, Richard. *Emlyn Williams.* Lon: Rockliff, 1957.

401 LAWSON, Robb. *The Story of the Scots Stage.* Paisley: Gardner, 1917.

402 MILLER, Anna I. "The Dramatic Awakening of Scotland and Wales." *The Independent Theatre in Europe,* **225**, 311–28.

403 *Scottish Drama Year Book.* Glasgow: Albyn Pr., 1948–.

404 WITTIG, Kurt. "Scottish Drama." *The Scottish Tradition in Literature.* Edinburgh: Oliver & Boyd, 1958, 311–22.

Modern Irish Drama

405 FREEDLEY, George. "England and Ireland," **152**, 216–32. (On Irish drama.)

406 KAVANAGH, Peter. *Irish Theatre: Being a History of the Drama in Ireland from the Earliest Period up to the Present Day.* Tralee: Kerryman, 1947. (Part 5.)

407 KENNY, Herbert A. "The Celtic Renaissance" and "Modern Times." *Literary Dublin: A History.* NY: Taplinger, 1974, 163–318.

408 KRAUSE, David. "The Barbarous Sympathies of Antic Irish Comedy." *Malahat Rev.,* No. 22 (1972), 99–117.

409 O'DRISCOLL, Robert, ed. *Theatre and Nationalism in Twentieth-Century Ireland.* Toronto: Univ. of Toronto Pr., 1971.*

410 O'HAODHA, Micheal. *Theatre in Ireland.* Oxford: Blackwell, 1974. (Cogent historical account, stressing 1899–1971.)†

411 POWER, Patrick C. *A Literary History of Ireland.* Cork: Mercier Pr., 1969.

412 RAFROIDI, Patrick, Raymonde POPOT, and William PARKER, eds. *Aspects of the Irish Theatre.* Paris: Eds. Universitaires, 1972.*

413 ROBINSON, Lennox, ed. *The Irish Theatre: Lectures* . . . Lon: Macmillan, 1939.

414 SADDLEMYER, Ann. " 'Worn out with Dreams': Dublin's Abbey Theatre." In **2313**, 104–32.

415 TRACY, Robert. "Ireland: The Patriot Game." In *The Cry of Home: Cultural Nationalism and the Modern Writer,* ed. H. Ernest Lewald. Knoxville: Univ. of Tennessee Pr., 1972, 39–57. (Focuses on modern dramatists up to Behan.)

1890s to 1920s

Under "Dramatists," see especially Carroll, Colum, Dunsany, Fitzmaurice, Gregory, Martyn, Moore, Robinson, Synge, and Yeats.

416 ANDREWS, Irene D. "The Irish Literary Theatre." *PoL,* 39 (1928), 94–100.

417 BOYD, Ernest. *The Contemporary Drama of Ireland.* Dub: Talbot, 1918.

418 CLARK, Barrett H. "The Irish Drama." *A Study of the Modern Drama,* **144**, 329–57.

419 CLARK, James M. "The Irish Literary Movement." *Englische Studien,* 49 (1915), 50–98.

420 ELLIS-FERMOR, Una. *The Irish Dramatic Movement.* 2nd ed. Lon: Methuen, 1954. (The standard account through 1920.)* †

421 FRASER, G. S. "The Irish Dramatic Revival." *The Modern Writer and His World,* **254**, 204–11.

422 GASSNER, John. "John Millington Synge and the Irish Muse." *Masters of the Drama,* **59**, 542–74.

423 GREGORY, Lady. *Our Irish Theatre: A Chapter of Autobiography.* New enl. ed., ed. Roger McHugh. NY: Oxford UP, 1973. (First publ. 1913.)* †

424 GWYNN, Denis. "The Irish Literary Theatre." *Edward Martyn and the Irish Revival.* Lon: Cape, 1930, 109–70.

425 HOGAN, Robert, and James KILROY. *The Modern Irish Drama: A Documentary History.* Vol. I: *The Irish Literary Theatre, 1899–1901;* Vol. II: *Laying the Foundations, 1902–1904.* Dub: Dolmen, 1975–. (In process.)*

426 McDERMOTT, Hubert. "The Background to Anglo-Irish Drama." *Topic,* 24 (Fall 1972), 69–76. (Developments in the 1890s.)

427 MALONE, Andrew E. *The Irish Drama.* NY: Blom, 1965 [c. 1929].*

428 MILLER, Anna I. "The National Theatre of Ireland." *The Independent Theatre in Europe,* **225**, 255–310.

429 MORRIS, Lloyd R. "The Drama." *The Celtic Dawn: A Survey of the Renascence in Ireland, 1889–1916.* NY: Cooper Square, 1970 [c. 1917], 88–172. (Superficial account.)

430 O'CONOR, Norreys J. *Changing Ireland: Literary Backgrounds of the Irish Free State, 1889–1922.* Cambridge, MA: Harvard UP, 1924.

431 SKELTON, Robin. "Themes and Attitudes in the Later Drama of Jack B. Yeats," *YeS,* No. 2 (1972), 100–20.

432 WEYGANDT, Cornelius. *Irish Plays and Playwrights.* Bos: Houghton, 1913. (The contemporary view of an American scholar.)

433 YEATS, W. B. "Dramatis Personae, 1896–1902." *Dramatis Personae, 1896–1902; Estrangement; The Death of Synge; The Bounty of Sweden.* NY: Macmillan, 1936, 3–82; also in his *Autobiographies,* **2177**.

434 YEATS, W. B. "The Irish Dramatic Movement: 1901–1919." *Explorations,* **2179**, 71–259.*

435 YEATS, W. B., ed. *Beltaine: The Organ of the Irish Literary Theatre. Numbers One to Three, May 1899–April 1900.* Facsimile reprint with intro. by B. C. Bloomfield. Lon: Cass, 1970.

436 YEATS, W. B., ed. *Samhain: October 1901–November 1908.* Facsimile reprint with intro. by B. C. Bloomfield. Lon: Cass, 1970.

1920s to 1970s

Under "Dramatists," see especially Beckett, Behan, Clarke, Friel, Johnston, and O'Casey.

437 CARROLL, Paul V. "The Irish Theatre (Post-war)." In *International Theatre*, **395**, 122–28.

438 CONLIN, Matthew T. "T. C. Murray: Ireland on the Stage." *Ren*, 13 (1961), 125–31.

439 "Drama in Ireland." *Iris Hibernia*, 4, No. 3 (1960). (Special number on the contemporary situation.)

440 DUKES, Ashley. "Dublin Plays and Playhouses." *TAM*, 14 (1930), 378–85.

441 FALLON, Gabriel. "Sitting at the Play." *Irish Monthly*, 64–82 (1936–54). (Uncollected essays and reviews, some with other titles, on the Irish theatre.)

442 GREGORY, Lady. *Journals, 1916–1930,* **1132**.

443 HOGAN, Robert. *After the Irish Renaissance: A Critical History of Irish Drama Since The Plough and the Stars.* Minneapolis: Univ. of Minnesota Pr., 1967.*

444 HOGAN, Robert. "The Experimental Theatre of the Poets." *After the Irish Renaissance*, **443**, 147–63.

445 "The Irish Theatre: Sick or Sound?" *Aquarius,* 4 (1971), 17–25. (Opinions of four theatre men.)

446 JORDAN, John. "The Irish Theatre: Retrospect and Premonition." In **100**, 165–83.

447 LANE, Temple. "The Dramatic Arrival of M. J. Molloy." *Irish Writing*, No. 11 (May 1950), 59–65.

448 LEVENTHAL, A. J. "Dramatic Commentary." *DM*, 18–33 (1943–58). (Uncollected essays and reviews, some with other titles.)

449 McHUGH, Roger. "Tradition and the Future of Irish Drama." *Stu*, 40 (1951), 469–74.

450 MALONE, Andrew E. [Annual reviews of Irish drama and theatre.] *DM*, 1–12 (1924–36). (Malone often used the pseudonym Lawrence P. Byrne.)

451 MILLER, Liam. "Eden and After: The Irish Theatre, 1945–1966." *Stu*, 55 (1966), 231–35.

452 O'MAHONY, T. P. "Theatre in Ireland." *Eire*, 4 (Summer 1969), 93–100. (Analyzes the roots of the present dismal state.)

453 PANNECOUCKE, Jean-Michel. "John Brendon Keane and the New Irish Rural Drama." In **412**, 137–48.

Theatre in Ireland
Since the 1890s

454 BELL, Sam H. *The Theatre in Ulster: A Survey of the Dramatic Movement in Ulster from 1902 Until the Present Day.* Totowa, NJ: Rowman & Littlefield, 1972.

455 BYRNE, Dawson. *The Story of Ireland's National Theatre: The Abbey Theatre, Dublin.* Dub: Talbot, 1929.

456 COLUM, Padraic. "Dublin Through the Abbey Theatre." *The Road Round Ireland,* **824**, 260–338.

457 FALLON, Gabriel. "The Achievements and Problems of the Irish Theatre." *ITA,* No. 2 (1957), 53–63.

458 FAUGHNAN, Leslie. "The Future of the Abbey Theatre: Towards a New Dynamic." *Stu,* 55 (1966), 236–46.

459 FAY, Frank J. *Towards a National Theatre: Dramatic Criticism,* ed. Robert Hogan. Dub: Dolmen, 1970.

460 FAY, Gerard. *The Abbey Theatre: Cradle of Genius.* Lon: Hollis & Carter, 1958.

461 FAY, William G., and Catherine CARSWELL. *The Fays of the Abbey Theatre: An Autobiographical Record.* Lon: Rich & Cowan, 1935.

461A FLANNERY, James W. *W. B. Yeats and the Idea of a Theatre: The Early Abbey Theatre in Theory and Practice.* New Haven, CT: Yale UP, 1976.

462 HICKEY, Des, and Gus SMITH. *Flight from the Celtic Twilight.* Indianapolis, IN: Bobbs-Merrill, 1973. (Interviews with theatre figures.)

463 HOGAN, Robert, and James KILROY. *The Modern Irish Drama,* **425**.

464 HOGAN, Robert, and Michael J. O'NEILL, eds. *Joseph Holloway's Irish Theatre.* Dixon, CA: Proscenium Pr., 1968–70. 3 vols. (Edited diaries of an avid theatregoer.)

465 KAVANAGH, Peter. *The Story of the Abbey Theatre, from Its Origins in 1899 to the Present.* NY: Devin-Adair, 1950.

466 KENNEDY, David. "The Drama in Ulster." In *The Arts in Ulster: A Symposium,* ed. Sam H. Bell et al. Lon: Harrap, 1951, 47–68.

467 MacLIAMMÓIR, Micheál. *All for Hecuba: An Irish Theatrical Autobiography.* Bos: Branden, 1967.

468 MOORE, George. *Hail and Farewell: A Trilogy.* Lon: Heinemann, 1911–14. 3 vols. (Vol. 3 recounts his theatrical affairs.)

469 O'SHIUBHLAIGH, Maire N. *The Splendid Years: Recollections of Maire Nic Shiubhlaigh, as Told to Edward Kenny.* Dub: Duffy, 1955. (By a founder of the Abbey.)

470 REID, Alec. "Dublin's Abbey Theatre Today." *DrS,* 3 (1964), 507–19.

471 ROBINSON, Lennox. *Ireland's Abbey Theatre: A History, 1899–1951.* Lon: Sidgwick & Jackson, 1951. (Chronological account, with many documents reprinted.)

472 SHAW, G. Bernard. "The Irish Players." *The Matter with Ireland,* ed. Dan H. Laurence and David H. Greene. NY: Hill & Wang, 1962, 61–68.

473 SIMPSON, Alan. *Beckett and Behan and a Theatre in Dublin.* Lon: Routledge, 1962. (Focuses on staging at the Pike Theatre.)

Modern British Dramatists

Under each dramatist, editions and nondramatic writings of significance are listed first, then bibliographic and reference material (if any), then scholarly, critical, and expository works.

Arden, John
(1930 –)

474 ARDEN, John. "Building the Play: An Interview with John Arden." *Encore,* 8 (July–Aug. 1961), 22–41; repr. in **137**, 581–606.

475 ARDEN, John. "Delusions of Grandeur." *TC,* 169 (1961), 200–206.

476 ARDEN, John, and Brendan HENNESSY. "John Arden Interviewed." *TrR* No. 40 (1971), 52–59.

477 ARDEN, John. "Some Thoughts upon Left-Wing Drama." *ITA,* 5 (1961), 187–203. (On some current British plays.)

478 ARDEN, John. "Telling a True Tale." In **308**, 125–29. (A cogent 1960 statement of dramatic theory.)

478A ARDEN, John. *To Present the Pretence: Essays on the Theatre and Its Public.* Lon: Eyre Methuen, 1977.

479 ARDEN, John. "Who's for a Revolution? Two Interviews with John Arden." *TDR,* 11 (Winter 1966), 41–53; the first repr. in **121**, 238–68.*

480 ADLER, Thomas P. "Religious Ritual in John Arden's *Serjeant Musgrave's Dance.*" *MD,* 16 (1973), 163–66.

481 ANDERSON, Michael. *Anger and Detachment,* **276**, 50-87.

482 BLINDHEIM, Joan T. "John Arden's Use of the Stage." *MD,* 11 (1968), 306–16.

483 BRANDT, G. W. "Realism and Parables (from Brecht to Arden)." In **100**, 49–54 (On *Musgrave.*)

484 BROWN, John R. "John Arden. Artificial Theatre: *Serjeant Musgrave's Dance, The Workhouse Donkey* and *The Hero Rises Up.*" *Theatre Language,* **281**, 190–234.*

485 CORRIGAN, Robert W. "The Theatre of John Arden." *The Theatre in Search of a Fix.* NY: Delacorte, 1973, 316–24.

486 DAY, Paul W. "Individual and Society in the Early Plays of John Arden." *MD,* 18 (1975), 239–49.

487 EPSTEIN, Arthur D. "John Arden's Fun House." *Univ Rev,* 36 (1970), 243–51. (On *The Happy Haven.*)

488 GASKILL, William. "Comic Masks and *The Happy Haven.*" *Encore,* 7 (Nov.–Dec. 1960), 15–19.

489 GILMAN, Richard. "Arden's Unsteady Ground." In **280**, 104–16.

JOHN ARDEN

490 HAHNLOSER-INGOLD, Margrit. *Das englische Theater und Bert. Brecht*, **296**, 174–253.

491 HAINSWORTH, J. D. "John Arden and the Absurd." *Rev of Eng Lit*, 7 (Oct. 1966), 42–49.

492 HAMPTON, Nigel. "Freedom and Order in Arden's *Ironhand.*" *MD*, 19 (1976), 129–33.

493 HAYMAN, Ronald. *John Arden.* Lon: Heinemann Educ., 1968. (77 pp.)

494 HUNT, Albert. *Arden: A Study of His Plays.* Lon: Eyre Methuen, 1974.* †

495 JACQUOT, Jean. "Présentation de John Arden." In *Le Théâtre moderne, II: Depuis la deuxième guerre mondiale*, ed. Jean Jacquot. Paris: Éds. du Centre National de la Recherche Scientifique, 1967, 133–56.

496 JORDAN, Robert. "Serjeant Musgrave's Problem." *MD*, 13 (1970), 54–62.

497 KENNEDY, Andrew K. *Six Dramatists in Search of a Language*, **158**, 213–29.

498 McMILLAN, Grant E. "The Bargee in *Serjeant Musgrave's Dance.*" *ETJ*, 25 (1973), 500–503.

499 MESSENGER, Ann P. "John Arden's Essential Vision: Tragical-Historical-Political." *QJS*, 58 (1972), 307–12.

500 MILLS, John. "Love and Anarchy in *Serjeant Musgrave's Dance.*" *DrS*, 7 (1968–69), 45–51.

501 MORGAN, Edwin. *"Armstrong's Last Goodnight."* *Encore*, 11 (July–Aug. 1964), 47–51.

502 O'CONNELL, Mary B. "Ritual Elements in John Arden's *Serjeant Musgrave's Dance.*" *MD*, 13 (1971), 356–59.

503 PAGE, Malcolm. "The Motives of Pacifists: John Arden's *Serjeant Musgrave's Dance.*" *DrS*, 66 (1967), 66–73.

504 PAGE, Malcolm, and Virginia EVANS. "Approaches to John Arden's *Squire Jonathan.*" *MD*, 13 (1971), 360–65.

505 SHRAPNEL, Susan. "John Arden and the Public Stage." *Cambridge Q*, 4 (1969), 225–36.

506 SKLOOT, Robert. "Spreading the Word: The Meaning of Musgrave's Logic." *ETJ*, 27 (1975), 208–19.

507 TAYLOR, John R. *Anger & After*, **318**, 83–105.*

508 THORNE, Barry. " 'Serjeant Musgrave's Dance': Form and Meaning." *QQ*, 78 (1971), 567–71.

509 TRUSSLER, Simon. *John Arden.* NY: Columbia UP, 1973. (Pamphlet.)†

510 TSCHUDIN, Marcus. *A Writer's Theatre*, **389**, 99–132. (Court Theatre production of *Musgrave.*)

511 WEIAND, Hermann J. *"Serjeant Musgrave's Dance."* In **173**, 14–25.

512 WEISE, Wolf-Dietrich. *Die "Neuen englischen Dramatiker" in ihrem Verhältnis zu Brecht*, **328**, 141–84.

513 WILLIAMS, Raymond. *Drama from Ibsen to Brecht*, **72**, 325–28. (On *Musgrave.*)

514 WORTH, Katharine J. "Avant Garde at the Royal Court Theatre: John Arden and N. F. Simpson." In **90**, 205–14.

Auden, W[ystan] H[ugh] (1907–1973) and Christopher Isherwood (1904–)

515 BLOOMFIELD, B. C., and Edward MENDELSON. *W. H. Auden: A Bibliography, 1924–1969.* 2nd ed. Charlottesville: Univ. of Virginia Pr., 1973.

516 BLAIR, John G. "Dramatic Indirections." *The Poetic Art of W. H. Auden.* Princeton, NJ: Princeton UP, 1965, 96–106.†

517 BRUEHL, William J. *"Polus Naufrangia:* A Key Symbol in *The Ascent of F6." MD,* 10 (1967), 161–64.

518 BUELL, Frederick. *W. H. Auden as a Social Poet.* Ithaca, NY: Cornell UP, 1973, 130–37. (On *Dog Beneath the Skin.*)

519 DONOGHUE, Denis. *"Drama à thèse:* Auden. . . ." *The Third Voice,* **251,** 62–70. (On *Ascent of F6.*)

520 FORSTER, E. M. *"The Ascent of F6." Two Cheers for Democracy.* Lon: Arnold, 1951, 271–73.

521 FULLER, John. "The Plays." In *A Reader's Guide to W. H. Auden.* NY: Farrar, 1970, 77–98.* †

522 GARRETT, John. *"The Dog Beneath the Skin." Criterion,* 14 (1935), 687–90.

523 GERSTENBERGER, Donna. "Poetry and Politics: The Verse Drama of Auden, Isherwood, and Spender." *The Complex Configuration,* **255,** 78–97.

524 HAHNLOSER-INGOLD, Margrit. *Das englische Theater und Bert. Brecht,* **296,** 84–119.

525 HAZARD, Forrest E. *"The Ascent of F6:* A New Interpretation." *Tennessee St in Lit,* 15 (1970), 165–75.

526 HOGGART, Richard. "The Plays with Christopher Isherwood." *Auden: An Introductory Essay.* Lon: Chatto & Windus, 1951, 71–86.

527 HOSKINS, Katharine B. "On the Left: Drama." *Today the Struggle,* **257,** 165–82.*

528 MARKEN, Ronald. "Power and Conflict in 'The Ascent of F6.' " *Discourse,* 7 (1964), 277–82.

528A MENDELSON, Edward. "The Auden-Isherwood Collaboration." *TCL,* 22 (1976), 276-85. (A documentary study.)

529 MITCHELL, Breon. "W. H. Auden and Christopher Isherwood: The 'German Influence.' " *Oxford German St,* 1 (1966), 163–72.

530 MULLIN, Donald. "The 'Decline of the West' as Reflected in Three Modern Plays." *ETJ,* 28 (1976), 363–75. (*Dog Beneath the Skin.*)

531 PRIOR, Moody E. *The Language of Tragedy,* **166,** 367–72.

532 REPLOGLE, Justin. "Auden's Marxism." *PMLA,* 80 (1965), 584–95. (Stresses the plays.)

533 SPEARS, Monroe K. "The Theatre." *The Poetry of W. H. Auden: The Disenchanted Island.* NY: Oxford UP, 1963, 90–105.

534 SPENDER, Stephen. "The Poetic Dramas of W. H. Auden and Christopher Isherwood." *New Writing* (Lon.), 6 (1938), 102–8.

535 VALGEMAE, Mardi. "Auden's Collaboration with Isherwood on *The Dog Beneath the Skin." Huntington Lib Q,* 31 (1968), 373–83.

536 WILLIAMS, Raymond. *Drama from Ibsen to Brecht*, **72**, 199–206.

537 WRIGHT, George T. "Plain Speech." *W. H. Auden*. NY: Twayne, 1969, 62–69.

Barrie, James M[atthew] (1860–1937)

538 BARRIE, J. M. *The Plays*, ed. A. E. Wilson. Definitive ed., rev. Lon: Hodder & Stoughton, 1942.

539 BARRIE, J. M. *Ibsen's Ghost: A Play in One Act*, ed. Penelope Griffin, pref. by Roger L. Green. Lon: C. Woolf, 1975. (From manuscripts.)

540 BARRIE, J. M. *Letters*, ed. Viola Meynell. NY: Scribner's, 1947.

541 BARRIE, J. M. *M'Connachie and J. M. B.: Speeches by J. M. Barrie*. Lon: Davies, 1938.

542 CUTLER, Bradley D. *Sir James M. Barrie: A Bibliography*. . . . NY: Greenberg, 1931.

543 ALSTON, Edwin F. "James Barrie's 'M'Connachie'—His 'Writing Half.' " *American Imago*, 29 (1972), 257–77.

544 BUTLER, Pierce. "Barrie: The Playwright." *SAQ*, 31 (1932), 222–41.

545 CHILD, Harold. "J. M. Barrie as Dramatist." *Essays and Reflections*, ed. S. C. Roberts. Cambridge, Eng.: Univ. Pr., 1948, 115–23.

546 DICKINSON, Thomas H. *The Contemporary Drama of England*, **148**, 135–56.

547 DUNBAR, Janet. *J. M. Barrie: The Man Behind the Image*. Bos: Houghton, 1970.

548 ELLEHAUGE, Martin O. M. *Striking Figures Among Modern English Dramatists*, **215**, 130–46.

549 GEDULD, Harry M. *Sir James Barrie*. NY: Twayne, 1971.*

550 GREEN, Roger L. *J. M. Barrie*. NY: Walck, 1961.

551 LAMACCHIA, Grace A. "Textual Variations for Act IV of *The Admirable Crichton*." *MD*, 12 (1970), 408–18.

552 McGRAW, William R. "Barrie and the Critics." *St in Scottish Lit*, 1 (1963), 111–30.*

553 McGRAW, William R. "J. M. Barrie's Concept of Dramatic Action." *MD*, 5 (1962), 133–41.

554 MACKAIL, Denis. *The Story of J. M. B.: A Biography*. Lon: Davies, 1941. (Authorized biography largely superseded by **547**.)

555 PHELPS, William L. "J. M. Barrie." *Essays on Modern Dramatists*. NY: Macmillan, 1921, 1–66.

556 ROY, James A. *James Matthew Barrie: An Appreciation*. Lon: Jarrolds, 1937.

557 WALBROOK, Henry M. *J. M. Barrie and the Theatre*. Lon: White, 1922.

558 WILLIAMS, David P. "Hook and Ahab: Barrie's Strange Satire on Melville." *PMLA*, 80 (1965), 483–88. (*Peter Pan*.)

Beckett, Samuel
(1906–)

9 BECKETT, Samuel. *I Can't Go on, I'll Go on: A Selection from Samuel Beckett's Work,* ed. with intro. by Richard W. Seaver. NY: Grove, 1976. (620-page collection.)

0 BECKETT, Samuel, and Tom F. DRIVER. "Beckett by the Madeleine." *Columbia Univ Forum,* 4 (Summer 1961), 21–25; repr. in *Drama in the Modern World: Plays and Essays,* ed. Samuel A. Weiss (Bos: Heath, 1964),† 505–8. (Interview with important theoretical statements.)

·1 BECKETT, Samuel. "Beckett's Letters on *Endgame* [to Alan Schneider]." In *The Village Voice Reader,* ed. Daniel Wolf and Edwin Fancher. Garden City, NY: Doubleday, 1962, 182–86.

2 BECKETT, Samuel, and Georges DUTHUIT. "Three Dialogues." In **611**, 16–22. (Aesthetic pronouncements.)

3 FEDERMAN, Raymond, and John FLETCHER. *Samuel Beckett, His Works and His Critics: An Essay in Bibliography.* Berkeley: Univ. of California Pr., 1970. (See also James Mays, "Samuel Beckett Bibliography: Comments and Corrections," *IUR,* 2 [1972], 189–208.)

4 BRYER, Jackson R. "Samuel Beckett: A Checklist of Criticism." In **638**, 219–59. (Valuable supplement to **563** because it analyzes books and articles by the works they treat.)

5 HOY, Peter C., ed. *Calepins de bibliographie, No. 2: Samuel Beckett,* comp. R. J. Davis, J. R. Bryer, and M. J. Friedman; rev. P. C. Hoy. Paris: Lettres Modernes, Minard, 1972.

6 ADMUSSEN, Richard L. "The Manuscripts of Beckett's *Play.*" *MD,* 16 (1973), 23–27.

7 ADORNO, Theodor W. "Towards an Understanding of *Endgame.*" In **604**, 82–114.

8 ALPAUGH, David J. "*Embers* and the Sea: Beckettian Intimations of Mortality." *MD,* 16 (1973), 317–28.

9 ALPAUGH, David J. "Negative Definition in Samuel Beckett's *Happy Days.*" *TCL,* 11 (1966), 202–10.

0 ALVAREZ, Alfred. *Samuel Beckett.* NY: Viking, 1973. (Introductory.)†

1 ANDERS, Günther. "Being Without Time: On Beckett's Play *Waiting for Godot.*" In **631**, 140–51.

2 ANDERSON, Irmgard Z. "Beckett's 'Tabernacle' in *Fin de partie.*" *Romance Notes,* 14 (1973), 417–20.

3 ASHMORE, Jerome. "Philosophical Aspects of *Godot.*" *Sym,* 16 (1962), 296–306.

4 ASMUS, Walter D. "Beckett Directs *Godot.*" *ThQ,* 5, No. 19 (1975), 19–26.

5 ATKINS, Anselm. "Lucky's Speech in Beckett's *Waiting for Godot:* A Punctuated Sense-Line Arrangement." *ETJ,* 19 (1967), 426–32.

6 AVIGAL, Shoshana. "Beckett's *Play:* The Circular Line of Existence." *MD,* 18 (1975), 251–58.

SAMUEL BECKETT

BEAUSANG, Michael. "Myth and Tragi-Comedy in Beckett's *Happy Days* *Mosaic,* 5 (Fall 1971), 59–77.

578 *Beckett at 60.* Lon: Calder & Boyars, 1967. (Includes comments by Pint Arrabal, Schneider, and others.)†

579 BEDIENT, Calvin. "Beckett and the Drama of Gravity." *SR,* 78 (197 143–55.

580 BENTLEY, Eric. "The Talent of Samuel Beckett [a 1956 review]" and "Pc script 1967." In **611**, 59–66.

581 BERMEL, Albert. "Hero and Heroine as Topographical Features." *C(tradictory Characters,* **43**, 159–84. (Treats *Krapp's Last Tape* as well *Happy Days*.)

582 BLAU, Herbert. *The Impossible Theater: A Manifesto.* NY: Macmilla 1964, 228–51. (Director's point of view on *Godot* and *Endgame*.)†

583 BRADBROOK, Muriel C. *"En attendant Godot." Literature in Actic Studies in Continental and Commonwealth Society.* NY: Barnes & Nob 1972, 13–33.

584 BRATER, Enoch. "The 'Absurd' Actor in the Theatre of Samuel Becket *ETJ,* 27 (1975), 197–207.

585 BRATER, Enoch. "Beckett, Ionesco, and the Tradition of Tragicomed) *College Lit,* 1 (Spring 1974), 113–27.

586 BRATER, Enoch. "The Empty Can: Samuel Beckett and Andy Warho *JML,* 3 (1974), 1255–64. (Stresses *Endgame*.)

587 BRATER, Enoch. "The 'I' in Beckett's *Not I*." *TCL,* 20 (1974), 189–20

588 BREUER, Rolf. "The Solution as Problem: Beckett's *Waiting for Godo MD,* 19 (1976), 225–36.

589 BRIDEL, Yves. "Sur le temps et l'espace dans le théâtre de S. Beckett: *attendant Godot–Oh les beaux jours." Études de Lettres,* 6 (April–June 197 59–73.

590 BRINK, A. W. "Universality in Samuel Beckett's *Endgame*." *QQ,* 78 (197 191–207.

591 BROOKS, Curtis M. "The Mythic Pattern in *Waiting for Godot*." *MD* (1966), 292–99.

592 BROWN, John R. "Mr. Beckett's Shakespeare." *CritQ,* 5 (1963), 310–2

593 BROWN, John R. *Theatre Language,* **281**, 238–47. (On *Godot*.)

594 BUSI, Frederick. "Creative Self-Deception in the Drama of Samuel Becket *Research St* (Wash.), 42 (1974), 153–60. (On *Godot*.)

595 BUSI, Frederick. "Joycean Echoes in *Waiting for Godot*." *Research* (Wash.), 43 (1975), 71–87.

596 BUTLER, Harry L. "Balzac and Godeau, Beckett and Godot: A Curi Parallel." *Romance Notes,* 3 (1962), 13–17.

597 CASE, Sue-Ellen. "Image and Godot." In **611**, 155–59.

598 CAVELL, Stanley. "Ending the Waiting Game: A Reading of Beckett's *E game." Must We Mean What We Say?* NY: Scribner's, 1969, 115–62.

599 CHADWICK, C. *"Waiting for Godot:* A Logical Approach." *Sym,* 14 (19(252–57.

600 CHAMBERS, Ross. "An Approach to *Endgame*." In **604**, 71–81.

601 CHAMBERS, Ross. "Beckett's Brinkmanship." In **631**, 152–68.

602 CHAMPIGNY, Robert. "Interprétation de *En attendant Godot*." *PMLA* (1960), 329–31; tr. in **611**, 137–44.

603 CHASE, N. C. "Images of Man: *Le Malentendu* and *En attendant Godot*." *WSCL*, 7 (1966), 295–302.

604 CHEVIGNY, Bell G., ed. *Twentieth Century Interpretations of Endgame: A Collection of Critical Essays*. Englewood Cliffs, NJ: Prentice-Hall, 1969.* †

605 CHIARI, Joseph. *Landmarks of Contemporary Drama*, **46**, 68–80. (Stresses *Godot*.)

606 CLEVELAND, Louise O. "Trials in the Soundscape: The Radio Plays of Samuel Beckett." *MD*, 11 (1968), 267–82.

607 COCKERHAM, Harry. "Bilingual Playwright." In *Beckett the Shape Changer*, **742**, 141–59.

608 COE, Richard N. *Samuel Beckett*. NY: Grove, 1964.†

609 COHEN, Robert S. "Parallels and the Possibility of Influence Between Simone Weil's *Waiting for God* and Samuel Beckett's *Waiting for Godot*." *MD*, 6 (1964), 425–36.

610 COHN, Ruby. "The Beginning of *Endgame*." *MD*, 9 (1966), 319–23. (Describes the two-act version.)

611 COHN, Ruby, ed. *Casebook on Waiting for Godot*. NY: Grove, 1967.* †

612 COHN, Ruby. "Grace Notes on Beckett's Environments." In *Break Out!*, **380**, 124–33.

613 COHN, Ruby. "The Laughter of Sad Sam Beckett." In **638**, 185–97. (Varieties of laughter in the plays.)

614 COHN, Ruby. "Plays Many Parts." *Back to Beckett*. Princeton, NJ: Princeton UP, 1973, 122–219.*

615 COHN, Ruby. *Samuel Beckett: The Comic Gamut*. New Brunswick, NJ: Rutgers UP, 1962, esp. 208–59.*

616 COHN, Ruby. "Shakespearean Embers in Beckett." *Modern Shakespeare Offshoots*, **48**, 375–88.

617 COHN, Ruby. "Tempest in an Endgame." *Sym*, 19 (1965), 328–34.

618 CORMIER, Ramona, and Janis L. PALLISTER. *Waiting for Death: The Philosophical Significance of Beckett's En attendant Godot*. University: Univ. of Alabama Pr., 1976.

619 DOHERTY, Francis. *Samuel Beckett*. Lon: Hutchinson, 1971. (Introductory.)†

620 DUBOIS, Jacques. "Beckett and Ionesco: The Tragic Awareness of Pascal and the Ironic Awareness of Flaubert," tr. Ruby Cohn. *MD*, 9 (1966), 283–91. (Stresses *Godot*.)

621 DUCKWORTH, Colin. *Angels of Darkness: Dramatic Effect in Samuel Beckett, with Special Reference to Eugene Ionesco*. Lon: Allen & Unwin, 1972.†

622 DUCKWORTH, Colin. "Introduction." *En attendant Godot*, ed. Colin Duckworth. Lon: Harrap, 1966, xvii–cxxxi; partly repr. in **611**, 89–100. (Detailed textual and critical study.)*

623 DUKORE, Bernard F. "Beckett's Play, *Play*." *ETJ*, 17 (1965), 19–23.

624 DUKORE, Bernard F. "Gogo, Didi, and the Absent Godot." *DrS*, 1 (1962), 301–7; see also Thomas B. Markus's response, "Controversy," *DrS*, 2 (1963), 360–63, and Dukore's retort, "A Non-Interpretation of *Godot*," *DrS*, 3 (1963), 117–19.

625 DUKORE, Bernard F. "*Krapp's Last Tape* as Tragicomedy." *MD*, 15 (1973), 351–54.

626 DUKORE, Bernard F. "The *Other* Pair in *Waiting for Godot*." *DrS*, 7 (1968–69), 133–37.

SAMUEL BECKETT

627 EASTHOPE, Anthony. "Hamm, Clov, and Dramatic Method in *Endgame*." *MD*, 10 (1968), 424–33; repr. in **604**, 61–70.

628 EASTMAN, Richard M. "Samuel Beckett and *Happy Days*." *MD*, 6 (1964), 417–24.

629 EASTMAN, Richard M. "The Strategy of Samuel Beckett's *Endgame*." *MD*, 2 (1959), 36–44.

630 ELIOPULOS, James. *Samuel Beckett's Dramatic Language*. The Hague: Mouton, 1975. (Linguistic analysis.)

631 ESSLIN, Martin, ed. *Samuel Beckett: A Collection of Critical Essays*. Englewood Cliffs, NJ: Prentice-Hall, 1965.* †

632 ESSLIN, Martin. "Samuel Beckett: The Search for the Self." *The Theatre of the Absurd*, **54**, 11–65.*

633 ESSLIN, Martin. "Voices, Patterns, Voices: Samuel Beckett's Later Plays." *Gambit*, 7, No. 28 (1976), 93–99.

634 FLETCHER, John. "The Art of the Dramatist." *Samuel Beckett's Art*. Lon: Chatto & Windus, 1967, 41–82.

635 FLETCHER, John, and John SPURLING. *Beckett: A Study of His Plays*. NY: Hill & Wang, 1972.* †

636 FLETCHER, John, ed. *Waiting for Godot, with an Afterword and Notes*. Lon: Faber, 1971.†

637 FRASER, G. S. "*Waiting for Godot*." In **611**, 133–37; also in **58**, 318–25.

638 FRIEDMAN, Melvin J., ed. *Samuel Beckett Now: Critical Approaches to His Novels, Poetry, and Plays*. Chicago: Univ. of Chicago Pr., 1970. (Based on a 1964 French volume of essays.)

639 FRISCH, Jack E. "*Endgame*: A Play as Poem." *DrS*, 3 (1963), 257–63.

640 GASKELL, Ronald. *Drama and Reality*, **57**, 147–54. (On *Endgame*.)

641 GASSNER, John. "*Avant-Garde*: Real or Fancied?" *Dramatic Soundings*, **104**, 683–95.

642 GASSNER, John. "Beckett: *Waiting for Godot*" and "Beckett's *Endgame* and Symbolism." *Theatre at the Crossroads: Plays and Playwrights of the Mid-Century American Stage*. NY: Holt, 1960, 252–61.

643 GILBERT, Sandra M. " 'All the Dead Voices': A Study of *Krapp's Last Tape*." *DrS*, 6 (1968), 244–57.

644 GILMAN, Richard. *The Making of Modern Drama: A Study of Büchner, Ibsen, Strindberg, Chekhov, Pirandello, Brecht, Beckett, Handke*. NY: Farrar, 1974, 234–66.*

645 GOLDMAN, Richard M. "*Endgame* and Its Scorekeepers." In **604**, 33–39.

646 GREGORY, Horace. "Beckett's Dying Gladiators." *The Dying Gladiators and Other Essays*. NY: Grove, 1961, 165–76.

647 GROSSVOGEL, David I. *Four Playwrights and a Postscript: Brecht, Ionesco, Beckett, Genet*. Ithaca, NY: Cornell UP, 1962, 87–131. (Alternative title: *Blasphemers*.)* †

648 GUICHARNAUD, Jacques, with June BECKELMAN. "Existence Onstage: Samuel Beckett." *Modern French Theatre from Giraudoux to Genet*. Rev. ed. New Haven, CT: Yale UP, 1967, 230–58.* †

649 HALLORAN, Stephen M. "The Anti-Aesthetics of *Waiting for Godot*." *CentR*, 16 (1972), 69–81.

650 HAMILTON, Kenneth. "Negative Salvation in Samuel Beckett." *QQ*, 69 (1962), 102–11. (Stresses *Godot*.)

31

SAMUEL BECKETT

651 HARVEY, Lawrence E. "Art and the Existential in *En attendant Godot*." *PMLA*, 75 (1960), 137–46; abridged in **611**, 144–54.

652 HASSAN, Ihab. "Acts Without Words." *The Literature of Silence: Henry Miller and Samuel Beckett*. NY: Knopf, 1967, 174–200.†

653 HAYWARD, Susan. "The Use of Refrain in Beckett's Plays." *Language and Style*, 8 (1975), 284–92.

654 HOFFMAN, Frederick J. *Samuel Beckett: The Language of Self*. Carbondale: Southern Illinois UP, 1962, 138–59.†

655 HOOKER, Ward. "Irony and Absurdity in the Avant-Garde Theatre." *KR*, 22 (1960), 436–54; repr. in **103**, 335–48; see also Martin Esslin's response, "The Absurdity of the Absurd," *KR*, 22 (1960), 670–73.

656 HOY, Cyrus. *The Hyacinth Room: An Investigation into the Nature of Comedy, Tragedy, & Tragicomedy*. NY: Knopf, 1964, 254–64.†

657 HUBERT, Renée R. "Beckett's *Play* Between Poetry and Performance." *MD*, 9 (1966), 339–46.

658 HUBERT, Renée R. "The Couple and the Performance in Samuel Beckett's Plays." *L'Esprit Créateur*, 2 (1962), 175–80.

659 ISER, Wolfgang. "Samuel Beckett's Dramatic Language." *MD*, 9 (1966), 251–59.

660 JACOBSEN, Josephine, and William R. MUELLER. *The Testament of Samuel Beckett*. NY: Hill & Wang, 1964.†

661 JOHNSTON, Denis. "Waiting with Beckett." *Irish Writing*, No. 34 (Spring 1956), 23–35.

662 JONES, Louisa. "Narrative Salvation in *Waiting for Godot*." *MD*, 17 (1974), 179–88.

663 *Journal of Beckett Studies*, 1–. (Biannual first publ. Dec. 1976.)

664 KENNEDY, Andrew K. *Six Dramatists in Search of a Language*, **158**, 130–64.*

665 KENNER, Hugh. *A Reader's Guide to Samuel Beckett*. NY: Farrar, 1973.†

666 KENNER, Hugh. *Samuel Beckett: A Critical Study*. Rev. ed. Berkeley: Univ. of California Pr., 1968.* †

667 KERN, Edith. "Beckett and the Spirit of the Commedia dell'Arte." *MD*, 9 (1966), 260–67. (In *Godot*.)

668 KERN, Edith. "Beckett's Knight of Infinite Resignation." *YFS*, 29 (1962), 49–56. (In *Happy Days*.)

669 KERN, Edith. "Drama Stripped for Inaction: Beckett's *Godot*." *YFS*, 14 (1954–55), 41–47.

670 KERN, Edith. "Structure in Beckett's Theatre." *YFS*, 46 (1971), 17–27.

671 KILLINGER, John. *World in Collapse*, **60**, 16–26.

672 KNAPP, Robert S. "Samuel Beckett's Allegory of the Uncreating Word." *Mosaic*, 6 (Winter 1973), 71–83.

673 KNOWLSON, James. "Beckett and John Millington Synge." *Gambit*, 7, No. 28 (1976), 65–81.

674 KNOWLSON, James. *Light and Darkness in the Theatre of Samuel Beckett*. Lon: Turret Books, 1972. (Pamphlet.)

675 KOLVE, V. A. "Religious Language in *Waiting for Godot*." *CentR*, 11 (1967), 102–27.

676 KOTT, Jan. "*King Lear* or *Endgame*." *Shakespeare Our Contemporary*, tr.

Boleslaw Taborski. Lon: Methuen, 1964, 101–37;† also in *Evergreen Rev*, 33 (Aug.–Sept. 1964), 53–65.*

677 KOTT, Jan. "A Note on Beckett's Realism." *Theatre Notebook*, 110, 241–45. (Stresses *Happy Days*.)

678 LAHR, John. "The Language of Silence." *Up Against the Fourth Wall*, 112, 50–77.

679 LAMONT, Rosette. "Beckett's Metaphysics of Choiceless Awareness." In 638, 199–217. (Stresses *Godot*.)

680 LAMONT, Rosette. "Death and Tragicomedy: Three Plays of the New Theatre." *MR*, 6 (1965), 381–402. (Part on *Happy Days*.)

681 LAMONT, Rosette. "The Metaphysical Farce: Beckett and Ionesco." *FR*, 32 (1959), 319–28. (Discusses *Endgame*.)

682 LAVIELLE, Émile. *"En attendant Godot," de Beckett*. Paris: Hachette, 1972.

683 LEVENTHAL, A. J. "Samuel Beckett: About Him and About." *Hermathena*, No. 114 (1972), 5–22.

684 LOWENKRON, David H. "A Case for 'The Tragicall Historie of Hamm.' " *ArQ*, 30 (1974), 217–28.

685 LUMLEY, Frederick. "The Case Against Beckett." *New Trends in 20th Century Drama*, 161, 202–8.

686 LYONS, Charles R. "Beckett's *Endgame*: An Anti-Myth of Creation." *MD*, 7 (1964), 204–9.

687 LYONS, Charles R. "Beckett's Major Plays and the Trilogy." *CoD*, 5 (1971–72), 254–68.

688 LYONS, Charles R. "Some Analogies Between the Epic Brecht and the Absurdist Beckett." *CoD*, 1 (1967–68), 297–304. (Compares *Mother Courage* and *Happy Days*.)

689 MacNEICE, Louis. *Varieties of Parable*. Cambridge, Eng.: Univ. Pr., 1965, 117–20. (On *Godot*.)

690 MAILER, Norman. "A Public Notice on *Waiting for Godot*." *Advertisements for Myself*. NY: Putnam, 1959, 320–25; repr. in 611, 69–74. (His second thoughts on the play.)

691 MATTHEWS, Honor. "Samuel Beckett: The Ambiguous Journey." *The Hard Journey: The Myth of Man's Rebirth*. Lon: Chatto & Windus, 1968, 139–68.

692 MAYOUX, Jean J. "The Theatre of Samuel Beckett." *Perspective*, 11 (1959), 142–55.

693 MÉLÈSE, Pierre. *Samuel Beckett*. Paris: Seghers, 1966. (Valuable detailed account of the plays and their performances in France.)*

694 MERCIER, Vivian. "Beckett's Anglo-Irish Stage Dialects." *JJQ*, 8 (1971), 311–17.

695 METMAN, Eva. "Reflections on Samuel Beckett's Plays." In 631, 117–39. (1960 article from a psychological journal.)

696 MONTGOMERY, Niall. "No Symbols Where None Intended." *New World Writing*, 5 (1954), 324–37.

697 MOORE, John R. "A Farewell to Something." *TDR*, 5 (Sept. 1960), 49–60. (On *Godot*.)

698 MUELLER, William R., and Josephine JACOBSEN. "Samuel Beckett's Long Saturday: To Wait or Not to Wait?" In 117, 76–97.

699 OBERG, Arthur K. *"Krapp's Last Tape* and the Proustian Vision." *MD*, 9 (1966), 333–38.

700 PACKARD, William. "Poetry in the Theatre. . . ." *Trace*, No. 66 (1967), 447–55.

701 PARKIN, Andrew. "Monologue into Monodrama: Aspects of Samuel Beckett's Plays." *Eire*, 9 (Winter 1974), 32–41.

702 PILLING, John. *Samuel Beckett*. Lon: Routledge & K. Paul, 1976.

703 POUNTNEY, Rosemary. "Samuel Beckett's Interest in Form: Structural Patterning in *Play*." *MD*, 19 (1976), 237–44.

704 PRONKO, Leonard C. *Avant-Garde: The Experimental Theater in France*. Berkeley: Univ. of California Pr., 1962, 22–58.†

705 RADKE, Judith J. "The Theater of Samuel Beckett: 'Une durée à animer.' " *YFS*, 29 (1962), 57–64.

706 RECHTIEN, John. "Time and Eternity Meet in the Present." *TSLL*, 6 (1964), 5–21. (On *Godot*.)

707 REID, Alec. *All I Can Manage, More Than I Could: An Approach to the Plays of Samuel Beckett*. Dub: Dolmen, 1968.†

708 REITER, Seymour. "Submerged Structure in Beckett's *Waiting for Godot*." *World Theater: The Structure and Meaning of Drama*. NY: Horizon, 1973, 214–28; also in *Cos*, 3 (1972), 181–96.

709 REXROTH, Kenneth. "Samuel Beckett and the Importance of Waiting." *Bird in the Bush: Obvious Essays*. NY: New Directions, 1959, 75–85.

710 RHODES, S. A. "From Godeau to Godot." *FR*, 36 (1963), 260–65.

711 ROBBE-GRILLET, Alain. "Samuel Beckett, or 'Presence' on the Stage." *For a New Novel: Essays on Fiction*, tr. Richard Howard. NY: Grove, 1965, 111–25; repr. in **611**, 108–16. (See also Bruce Morrissette, "Robbe-Grillet as a Critic of Samuel Beckett," in **638**, 59–71.)*

712 ROBINSON, Michael. "The Theatre." *The Long Sonata of the Dead: A Study of Samuel Beckett*. NY: Grove, 1970, 229–97.* †

713 ROSEN, Steven J. *Samuel Beckett and the Pessimistic Tradition*. New Brunswick, NJ: Rutgers UP, 1976.

714 SASTRE, Alfonso. "Seven Notes on *Waiting for Godot*," tr. Leonard C. Pronko. In **611**, 101–7.

715 SCHECHNER, Richard. "There's Lots of Time in *Godot*." *Public Domain: Essays on the Theatre*. Indianapolis, IN: Bobbs-Merrill, 1969, 109–19; repr. in **611**, 175–87. (A 1966 *MD* essay.)*

716 SCHNEIDER, Alan. "Waiting for Beckett: A Personal Chronicle." *Chelsea Rev*, 2 (Sept. 1958), 3–20; abridged in **604**, 14–21.

717 SCHOELL, Konrad. "The Chain and the Circle: A Structural Comparison of *Waiting for Godot* and *Endgame*." *MD*, 11 (1968), 48–53.

718 SCOTT, Nathan A. *Samuel Beckett*. NY: Hillary House, 1965, 80–123.

719 SERREAU, Geneviève. *Histoire du "Nouveau Théâtre."* Paris: Gallimard, 1966, 83–116.

720 SHEEDY, John J. "The Comic Apocalypse of King Hamm." *MD*, 9 (1966), 310–18.

721 SHEEDY, John J. "The Net [in *Godot*]." In **611**, 159–66.

722 SIMPSON, Alan. *Beckett and Behan and a Theatre in Dublin*, **473**.

723 SMITH, H. A. "Dipsychus Among the Shadows." In **100**, 156–63.

724 SMITH, Stephani P. "Between Pozzo and Godot: Existence as Dilemma." *FR*, 47 (1974), 889–903.

725 STEMPEL, Daniel. "History Electrified into Anagogy: A Reading of *Waiting for Godot*." *ConL*, 17 (1976), 263–78.

726 STRAUSS, Walter A. "Dante's Belacqua and Beckett's Tramps." *CL*, 11 (1959), 250–61.

727 STYAN, J. L. "Beckett and the Absurd" and " 'Waiting for Godot': An Analytic Note on Performance." *The Dark Comedy*, **70**, 217–34.*

728 SUVIN, Darko. "Beckett's Purgatory of the Individual, or the 3 Laws of Thermodynamics: Notes for an Incamination Towards a Presubluminary Exagmination Round Beckett's Factification." *TDR*, 11 (Summer 1967), 23–36; repr. in **611**, 121–32.

729 SZANTO, George H. "Samuel Beckett: Dramatic Possibilities." *MR*, 15 (1974), 735–61.*

730 TODD, Robert E. "Proust and Redemption in *Waiting for Godot*." *MD*, 10 (1967), 175–81.

731 TORRANCE, Robert M. "Modes of Being and Time in the World of *Godot*." *MLQ*, 28 (1967), 77–95.

732 TROUSDALE, Marion. "Dramatic Form: The Example of *Godot*." *MD*, 11 (1968), 1–9.

733 WALKER, Roy. "Samuel Beckett's Double Bill: Love, Chess and Death." *TC*, 164 (1958), 533–44. (On *Endgame* and *Krapp*.)

734 WARNER, Francis. "The Absence of Nationalism in the Work of Samuel Beckett." In **409**, 179–204.

735 WEALES, Gerald. "The Language of *Endgame*." *TDR*, 6 (June 1962), 107–17.

736 WEBB, Eugene. *The Plays of Samuel Beckett*. Lon: Owen, 1972.* †

737 WEBNER, Hélène L. "*Waiting for Godot* and the New Theology." *Ren*, 21 (1968), 3–9, 31.

738 WELLWARTH, George E. "Samuel Beckett: Life in the Void." *The Theater of Protest and Paradox*, **329**, 41–56.

739 WHITAKER, Thomas R. "Notes on Playing the Player." *CentR*, 16 (1972), 1–22. (Part on *Happy Days*.)

740 WILCHER, Robert. " 'What's It Meant to Mean?': An Approach to Beckett's Theatre." *CritQ*, 18 (1976), 9–37.

741 WILLIAMS, Raymond. *Drama from Ibsen to Brecht*, **72**, 299–305. (On *Godot*.)

742 WORTH, Katharine J. "The Space and the Sound in Beckett's Theatre." In *Beckett the Shape Changer*, ed. K. J. Worth. Lon: Routledge & K. Paul, 1975, 185–218.

743 WORTH, Katharine J. "Yeats and the French Drama." *MD*, 8 (1966), 382–91. (Influences on *Happy Days*.)

744 ZILLIACUS, Clas. "Samuel Beckett's *Embers*: 'A Matter of Fundamental Sounds.' " *MD*, 13 (1970), 216–25.

745 ZILLIACUS, Clas. "Three Times *Godot*: Beckett, Brecht, Bulatovic." *CoD*, 4 (1970), 3–17.

Behan, Brendan
(1923–1964)

746 BEHAN, Brendan. *Borstal Boy*. Lon: Hutchinson, 1958.†

747 BEHAN, Brendan. *Confessions of an Irish Rebel*. Lon: Hutchinson, 1965.†

748 ARMSTRONG, William A. "The Irish Point of View: The Plays of Sean O'Casey, Brendan Behan, and Thomas Murphy." In **90**, 93–98 on Behan.

749 BOREL, Françoise. "Alas, Poor Brendan!" In **412**, 119–36.

750 BOYLE, Ted E. *Brendan Behan*. NY: Twayne, 1969.

751 GERDES, Peter R. *The Major Works of Brendan Behan*. Bern: Lang, 1973.

752 HOGAN, Robert. "The Short Happy World of Brendan Behan." *After the Irish Renaissance*, **443**, 198–207.

753 JEFFS, Rae. *Brendan Behan, Man and Showman*. Lon: Hutchinson, 1966. (Memoirs of Behan from 1957 to his death.)

754 KLEINSTÜCK, Johannes. "Brendan Behan's 'The Hostage.' " *E&S*, 24 (1971), 69–83.

755 LEVITT, Paul M. "Hostages to History: Title as Dramatic Metaphor in 'The Hostage.' " *NS*, 5 (1975), 401–6.

756 McCANN, Sean, ed. *The World of Brendan Behan*. Lon: New Eng. Lib., 1965. (Memoirs and impressions.)

757 MacINNES, Colin. "The Writings of Brendan Behan." *LonM*, 2 (Aug. 1962), 53–61.

758 McMAHON, Seán. "*The Quare Fellow*." *Eire*, 4 (Winter 1969), 143–57.

759 MARTIN, Augustine. "Brendan Behan." *Threshold*, No. 18 (1963), 22–28. (Behan as satirical dramatist.)

760 O'CONNOR, Ulick. *Brendan Behan*. Lon: Hamilton, 1970. (Detailed biography. For material on plays, see especially chapters 15–17.)

761 PORTER, Raymond J. *Brendan Behan*. NY: Columbia UP, 1973. (Pamphlet.)†

762 SIMPSON, Alan. *Beckett and Behan and a Theatre in Dublin*, **473**.

763 TAYLOR, John R. *Anger & After*, **318**, 123–30.

764 TRACY, Robert. "Ireland: The Patriot Game," **415**, 44–48. (On Behan.)

765 WALL, Richard. "*An Giall* and *The Hostage* Compared." *MD*, 18 (1975), 165–72.

766 WICKSTROM, Gordon M. "The Heroic Dimension in Brendan Behan's *The Hostage*." *ETJ*, 22 (1970), 406–11.

Bolt, Robert
(1924–)

767 BOLT, Robert. "English Theatre Today: The Importance of Shape." *ITA*, 3 (1958), 140–45.

768 BOLT, Robert, and Richard A. DUPREY. "Interview with Robert Bolt." *CathW*, 195 (1962), 364–69.

769 ANDEREGG, Michael A. "A Myth for All Seasons: Thomas More." *Colorado Q*, 23 (1975), 293–306. (Play and film.)

770 ATKINS, Anselm. "Robert Bolt: Self, Shadow, and the Theater of Recognition." *MD*, 10 (1967), 182–88.

771 BARNETT, Gene A. "The Theatre of Robert Bolt." *DR*, 48 (1968), 13–23.

772 FOSBERY, M. W. "*A Man for All Seasons.*" *Eng St in Africa*, 6 (1963), 164–72.

773 HAYMAN, Ronald. *Robert Bolt*. Lon: Heinemann Educ., 1969. (Includes interviews.)†

774 McELRATH, Joseph. "The Metaphoric Structure of *A Man for All Seasons.*" *MD*, 14 (1971), 84–92.

775 REYNOLDS, E. E. "The Significance of *A Man for All Seasons.*" *Moreana*, No. 23 (1969), 34–39.

776 TEES, Arthur T. "The Place of the Common Man: Robert Bolt: *A Man for All Seasons.*" *Univ Rev*, 36 (1969), 67–71.

777 TREWIN, John C. "Two Morality Playwrights: Robert Bolt and John Whiting." In **90**, 119–27.

778 TYNAN, Kenneth. *Tynan Right & Left: Plays, Films, People, Places and Events*. NY: Atheneum, 1967, pp. 26–32. (Review of *Seasons*, with retort by Bolt and reply by Tynan.)

Bond, Edward
(1935–)

779 BOND, Edward. "A Discussion with Edward Bond." *Gambit*, 5, No. 17 (1970), 5–38.

780 BOND, Edward. "Drama and the Dialectics of Violence." *ThQ*, 2 (Jan.–March 1972), 4–14. (Interview.)

781 BOND, Edward. "Edward Bond: An Interview by Giles Gordon." *TrR*, No. 22 (1966), 7–15; repr. in **114**, 125–36.

782 ARNOLD, Arthur. "Lines of Development in Bond's Plays." *ThQ*, 2 (Jan.–March 1972), 15–19. (Retort by Bond in following issue, p. 105.)

783 BABULA, William. "Scene Thirteen of Bond's *Saved.*" *MD*, 15 (1972), 147–49.

784 BARTH, Adolf K. H. "The Aggressive 'Theatrum Mundi' of Edward Bond: *Narrow Road to the Deep North.*" *MD*, 18 (1975), 189–200.

785 COHN, Ruby. *Modern Shakespeare Offshoots*, **48**, 254–66. (On *Lear*.)

786 DURBACH, Errol. "Herod in the Welfare State: *Kindermord* in the Plays of Edward Bond." *ETJ*, 27 (1975), 480–87. (*Saved* and *Narrow Road*.)

787 ESSLIN, Martin. "Edward Bond's Three Plays." *Brief Chronicles*, **102**, 174–80.

788 OPPEL, Horst, and Sandra CHRISTENSON. *Edward Bond's Lear and Shakespeare's King Lear*. Wiesbaden: Steiner, 1974. (42 pp.)

789 PASQUIER, Marie C. "La Place d'Edward Bond dans le nouveau théâtre anglais" and "Edward Bond: Cohérence naissante d'une oeuvre." *Cahiers de la Compagnie Madeleine Renaud-Jean Louis Barrault*, 74 (1970), 21–57.

790 SCHARINE, Richard. *The Plays of Edward Bond*. Lewisburg, PA: Bucknell UP, 1975.*

791 TAYLOR, John R. *The Second Wave*, **319**, 77–93.

792 TRUSSLER, Simon. *Edward Bond*. Harlow: Longman for the British Council, 1976. (Pamphlet.)†

792A WOLFENSPERGER, Peter. *Edward Bond: Dialektik des Weltbildes und dramatische Gestaltung*. Bern: Francke, 1976.

793 WORTHEN, John. "Endings and Beginnings: Edward Bond and the Shock of Recognition." *ETJ*, 27 (1975), 466–79.

Bridie, James (pseud. of Osborne Henry Mavor) (1888–1951)

794 BRIDIE, James. *One Way of Living*. Lon: Constable, 1939.

795 BRIDIE, James. *Some Talk of Alexander*. Lon: Methuen, 1926. (With the above volume, Bridie's autobiography.)

796 BRIDIE, James. *Tedious and Brief*. Lon: Constable, 1945. (Essays, lectures, and dramatic fragments.)

797 BANNISTER, Winifred. *James Bridie and His Theatre*. Lon: Rockliff, 1955.

798 ELLIOT, Walter. "Bridie's Last Play." In *The Baikie Charivari; or, The Seven Prophets: A Miracle Play*. Lon: Constable, 1953, v-xii.

799 GERBER, Ursula. *James Bridies Dramen*. Bern: Francke, 1961.

800 GREENE, Anne. "Bridie's Concept of the Master Experimenter." *St in Scottish Lit*, 2 (1964), 96–110.

801 LINKLATER, Eric. "James Bridie." *The Art of Adventure*. Lon: Macmillan, 1947, 25–43.

802 LUYBEN, Helen L. *James Bridie: Clown and Philosopher*. Phila: Univ. of Pennsylvania Pr., 1965.*

803 MARCEL, Gabriel. "Le Théâtre de James Bridie." *Études Anglaises*, 10 (1957), 291–303.

804 MARDON, Ernest G. *The Conflict Between the Individual and Society in the Plays of James Bridie*. Glasgow: MacLellan, 1972.

805 MICHIE, James A. "Educating the Prophets." *MD*, 11 (1969), 429–31. (His Jonah play.)

806 MORGAN, Edwin. "James Bridie." *Essays*. Cheadle: Carcanet New Pr., 1974, 232–41.

806A NENTWICH, Michael. *Der "schottische Shaw": Untersuchungen zum dramatischen Werk von James Bridie*. Bern: Lang, 1975.

807 WALTER, Marie. "The Grateful Dead: An Old Tale Newly Told." *SFQ*, 23 (1959), 190–95. (*Tobias and the Angel*.)

808 WEALES, Gerald. *Religion in Modern English Drama*, **172**, 79–90.

Carroll, Paul Vincent
(1900–1968)

809 CARROLL, Paul Vincent. "Paul Vincent Carroll Number." *JIL*, 1 (Jan. 1972). (Includes an interview, some letters to Robert Hogan, and the play *We Have Ceased to Live*.)

810 COLEMAN, Sister Anne. "Paul Vincent Carroll's View of Irish Life." *CathW*, 192 (1960), 87–93.

811 CONWAY, John D. "Paul Vincent Carroll's Major Dramatic Triumphs." *Connecticut Rev*, 6 (April 1973), 61–69. (*Shadow and Substance* and *The White Steed*.)

812 CONWAY, John D. "The Satires of Paul Vincent Carroll." *Eire*, 7 (Fall 1972), 13–23.

813 DOYLE, Paul A. *Paul Vincent Carroll*. Lewisburg, PA: Bucknell UP, 1971.* †

814 FALLON, Gabriel. "Greatness and Paul Vincent Carroll." *Irish Monthly*, 70 (May 1942), 196–202.

815 HOGAN, Robert. "Paul Vincent Carroll: The Rebel as Prodigal Son." *After the Irish Renaissance*, **443**, 52–63.

816 McMAHON, Seán. "Oisín's Return: The Protest Plays of Paul Vincent Carroll." *Eire*, 2 (Autumn 1967), 49–64.

817 PALLETTE, Drew B. "Paul Vincent Carroll—Since *The White Steed*." *MD*, 7 (1965), 375–81.

Clarke, Austin
(1896–1974)

818 CLARKE, Austin. *Collected Plays*. Dub: Dolmen, 1963.

818A CLARKE, Austin. *The Celtic Twilight and the Nineties*. Dub: Dolmen, 1969. (Incl. essay on verse drama.)

819 CLARKE, Austin. *Twice Round the Back Church*. Lon: Routledge, 1962. (Autobiography.)

819A HALPERN, Susan. *Austin Clarke: His Life and Works*. Dub: Dolmen, 1974.

820 McHUGH, Roger. "The Plays of Austin Clarke." *IUR*, 4 (1974), 52–64.

821 MERCIER, Vivian. "Austin Clarke—the Poet in the Theatre." *Chimera*, 5 (Spring 1947), 25–36.

822 MERCIER, Vivian. "The Verse Plays of Austin Clarke." *DM*, 19 (April–June 1944), 39–47.

Colum, Padraic
(1881–1972)

823 COLUM, Padraic. *Three Plays*. Dub: Figgis, 1963. (Includes a brief preface by Colum.)

824 COLUM, Padraic. *The Road Round Ireland*. NY: Macmillan, 1926. (Memoirs.)

825 COLUM, Padraic. "Padraic Colum Number." *JIL*, 2 (Jan. 1973). (Includes a long interview, memorials, and selections from his work.)

826 COLUM, Padraic. [Interview] In **462**, 13–22.

827 BOWEN, Zack. *Padraic Colum: A Biographical-Critical Introduction*. Carbondale: Southern Illinois UP, 1970, 60–89.

828 BOWEN, Zack. "Padraic Colum and Irish Drama." *Eire*, 5 (Winter 1970), 71–82.

829 BURGESS, Charles. "A Playwright and His Work." *JIL*, 2 (Jan. 1973), 40–58.

830 WEYGANDT, Cornelius. *Irish Plays and Playwrights*, **432**, 198–208.

Coward, Noël
(1899–1973)

831 COWARD, Noël. *Play Parade*. Lon: Heinemann, 1950–62. 6 vols. (With intros. by Coward.)

832 COWARD, Noël. *Future Indefinite*. NY: Doubleday, 1954.

833 COWARD, Noël. *Present Indicative*. NY: Doubleday, 1937. (With the preceding title, his autobiography.)

834 ALBEE, Edward. "Introduction." In *Three Plays* [*by*] *Noël Coward: Blithe Spirit, Hay Fever, Private Lives*. Boulder: Delta, 1965, 3–6.†

835 CASTLE, Charles. *Noël*. Lon: Allen, 1972.†

836 ERVINE, St. John. "The Plays of Mr. Noel Coward." *QQ*, 43 (1935), 1–21; also in *Essays by Divers Hands*, 14 (1935), 67–98.

837 FULTON, A. R. "*Blithe Spirit*." *Drama and Theatre, Illustrated by Seven Modern Plays*. NY: Holt, 1946, 456–64.

838 GREACEN, Robert. *The Art of Noel Coward*. Aldington: Hand & Flower Pr., 1953. (Brief study.)

839 LESLEY, Cole. *The Life of Noël Coward*. Lon: Cape, 1976. (Biography by an intimate friend.)

840 LEVIN, Milton. *Noel Coward*. NY: Twayne, 1968.*

841 MANDER, Raymond, and Joe MITCHENSON. *Theatrical Companion to Coward*. Lon: Rockliff, 1957. (Includes an overview by Terence Rattigan.)

842 MORLEY, Sheridan. *A Talent to Amuse: A Biography of Noël Coward*. Garden City, NY: Doubleday, 1969.†

843 MORSE, Clarence R. *Mad Dogs and Englishmen: A Study of Noel Coward*.

Emporia State Research St., Vol. 21, No. 4. Emporia: Kansas State Teachers College, 1971. (Brief study.)

844 O'CASEY, Sean. "Coward Codology [I, II, III]." *The Green Crow*, **1281**, 87–115. (Critical attack, stressing *Cavalcade* and *Design for Living*.)

845 STOKES, Sewell. "Noel Coward." *TAM*, 28 (1944), 29–39.

846 SWINNERTON, Frank. "Post-War Pessimism." *The Georgian Scene*. NY: Farrar, 1934, 433–59.

847 TAYLOR, John R. *The Rise and Fall of the Well-Made Play*, **170**, 124–45.*

848 WOODBRIDGE, Homer E. "Noel Coward." *SAQ*, 37 (1938), 239–51.

Delaney, Shelagh
(1939–)

849 DELANEY, Shelagh. *Sweetly Sings the Donkey*. NY: Putnam's, 1963. (Memoirs.)

850 IPPOLITO, G. J. "Shelagh Delaney." *DrS*, 1 (1961), 86–91.

851 NOEL, J. "Some Aspects of Shelagh Delaney's Use of Language in *A Taste of Honey*." *Revue des Langues Vivantes*, 26 (1960), 284–90.

852 OBERG, Arthur K. "*A Taste of Honey* and the Popular Play." *WSCL*, 7 (1966), 160–67.

853 TAYLOR, John R. *Anger & After*, **318**, 130–40.

Duncan, Ronald
(1914–)

854 DUNCAN, Ronald. *Collected Plays*. Lon: Hart-Davis, 1971. (Includes a brief intro. by Duncan.)

855 DUNCAN, Ronald. "Write with Both Hands." *Drama*, No. 31 (Winter 1953), 17–20. (On writing poetic drama.)

856 DUNCAN, Ronald. *All Men Are Islands: An Autobiography*. Lon: Hart-Davis, 1964.

857 DUNCAN, Ronald. *How to Make Enemies*. Lon: Hart-Davis, 1968. (Sequel to above title.)

858 DUNCAN, Ronald. *Ronald Duncan: Verse Dramatist and Poet, Interviewed by William B. Wahl*. Salzburg: Univ. Salzburg, 1973.

859 HAUETER, Max W. *Ronald Duncan: The Metaphysical Content of His Plays*. Lon: Rebel Pr., 1969.

860 SPANOS, William V. *The Christian Tradition in Modern British Verse Drama*, **268**, 282–93. (On *This Way to the Tomb*.)

861 WAHL, William B. *A Lone Wolf Howling: The Thematic Content of Ronald Duncan's Plays*. Salzburg: Univ. Salzburg, 1973.

862 WEALES, Gerald. *Religion in Modern English Drama*, **172**, 233–39.

863 WELLAND, Dennis. "Some Post-War Experiments in Poetic Drama." In **90**, 38–43. (On *This Way to the Tomb*.)

Dunsany, Lord [Edward J. M. D. Plunkett, 18th Baron] (1878–1957)

864 DUNSANY, Lord. *Patches of Sunlight*. Lon: Heinemann, 1938. (Autobiography.)

865 AMORY, Mark. *Biography of Lord Dunsany*. Lon: Collins, 1972.

866 BIERSTADT, Edward H. *Dunsany the Dramatist*. Bos: Little, Brown, 1917.

867 BOYD, Ernest A. "Lord Dunsany, Fantaisiste." *Appreciations and Depreciations: Irish Literary Studies*. Dub: Talbot, 1917, 71–100, esp. 88–98.

868 GOGARTY, Oliver S. J. "Lord Dunsany." *Atlantic Monthly*, 195 (March 1955), 67–72. (The "liturgic" quality of his plays.)

869 MALONE, Andrew E. *The Irish Drama*, **427**, 246–56.

870 WEYGANDT, Cornelius. "Dramas of Dunsany." *Tuesdays at Ten*. Phila.: Univ. of Pennsylvania Pr., 1928, 13–42.

Eliot, T[homas] S[tearns] (1888– 1965)

In this section Eliot's full-length plays are referred to in the notes by the abbreviations *MC*, *FR*, *CP*, *CC*, and *ES*.

871 ELIOT, T. S. *Complete Poems and Plays*. NY: Harcourt, 1962.

872 ELIOT, T. S. "The Aims of Poetic Drama." *Adam: International Rev*, No. 200 (1949), 10–16.

873 ELIOT, T. S. *Poetry and Drama*. Cambridge, MA: Harvard UP, 1951; repr. in his *On Poetry and Poets* (Lon: Faber, 1957), 72–88;† mostly repr. in **99**, 250–60. (On his own theory and drama.)*

874 ELIOT, T. S. "Religious Drama: Mediaeval and Modern." *Univ of Edinburgh J*, 9 (Autumn 1937), 8–17.

875 BEARE, Robert L. "Notes on the Text of T. S. Eliot: Variants from Russell Square." *St in Bibl*, 9 (1957), 21–49.

876 CARPENTER, Charles A. "T. S. Eliot as Dramatist: Critical Studies in English, 1933–1975." *BB*, 33 (1976), 1–12.

877 GALLUP, Donald. *T. S. Eliot: A Bibliography*. Rev. ed. NY: Harcourt, 1969. (Descriptive bibl. of Eliot's writings.)

878 MARTIN, Mildred. *A Half-Century of Eliot Criticism: An Annotated Bibliography of Books and Articles in English, 1916–1965*. Lewisburg, PA: Bucknell UP, 1972.*

879 ADAIR, Patricia M. "Mr. Eliot's 'Murder in the Cathedral.' " *Cambridge J*, 4 (Nov. 1950), 83–95.

880 ADAMS, John F. "The Fourth Temptation in *Murder in the Cathedral*." *MD*, 5 (1963), 381–88.

881 ARROWSMITH, William. "Notes on English Verse Drama (II): 'The Cocktail Party.' " *HudR*, 3 (1950), 411–30.*

882 ARROWSMITH, William. "Transfiguration in Eliot and Euripides." *SR*, 63 (1955), 421–42; repr. as "The Comedy of T. S. Eliot" in **122**, 148–72; repr. in **93**, 134–51.*

883 AVERY, Helen P. "*The Family Reunion* Reconsidered." *ETJ*, 17 (1965), 10–18.

884 AYLEN, Leo. *Greek Tragedy and the Modern World*. Lon: Methuen, 1964, 320–37. (Stresses *MC*.)

885 BARBER, C. L. "The Power of Development . . . in a Different World." In **942**, 213–43. (On *CP* and *CC*.)

886 BARBER, C. L. "T. S. Eliot After Strange Gods." *SoR*, 6 (1940), 387–416; repr. in **973**, 415–43. (On *FR*.)

887 BATTENHOUSE, Roy W. "Eliot's 'The Family Reunion' as Christian Prophecy." *Christendom*, 10 (1945), 307–21.

888 BELLI, Angela. *Ancient Greek Myths and Modern Drama: A Study in Continuity*. NY: New York UP, 1969, 51–70. (On *FR*.)†

889 BLACKMUR, R. P. "T. S. Eliot: From *Ash Wednesday* to *Murder in the Cathedral*." *The Double Agent*. NY: Arrow, 1935, 184–218; repr. in **973**, 236–62.

890 BODKIN, Maud. *The Quest for Salvation in an Ancient and a Modern Play*. Lon: Oxford UP, 1941. (54-page comparison of *FR* and Aeschylus's *Eumenides*.)*

891 BRADBROOK, Muriel C. "Eliot as Dramatist." *English Dramatic Form*, **142**, 162–78.

892 BRAINERD, Barron, and Victoria NEUFELDT. "On [Solomon] Marcus' Methods for the Analysis of the Strategy of a Play." *Poetics*, No. 10 (1974), 31–74. (Treats *CP* at length.)

893 BROUSSARD, Louis. *American Drama: Contemporary Allegory from Eugene O'Neill to Tennessee Williams*. Norman: Univ. of Oklahoma Pr., 1962, 69–91.

894 BROWNE, E. Martin. *The Making of T. S. Eliot's Plays*. Lon: Cambridge UP, 1969. (Based on the director's memories and letters.)*

895 CARNE-ROSS, Donald. "The Position of 'The Family Reunion' in the Work of T. S. Eliot." *Rivista di Letterature Moderne*, 2 (Oct. 1950), 125–39.

896 CHIARI, Joseph. *T. S. Eliot: Poet and Dramatist*. Lon: Vision Pr., 1972.

897 CLARK, David R., ed. *Twentieth Century Interpretations of Murder in the Cathedral: A Collection of Critical Essays*. Englewood Cliffs, NJ: Prentice-Hall, 1971* †

898 COGHILL, Nevill, ed. *T. S. Eliot's 'The Cocktail Party.'* Lon: Faber, 1974. (Voluminous notes and commentary.)*†

899 COLBY, Robert A. "Orpheus in the Counting House: *The Confidential Clerk*." *PMLA*, 72 (1957), 791–802.

900 COLBY, Robert A. "The Three Worlds of *The Cocktail Party*: The Wit of T. S. Eliot." *UTQ*, 24 (1954), 56–69.

901 CUTTS, John P. "Evidence for Ambivalence of Motives in *Murder in the Cathedral*." *CoD*, 8 (1974), 199–210.

902 DAVENPORT, Gary T. "Eliot's *The Cocktail Party*: Comic Perspective as Salvation." *MD*, 17 (1974), 301–6.

903 DOBRÉE, Bonamy. " 'The Confidential Clerk' " and " 'The Elder Statesman.' " *The Lamp and the Lute*. 2nd ed. Lon: Cass, 1964, 122–49.

904 DONOGHUE, Denis. *The Third Voice*, **251**, 76–179.*

905 FERGUSSON, Francis. *"Murder in the Cathedral*: The Theological Scene." *The Idea of a Theater*. Garden City, NY: Doubleday, 1949, 222–34†; repr. in **897**, 27–37.

906 FINDLATER, Richard. *The Unholy Trade*, **253**, 130–46.

907 FRYE, Northrop. *T. S. Eliot*. NY: Grove, 1963, 89–99.†

908 GARDNER, Helen. "The Comedies of T. S. Eliot." *SR*, 74 (1966), 153–75; also in *Essays by Divers Hands*, 34 (1966), 55–73; repr. in *T. S. Eliot: The Man and His Work*, ed. Allen Tate (NY: Delacorte, 1966), 159–81.*

909 GARDNER, Helen. "The Language of Drama." *The Art of T. S. Eliot*. NY: Dutton, 1959 [c. 1949], 127-57. †

910 GASKELL, Ronald. "*The Family Reunion*." *Drama and Reality*, **57**, 128–38.

911 GASSNER, John. "T. S. Eliot: The Poet as Anti-Modernist." *The Theatre in Our Times*, **105**, 267–81.(Stresses *CP*.)

912 GERALDINE, Sister M. "The Rhetoric of Repetition in *Murder in the Cathedral*." *Ren*, 19 (1967), 132–41.

913 GERSTENBERGER, Donna. "T. S. Eliot: Toward Community." *The Complex Configuration*, **255**, 41–77.

914 GOLDMAN, Michael. "Fear in the Way: The Design of Eliot's Drama." In *Essays on the Occasion of the Fiftieth Anniversary of The Waste Land*, ed. A. Walton Litz. Princeton, NJ: Princeton UP, 1973, 155–80.

915 HAMALIAN, Leo. "Mr. Eliot's Saturday Evening Service." *Accent*, 10 (1950), 195–212. (On *CP*.)

916 HARDING, D. W. "Progression of Theme in Eliot's Modern Plays." *Experience into Words: Essays on Poetry*. NY: Horizon, 1964, 132–62.

917 HARDY, John E. "An Antic Disposition." *SR*, 65 (1957), 50–60. (On *CP*.)

918 HATHORN, Richmond Y. "Eliot's *Murder in the Cathedral*: Myth and History." *Tragedy, Myth, and Mystery*. Bloomington: Indiana UP, 1962, 195–216.†

919 HEADINGS, Philip R. *T. S. Eliot*. NY: Twayne, 1964, 100–18, 143–67.†

920 HEILMAN, Robert B. "*Alcestis* and *The Cocktail Party*." *CL*, 5 (1953), 105–16.

921 HENN, T. R. "Mr. Eliot's Compromise." *The Harvest of Tragedy*. Lon: Methuen, 1956, 217–32.

922 HOLT, Charles L. "On Structure and *Sweeney Agonistes*." *MD*, 10 (1967),43–47.

923 HOMAN, Richard L. "T. S. Eliot's *The Confidential Clerk*: Prelude to Pinter?" *ETJ*, 28 (1976), 398–404.

924 HOWARTH, Herbert. "Drama."In *Notes on Some Figures Behind T. S. Eliot*. Bos: Houghton, 1964, 300–340. (Backgrounds, esp. of *MC*, *FR*, and *CP*.)

925 JAYNE, Sears. "Mr. Eliot's Agon." *PQ*, 34 (1955), 395–414. (On *Sweeney Agonistes*.)

926 JONES, David E. *The Plays of T. S. Eliot*. Toronto: Univ. of Toronto Pr., 1960.* †

927 KENNEDY, Andrew K. *Six Dramatists in Search of a Language*, **158**, 87–129.

928 KENNER, Hugh. "For Other Voices." *Poetry*, 94 (1959), 36–40; repr. in *T. S. Eliot: A Collection of Critical Essays*, ed. Hugh Kenner (Englewood Cliffs, NJ: Prentice-Hall, 1962), 187–91. (On *ES*.)

929 KENNER, Hugh. "Sweeney and the Voice" and *"Murder in the Cathedral."* *The Invisible Poet: T. S. Eliot.* NY: Obolensky, 1959, 222–35, 276–85.†

930 KIRK, Russell. *Eliot and His Age: T. S. Eliot's Moral Imagination in the Twentieth Century.* NY: Random, 1972.

931 KLINE, Peter. "The Spiritual Center in Eliot's Plays." *KR*, 21 (1959), 457–72. (Stresses *MC*.)

932 KNUST, Herbert. "What's the Matter with One-Eyed Riley?" *CL*, 17 (1965), 289–98.

933 KRIEGER, Murray. *"Murder in the Cathedral*: The Limits of Drama and the Freedom of Vision." *The Classic Vision.* Baltimore, MD: Johns Hopkins UP, 1971, 337–62;† also in *The Shaken Realist*, ed. Melvin J. Friedman and John B. Vickery (Baton Rouge: Louisiana State UP, 1970), 72–99.

934 LANGBAUM, Robert." The Mysteries of Identity as a Theme in T. S. Eliot's Plays." *VQR*, 49 (1973), 560–80. (On *CP* and after.)

935 LAWLOR, John. "The Formal Achievement of 'The Cocktail Party.' " *VQR*, 30 (1954), 431–51.

936 LIGHTFOOT, Marjorie J. "Charting Eliot's Course in Drama." *ETJ*, 20 (1968), 186–97.

937 LIGHTFOOT, Marjorie J. "The Uncommon Cocktail Party." *MD*, 11 (1969), 382–95.

938 McLAUGHLIN, John J. "A Daring Metaphysic: *The Cocktail Party." Ren*, 3 (1950), 15–28.

939 MARTZ, Louis L. "The Saint as Tragic Hero: *Saint Joan* and *Murder in the Cathedral."* In *Tragic Themes in Western Literature*, ed. Cleanth Brooks. New Haven, CT: Yale UP, 1955, 150–78.

940 MARTZ, Louis L. "T. S. Eliot: The Wheel and the Point." *The Poem of the Mind*. NY: Oxford UP, 1966, 105–24; repr. in **973**, 444–62; abridged in **897**, 15–26. (On *MC*.)

941 MASON, William H. *Murder in the Cathedral.* Oxford: Blackwell, 1962. (73-page intro. to the play.)

942 MATTHIESSEN, F. O. "The Plays." *The Achievement of T. S. Eliot.* 3rd ed. NY: Oxford UP, 1958, 155–76. (On *MC* and *FR* only; note **885**.)* †

943 MAXWELL, Desmond E. S. "Realism and Poetic Drama." *The Poetry of T. S. Eliot.* Lon: Routledge, 1952, 181–213.

944 MELCHIORI, Giorgio. "Eliot and the Theatre." *The Tightrope Walkers: Studies of Mannerism in Modern English Literature.* Lon: Routledge, 1956, 104–49 (see also 248–55).

945 MUDFORD, P. G. "T. S. Eliot's Plays and the Tradition of 'High Comedy.' " *CritQ*, 16 (1974), 127–40.

946 MURRY, John M. "The Plays of T. S. Eliot." *Unprofessional Essays.* Lon: Cape, 1956, 151–91.*

947 OLSHIN, Toby A. "A Consideration of *The Rock." UTQ*, 39 (1970), 310–23.

948 PANKOW, Edith. "The 'Eternal Design' of *Murder in the Cathedral." PLL*, 9 (1973), 35–47.

949 PEACOCK, Ronald. *The Poet in the Theatre*, **67**, 1–20.

950 PETER, John. " 'The Family Reunion.' " *Scrutiny*, 16 (1949), 219–30.

951 PETER, John. " 'Murder in the Cathedral.' " *SR*, 61 (1953), 362–83; repr. in *T. S. Eliot*, **928, 155**–72.

952 PICKERING, Jerry V. "Form as Agent: Eliot's *Murder in the Cathedral."* *ETJ*, 20 (1968), 198–207.

953 PORTER, Thomas E. "The Old Woman, the Doctor and the Cook: *The Cocktail Party.*" *Myth and Modern American Drama*. Detroit, MI: Wayne State UP, 1969, 53–76.

954 PRIOR, Moody E. *The Language of Tragedy*, **166**, 353–67.

955 RANSOM, John Crowe. "A Cathedralist Looks at Murder." *The World's Body*. New ed. Baton Rouge: Louisiana State UP, 1968, 166–72. (See also "Postscript," 351–75.)†

956 RECKFORD, Kenneth J. "Heracles and Mr. Eliot." *CL*, 16 (1964), 1–18. (On *CP*.)

957 REHAK, Louise R. "On the Use of Martyrs: Tennyson and Eliot on Thomas Becket." *UTQ*, 33 (1963), 43–60.

958 RILLIE, John A. M. "Melodramatic Device in T. S. Eliot." *Rev of Eng St*, 13 (1962), 267–81. (Stresses *MC* and *FR*.)

958A ROBERTS, Patrick. "Orestes in Modern Drama: *The Family Reunion.*" *The Psychology of Tragic Drama*. Lon: Routledge & K. Paul, 1975, 183–99.

959 SARKAR, Subhas. *T. S. Eliot the Dramatist*. Calcutta: Minerva, 1972.

960 SENA, Vinod. "The Ambivalence of *The Cocktail Party.*" *MD*, 14 (1972), 392–404.

961 SENA, Vinod. "Eliot's *The Family Reunion*: A Study in Disintegration." *SoR*, 3 (1967), 895–921.

962 SHARONI, Edna G. " 'Peace' and 'Unbar the Door': T. S. Eliot's *Murder in the Cathedral* and Some Stoic Forebears." *CoD*, 6 (1972), 135–53.

963 SHORTER, Robert N. "Becket as Job: T. S. Eliot's *Murder in the Cathedral.*" *SAQ*, 67 (1968), 627–35; repr. in **897**, 86–93.

964 SMITH, Carol H. *T. S. Eliot's Dramatic Theory and Practice from Sweeney Agonistes to The Elder Statesman*. Princeton, NJ: Princeton UP, 1963.* †

965 SMITH, Grover. *T. S. Eliot's Poetry and Plays: A Study in Sources and Meaning*. 2nd ed. Chicago: Univ. of Chicago Pr., 1974, 110–18, 171–248.* †

966 SPANOS, William V. *The Christian Tradition in Modern British Verse Drama*, **268**, 63–68, 81–104, 184–251.*

967 SPANOS, William V. " 'Wanna Go Home, Baby?': *Sweeney Agonistes* as Drama of the Absurd." *PMLA*, 85 (1970), 8–20.

968 SPENDER, Stephen. "Poetic Drama." *T. S. Eliot*. NY: Viking, 1976, 185–223.

969 STEIN, Walter. "After the Cocktails." *EIC*, 3 (1953), 85–104.

970 STELZMANN, Rainulf A. "The Theology of T. S. Eliot's Dramas." *Xavier Univ St*, 1 (April 1961), 7–17.

971 STYAN, J. L. *The Elements of Drama*, **71**, 135–40, 274–84. (On *MC* and *CP*.)

972 UNGER, Leonard. "Laforgue, Conrad, and T. S. Eliot." *The Man in the Name*. Minneapolis: Univ. of Minnesota Pr., 1956, 190–242 (esp. 211–26 on *CP* and *CC*); repr. in his *T. S. Eliot: Moments and Patterns* (Minneapolis: Univ. of Minnesota Pr., 1966), 103–56.†

973 UNGER, Leonard, ed. *T. S. Eliot: A Selected Critique*. NY: Rinehart, 1948.

974 WARD, David. " 'Strife with Shadows': The Plays." *T. S. Eliot Between Two Worlds*. Lon: Routledge, 1973, 172–222.

975 WASSON, Richard. "The Rhetoric of Theatre: The Contemporaneity of T. S. Eliot." *DrS*, 6 (1968), 231–43.

976 WEALES, Gerald. *Religion in Modern English Drama*, **172**, 183–206.

977 WILLIAMS, Raymond. *Drama from Ibsen to Brecht*, **72**, 174–98.

978 WILLIAMS, Raymond. "Tragic Resignation and Sacrifice: Eliot and Pasternak." *Modern Tragedy*, **73**, 156–67. (On *MC* and *CP*.)

979 WIMSATT, W. K. "Eliot's Comedy." *Hateful Contraries*. Lexington: Univ. of Kentucky Pr., 1965, 184–200. (1950 *SR* essay on *CP*.)*

980 WINTER, Jack. " 'Prufrockism' in *The Cocktail Party*." *MLQ*, 22 (1961), 135–48.

981 WORTH, KATHARINE J. *Revolutions in Modern English Drama*, **174**, 55–66.

982 WYMAN, Linda. "*Murder in the Cathedral*: The Plot of Diction." *MD*, 19 (1976), 135–45.

Fitzmaurice, George
(1877–1963)

983 FITZMAURICE, George. *The Plays*. Dub: Dolmen, 1967–70. 3 vols. (Intros. by Austin Clarke and Howard K. Slaughter.)

984 HENDERSON, Joanne L. "Checklist of Four Kerry Writers: George Fitzmaurice [etc.]." *JIL*, 1 (May 1972), 101–19.

985 CLARKE, Austin. "The Dramatic Fantasies of George Fitzmaurice." *DM*, 15 (April–June 1940), 9–14.

986 CONBERE, John P. "The Obscurity of George Fitzmaurice." *Eire*, 6 (Spring 1971), 17–26.

987 COUGHLIN, Matthew N. "Farce Transcended: George Fitzmaurice's *The Toothache*." *Eire*, 10 (Winter 1975), 85–100.

988 HOGAN, Robert. "The Genius of George Fitzmaurice." *After the Irish Renaissance*, **443**, 164–75.

989 McGUINNESS, Arthur E. *George Fitzmaurice*. Lewisburg, PA: Bucknell UP, 1974.* †

990 RILEY, J. D. "The Plays of George Fitzmaurice." *DM*, 30 (Jan.–March 1955), 5–19.

991 SLAUGHTER, Howard K. *George Fitzmaurice and His Enchanted Land*. Dub: Dolmen, 1972. (Brief survey.)

Friel, Brian
(1929–)

992 FRIEL, Brian. "The Theatre of Hope and Despair." *Everyman*, No. 1 (1968), 17–22.

993 FRIEL, Brian. [Interview.] In **462**, 220–25.

994 COAKLEY, James. "Chekov in Ireland: Brief Notes on Friel's Philadelphia." *CoD*, 7 (1973), 191–97.

995 LEVIN, Milton. "Brian Friel: An Introduction." *Eire*, 7 (Summer 1972), 132–36.

996 MAXWELL, Desmond E. S. *Brian Friel*. Lewisburg, PA: Bucknell UP, 1973.* †

Fry, Christopher
(1907–)

997 FRY, Christopher. *Plays*. Lon: Oxford UP, 1969–71. 3 vols.†

998 FRY, Christopher. "An Experience of Critics." In *An Experience of Critics, and The Approach to Dramatic Criticism*, by Ivor Brown et al., eds. Kaye Webb. Lon: Oxford UP, 1953, 11–32.

999 FRY, Christopher. "Why Verse?" *World Theatre*, 4, No. 4 (1955), 51–61; repr. in **99**, 125–30.

000 FRY, Christopher. "Poetry and the Theatre." *Adam: International Rev*, Nos. 214–15 (1951), 2–10.

1001 FRY, Christopher. "Talking of Henry." *TC*, 169 (1961), 185–90. (On *Curtmantle*.)

1002 ADLER, Jacob H. "Shakespeare and Christopher Fry." *ETJ*, 11 (1959), 85–98.

1003 ARROWSMITH, William. "Notes on English Verse Drama: Christopher Fry." *HudR*, 3 (1950), 203–16.*

1004 BARNES, Lewis W. "Christopher Fry: The Chestertonian Concept of Comedy." *Xavier Univ St*, 2 (March 1963), 30–47.

1005 BEWLEY, Marius. "The Verse of Christopher Fry." *Scrutiny*, 18 (1951), 78–84.

1006 BROWNE, E. Martin. "Henry II as Hero: Christopher Fry's New Play, *Curtmantle*." *DrS*, 2 (1962), 63–71.

1007 BULLOUGH, Geoffrey. "Christopher Fry and the 'Revolt' Against Eliot." In **90**, 56–78.

1008 COLLINS, J. A. "Poet of Paradox: The Dramas of Christopher Fry." *Literary Half-Yearly*, 12, No. 2 (1971), 62–75.

1009 DONOGHUE, Denis. "Christopher Fry's Theatre of Words." *The Third Voice*, **251**, 180–92.

1010 ELDER, Walter. "Venus Attended by Muses." *KR*, 12 (1950), 712–17.

1011 FERGUSON, John. "*The Boy with a Cart*." *MD*, 8 (1965), 284–92.

1012 FERGUSON, John. "Christopher Fry's *A Sleep of Prisoners*." *English*, 10 (1954), 42–47.

1013 FINDLATER, Richard. "The Two Countesses." *TC*, 156 (1954), 175–83. (*The Dark Is Light Enough* and Priestley's *The White Countess*.)

1014 FINDLATER, Richard. *The Unholy Trade*, **253**, 154–69.

1015 GERSTENBERGER, Donna. "Christopher Fry: An Antic Disposition." *The Complex Configuration*, **255**, 98–125.

1016 GREENE, Anne. "Fry's Cosmic Vision." *MD*, 4 (1962), 355–64.

1017 HIGHET, Gilbert. "The Poet and the Modern Stage: Christopher Fry." *People, Places and Books*. NY: Oxford UP, 1953, 61–68.

1018 ITSCHERT, Hans. *Studien zur Dramaturgie des "Religious Festival Play" bei Christopher Fry*. Tübingen: Niemeyer, 1963. (254 pp.)

1019 LECKY, Eleazer. "Mystery in the Plays of Christopher Fry." *TDR*, 4 (March 1960), 80–87.

CHRISTOPHER FRY

1020 LUTYENS, David B. "The Dilemma of the Christian Dramatist: Paul Claudel and Christopher Fry." *TDR*, 6 (June 1962), 118–24.

1021 MANDEL, Oscar. "Themes in the Drama of Christopher Fry." *Études Anglaises*, 10 (1958), 335–49.

1022 MAURA, Sister M. "Christopher Fry: An Angle of Experience." *Ren*, 8 (1955), 3–11, 36.

1023 MELCHIORI, Giorgio. *The Tightrope Walkers*, **944**, 150–74, 257–65.*

1024 MERCHANT, W. Moelwyn. *Creed and Drama*. Phila., PA: Fortress Pr., 1965, 98–109.

1025 PARKER, Gerald. "A Study of Christopher Fry's *Curtmantle*." *DR*, 43 (1963), 200–211.

1026 REDMAN, Ben Ray. "Christopher Fry: Poet-Dramatist." *CE*, 14 (1953), 191–97; also in *Eng J*, 42 (Jan. 1953), 1–7.

1027 ROSTON, Murray. *Biblical Drama in England*, **168**, 299–306.

1028 ROY, Emil. *Christopher Fry*. Carbondale: Southern Illinois UP, 1968.*

1029 SPANOS, William V. "Charles Williams and Christopher Fry: The Figure of the Dance." *The Christian Tradition in Modern British Verse Drama*, **268**, 304–24. (On *A Sleep of Prisoners*.)*

1030 SPEARS, Monroe K. "Christopher Fry and the Redemption of Joy." *Poetry*, 78 (1951), 28–43.*

1031 STAMM, Rudolf. "Christopher Fry and the Revolt Against Realism in Modern English Drama." In *The Shaping Powers at Work*. Heidelberg: Carl Winter, 1967, 277–309; repr. from *Anglia*, 72 (1954), 78–109.

1032 STANFORD, Derek. *Christopher Fry: An Appreciation*. Lon: Nevill, 1951.

1033 STANFORD, Derek. "God in the Drama of Christopher Fry." *Lon Q and Holborn Rev*, 26 (1957), 124–30.

1034 STYAN, J. L. *The Elements of Drama*, **71**, 39–44, 263–67. (On *A Sleep of Prisoners* and *The Lady's Not for Burning*.)

1035 URANG, Gunnar. "The Climate Is the Comedy: A Study of Christopher Fry's *The Lady's Not for Burning*." *Christian Scholar*, 46 (Spring 1963), 61–86.

1036 VOS, Nelvin. "The Comic Victim-Victor: His Passionate Action in the Drama of Christopher Fry." *The Drama of Comedy*. Richmond: John Knox Pr., 1966, 74–99.

1037 WEALES, Gerald. *Religion in Modern English Drama*, **172**, 206–24.

1038 WIERSMA, Stanley M. *Christopher Fry: A Critical Essay*. Grand Rapids, MI: Eerdmans, 1970. (Brief study.)†

1039 WIERSMA, Stanley M. "Christopher Fry's *A Phoenix Too Frequent*: A Study in Source and Symbol." *MD*, 8 (1965), 293–302.

1040 WIERSMA, Stanley M. "Christopher Fry's Definition of the Complete Pacifist in *The Dark Is Light Enough*." *Ariel*, 6 (October 1975), 3–28.

1041 WIERSMA, Stanley M. "Spring and the Apocalypse, Law and Prophets: A Reading of Fry's *The Lady's Not for Burning*." *MD*, 13 (1971), 432–47.

1042 WOODBURY, John. "The Witch and the Nun: A Study of 'The Lady's Not for Burning.' " *Manitoba Arts Rev*, 10 (Winter 1956), 41–54.

1043 WOODFIELD, J. "Christopher Fry's *Curtmantle*: The Form of Unity." *MD*, 17 (1974), 307–18.

Galsworthy, John
(1867–1933)

1044 GALSWORTHY, John. *The Plays*. Lon: Duckworth, 1929. (1150-page complete edition.)

1045 GALSWORTHY, John. *Works: Manaton Edition*. Lon: Heinemann, 1922–36. 30 vols. (Vols. 18–22 contain the plays, with prefaces by Galsworthy.)

1046 GALSWORTHY, John. "Some Platitudes Concerning Drama." *The Inn of Tranquillity: Studies and Essays*. NY: Scribner's, 1912, 189–202; repr. in **99**, 45–52.*

1047 GALSWORTHY, John. *Letters from John Galsworthy, 1900–1932*, ed. Edward Garnett. Lon: Cape, 1934.

1048 GALSWORTHY, John. *Letters to Leon Lion*, ed. Asher B. Wilson. NY: Humanities, 1968. (Concerns theatrical matters, 1921–32.)

1049 GALSWORTHY, John. *Glimpses and Reflections*. Lon: Heinemann, 1937.

1050 MARROT, Harold V. *Bibliography of the Works of John Galsworthy*. Lon: Mathews, 1928.

1051 MIKHAIL, Edward H. *John Galsworthy the Dramatist: A Bibliography of Criticism*. Troy, NY: Whitston, 1971.*

1052 ALEXANDER, Henry. "Galsworthy as Dramatist." *QQ*, 40 (1933), 177–88.

1053 BACHE, William B. "*Justice*: Galsworthy's Dramatic Tragedy." *MD*, 3 (1960), 138–42.

1054 BARKER, Dudley. *The Man of Principle: A Biography of John Galsworthy*. NY: Stein, 1969.

1055 CHOUDHURI, Asoke D. *Galsworthy's Plays: A Critical Survey*. New Delhi: Orient Longmans, 1961.

1056 COATS, Robert H. *John Galsworthy as a Dramatic Artist*. NY: Scribner's, 1926.

1057 CUNLIFFE, John W. *Modern English Playwrights*, **146**, 95–112.

1058 DICKINSON, Thomas H. *The Contemporary Drama of England*, **148**, 201–19.

1059 DUPONT, Victor. *John Galsworthy: The Dramatic Artist*. Paris: Didier, 1942.

1060 DUPRÉ, Catherine. *John Galsworthy: A Biography*. NY: Coward, McCann & Geoghegan, 1976.

1061 EASTMAN, Fred. "The Dramatist and the Minister." In *The Arts and Religion*, ed. Albert E. Bailey. NY: Macmillan, 1944, 141–50. (On *Loyalties*.)

1062 ELLEHAUGE, Martin O. M. *Striking Figures Among Modern English Dramatists*, **215**, 30–46.

1063 ERVINE, St. John. "The Later Plays of Mr. John Galsworthy." *FortR*, 110 (1918), 83–92.

1064 ERVINE, St. John. "The Realistic Test in Drama." *YR*, 11 (1922), 285–303. (On *The Fugitive*.)

1065 GARY, Franklin. "Galsworthy and the *Poetics*." *Symposium: A Critical Rev*, 1 (1930), 72–81. (On his plays as imitations of the surfaces of life.)

1066 KAYE-SMITH, Sheila. "The Plays." *John Galsworthy*. Lon: Nisbet, 1916, 17–51.

1067 MARROT, Harold V. *The Life and Letters of John Galsworthy*. Lon: Heinemann, 1935.

1068 OULD, Hermann. *John Galsworthy*. Lon: Chapman & Hall, 1934.

1069 PHELPS, William L. *Essays on Modern Dramatists*. NY: Macmillan, 1921, 99–141.

1070 SCHALIT, Leon. "The Plays." *John Galsworthy: A Survey*, tr. E. E. Coe and Therese Harbury. NY: Scribner, 1929, 219–333.*

1071 SCHEICK, William J. "Chance and Impartiality: A Study Based on the Manuscript of Galsworthy's *Loyalties*." *TSLL*, 17 (1975), 653–72.

1072 SCRIMGEOUR, Gary J. "Naturalist Drama and Galsworthy." *MD*, 7 (1964), 65–78.

1073 SIMRELL, V. E. "John Galsworthy: The Artist as Propagandist." *Q J of Speech Education*, 13 (1927), 225–36.

1074 SKEMP, Arthur R. "The Plays of Mr. John Galsworthy." *E&S*, 4 (1913), 151–71.

1075 WILSON, Asher. "Oscar Wilde and *Loyalties*." *ETJ*, 11 (1959), 208–11.

Gilbert, W[illiam] S[chwenck] (1836–1911)

1076 GILBERT, W. S. *Original Plays*. Series 1–4. NY: Scribner, Armstrong, 1876–1911. 4 vols.

1077 GILBERT, W. S. *The Complete Plays of Gilbert and Sullivan*. NY: Modern Lib., 1936.

1078 BERLIN, Normand. "*Patience*: A Study in Poetic Elaboration." *Studia Neophilologica*, 33 (1961), 80–85.

1079 CHESTERTON, G. K. "Gilbert and Sullivan." In *The Eighteen-Eighties*, **185**, 136–58; repr. in **1088**, 183–205.

1080 DANTON, George H. "Gilbert's *Gretchen*." *Germanic Rev*, 21 (1946), 132–42.

1081 DARK, Sidney, and Rowland GREY. *W. S. Gilbert: His Life and Letters*. Lon: Methuen, 1923.

1082 DICKINSON, Thomas H. *The Contemporary Drama of England*, **148**, 64–77.

1083 DuBOIS, Arthur E. "W. S. Gilbert, Practical Classicist." *SR*, 37 (1929), 94–107.

1084 GARSON, Ronald W. "The English Aristophanes." *Revue de Littérature Comparée*, 46 (1972), 177–93.

1085 GRANVILLE-BARKER, Harley. "Exit Planché—Enter Gilbert," **186**.

1086 HALL, Robert A. "The Satire of *The Yeoman of the Guard*." *Modern Language Notes*, 73 (1958), 492–97; repr. in **1088**, 217–25.

1087 JONES, John B. "In Search of Archibald Grosvenor: A New Look at Gilbert's *Patience*." *Victorian Poetry*, 3 (1965), 45–53; repr. in **1088**, 243–56.

1088 JONES, John B., ed. *W. S. Gilbert: A Century of Scholarship and Commentary*. NY: New York UP, 1970.*

1089 LAUTERBACH, Charles E. "Taking Gilbert's Measure." *Huntington Lib Q*, 19 (1956), 196–202; repr. in **1088**, 207–15.

1090 NICOLL, Allardyce. "The Fantastic and Satiric Comedy." *A History of English Drama*, **192**, 132–47.

1091 PEARSON, Hesketh. *Gilbert: His Life and Strife*. Lon: Methuen, 1957.

1092 PERRY, Henry T. E. "The Victorianism of W. S. Gilbert." *SR*, 36 (1928), 302–9; repr. in **1088**, 147–56.

1093 QUILLER-COUCH, Arthur. "W. S. Gilbert." *Studies in Literature, Third Series*. Cambridge, Eng.: Univ. Pr., 1930, 216–38; repr. in **1088**, 157–81.

1094 REVITT, Paul J. "Gilbert and Sullivan: More Seriousness Than Satire." *Western Humanities Rev*, 19 (1965), 19–34. (On the Savoy operas as serious works of art.)

1095 SICHEL, Walter. "The English Aristophanes." *FortR*, 96 (1911), 681–704; repr. in **1088**, 69–109.

1096 STANTON, Stephen S. "Ibsen, Gilbert, and Scribe's *Bataille de dames*." *ETJ*, 17 (1965), 24–30. (On *Engaged*.)

1097 STEDMAN, Jane W. "From Dame to Woman: W. S. Gilbert and Theatrical Transvestism." In *Suffer and Be Still: Women in the Victorian Age*, ed. Martha Vicinus. Bloomington: Indiana UP, 1972, 20–37.

1098 STEDMAN, Jane W. "The Genesis of *Patience*." *Modern Philology*, 66 (1968), 48–58; repr. in **1088**, 285–318.

1099 SUTTON, Max K. *W. S. Gilbert*. Bos: Twayne, 1975.

1100 THORNDIKE, Ashley H. "Sir William Schwenk Gilbert." *English Comedy*. NY: Cooper Square, 1965 [c. 1929], 540–59.

1101 WEISINGER, Herbert. "The Twisted Cue." *The Agony and the Triumph: Papers on the Use and Abuse of Myth*. East Lansing: Michigan State UP, 1964, 159–71; repr. in **1088**, 227–41.

Granville-Barker, Harley (1877–1946)

1102 GRANVILLE-BARKER, Harley. *Collected Plays*. Watergate Edition. Lon: Sidgwick & Jackson, 1967–.†

1103 GRANVILLE-BARKER, Harley. *The Exemplary Theatre*. Lon: Chatto & Windus, 1922.

1104 GRANVILLE-BARKER, Harley. *The Use of the Drama*. Princeton, NJ: Princeton UP, 1945. (See also *On Dramatic Method*, 1931.)

1105 ELLEHAUGE, Martin O. M. *Striking Figures Among Modern English Dramatists*, **215**, 47–60.

1106 EVANS, T. F. "Granville Barker: Shavian Disciple." *Shaw Bul*, 2 (May 1958), 1–19.

1107 HOWE, Percival P. *Dramatic Portraits*, **155**, 185–208.

1108 MORGAN, Margery M. "Bernard Shaw on the Tightrope." *MD*, 4 (1962), 343–54. (Compares *Madras House* with Shaw's *Misalliance*.)

1109 MORGAN, Margery M. *A Drama of Political Man: A Study in the Plays of Harley Granville Barker*. Lon: Sidgwick & Jackson, 1961. (Full, perceptive study.)*

1110 MORGAN, Margery M. "Two Varieties of Political Drama: 'The Apple Cart' and Granville-Barker's 'His Majesty.' " *Shavian*, 2 (April 1962), 9–16.

1111 NICKSON, Richard. "Granville-Barker as Playwright." *TA*, 27 (1971–72), 22–39.

1112 NORTON, Roger C. "Hugo von Hofmannsthal's *Die Schwierige* and Granville-Barker's *Waste*." *CL*, 14 (1962), 272–79.

1113 PURDOM, C. B. *Harley Granville Barker: Man of the Theatre, Dramatist and Scholar*. Cambridge, MA: Harvard UP, 1956.

1114 RITCHIE, Harry M. "Harley Granville Barker's *The Madras House* and the Sexual Revolution." *MD*, 15 (1972), 150–58.

1115 SHAW, G. Bernard. "Barker's Wild Oats." *Harper's*, 194 (Jan. 1947), 49–53; also in *Drama*, 3 (Winter 1946), 7–14.

1116 WEALES, Gerald. "The Edwardian Theater and the Shadow of Shaw." In *Edwardians and Late Victorians*, ed. Richard Ellmann. English Inst. Essays, 1959. NY: Columbia UP, 1960, 160–87.*

Greene, Graham (1904–)

1117 GREENE, Graham. *A Sort of Life*. NY: Simon & Schuster, 1970.

1118 VANN, Jerry D. *Graham Greene: A Checklist of Criticism*. Kent, OH: Kent State UP, 1970.

1119 ADLER, Jacob H. "Graham Greene's Plays: Technique Versus Value." In *Graham Greene: Some Critical Considerations*, ed. Robert O. Evans. Lexington: Univ. of Kentucky Pr., 1963, 219–30.†

1120 BOYD, John D. "Earth Imagery in Graham Greene's *The Potting Shed*." *MD*, 16 (1973), 69–80.

1121 COTTRELL, Beekman W. "Second Time Charm: The Theatre of Graham Greene." *MFS*, 3 (1957), 249–55.

1122 DeVITIS, A. A. "The Drama." *Graham Greene*. NY: Twayne, 1964, 126–38.

1123 KUNKEL, Francis L. "The Plays." *The Labyrinthine Ways of Graham Greene*. NY: Sheed & Ward, 1959, 153–72.

1124 MURPHY, John P. "*The Potting Shed*." *Ren*, 12 (1959), 43–49.

1125 ROBERTSON, Roderick. "Toward a Definition of Religious Drama." *ETJ*, 9 (1957), 99–105. (*The Living Room* is the central example.)

1126 STRATFORD, Philip. "The Novelist as Playwright." *Faith and Fiction: Creative Process in Greene and Mauriac*. South Bend, IN: Univ. of Notre Dame Pr., 1964, 243–82.

1127 STRATFORD, Philip. "The Uncomplacent Dramatist." In *Graham Greene: A Collection of Critical Essays*, ed. Samuel Hynes. Englewood Cliffs, NJ: Prentice-Hall, 1973, 138–53. (A 1961 *WSCL* article.)†

1128 STRATFORD, Philip. "Unlocking the Potting Shed." *KR*, 24 (1962), 129–43.

Gregory, Lady
[Isabella Augusta P.] (1852–1932)

1129 GREGORY, Lady. *The Collected Plays*, ed. Ann Saddlemyer. Coole Edition, Vols. 5–8. NY: Oxford UP, 1970. 4 vols.

1130 GREGORY, Lady. *Selected Plays*, ed. with intro. by Elizabeth Coxhead; foreword by Sean O'Casey. Lon: Putnam's, 1962.

1131 GREGORY, Lady. "The Lady Gregory Letters to Sean O'Casey," ed. A. C. Edwards. *MD*, 8 (1965), 95–111.

1132 GREGORY, Lady. *Journals, 1916-1930*, ed. Lennox Robinson. Lon: Putnam's, 1946.

1133 GREGORY, Lady. *Seventy Years: Being the Autobiography of Lady Gregory*, ed. Colin Smythe. Coole Edition, Vol. 13. Gerrards Cross: Smythe, 1974; see also **423**.

1134 MIKHAIL, Edward H. "The Theatre of Lady Gregory." *BB*, 27 (Jan.–March 1970), 10, 9. (Bibl.)

1135 ADAMS, Hazard. *Lady Gregory*. Lewisburg, PA: Bucknell UP, 1973.* †

1136 BOWEN, Anne. "Lady Gregory's Use of the Proverbs in Her Plays." *SFQ*, 3 (1939), 231–43.

1137 BOYD, Ernest. *The Contemporary Drama of Ireland*, **417**, 121–38.

1138 COXHEAD, Elizabeth. *J. M. Synge and Lady Gregory*. Lon: Longmans, 1962. (Pamphlet.)†

1139 COXHEAD, Elizabeth. *Lady Gregory: A Literary Portrait*. Lon: Macmillan, 1961.

1140 DEDIO, Anne. *Das dramatische Werk von Lady Gregory*. Bern: Francke, 1967.

1141 ELLIS-FERMOR, Una. *The Irish Dramatic Movement*, **420**, 136–62.*

1142 HOWARTH, Herbert. *The Irish Writers, 1880–1940: Literature Under Parnell's Star*. Lon: Rockliff, 1958, 83–109.

1143 KOPPER, Edward A. *Lady Isabella Persse Gregory*. Bos: Twayne, 1976.

1144 MALONE, Andrew E. *The Irish Drama*, **427**, 52–60, 156–64.

1145 MURPHY, Daniel J. "Lady Gregory, Co-author and Sometimes Author of the Plays of W. B. Yeats." In *Modern Irish Literature* [by several authors]. New Rochelle: Iona College Pr., 1972, 43–52.

1146 SADDLEMYER, Ann. *In Defense of Lady Gregory, Playwright*. Dub: Dolmen, 1966.*

1147 WEYGANDT, Cornelius. *Irish Plays and Playwrights*, **432**, 138–59.

Hankin, St. John
(1869–1909)

1148 HANKIN, St. John. *The Dramatic Works*, with intro. by John Drinkwater. NY: Kennerley, 1912. 3 vols.

1149 HANKIN, St. John. "A Note on Happy Endings" and "Puritanism and the English Stage." *The Dramatic Works*, **1148**, III, 119–48.

1150 ERVINE, St. John. "Introduction." *The Return of the Prodigal*. Lon: Richards, 1949.

1151 HOWE, Percival P. *Dramatic Portraits*, **155**, 163–84.

1152 PHILLIPS, William H. "The Individual and Society in the Plays of St. John Hankin." *Shavian*, 4 (Spring 1972), 170–74.

Jellicoe, Ann
(1928–)

1153 JELLICOE, Ann. [Interview.] In **114**, 244–49.

1154 JELLICOE, Ann. "Question and Answer: An Interview." *NTM*, 1 (July 1960), 24–28.

1155 JELLICOE, Ann. *Some Unconscious' Influences in the Theatre*. Cambridge, Eng.: Univ. Pr., 1967. (Pamphlet.)†

1156 TAYLOR, John R. *Anger & After*, **318**, 73–83.

1157 TSCHUDIN, Marcus. *A Writer's Theatre*, **389**, 69–97. (Court Theatre production of *The Sport of My Mad Mother*.)

Johnston, Denis
(1901–)

1158 JOHNSTON, Denis. *Collected Plays*. Lon: Cape, 1960. 2 vols. (Intros. by Johnston.)

1159 JOHNSTON, Denis, and Gordon HENDERSON. "An Interview with Denis Johnston." *JIL*, 2 (May–Sept. 1973), 30–44.

1160 JOHNSTON, Denis. [Interview.] In **462**, 60–72.

1161 FERRAR, Harold. *Denis Johnston's Irish Theatre*. Dub: Dolmen, 1973.* †

1162 HOGAN, Robert. "The Adult Theatre of Denis Johnston." *After the Irish Renaissance*, **443**, 133–46.

1163 HOGAN, Thomas. "Denis Johnston: Last of the Anglo-Irish." *Envoy*, 3 (Aug. 1950), 33–46.

1164 JORDAN, John. "The Irish Theatre: Retrospect and Premonition." In **100**, 171–75 on Johnston.

1165 SPINNER, Kaspar. *Die alte Dame sagt Nein! Drei irische Dramatiker: Lennox Robinson, Sean O'Casey, Denis Johnston*. Bern: Francke, 1961, 158–91.

Jones, Henry Arthur
(1851–1929)

1166 JONES, Henry Arthur. *Representative Plays*, ed. with intros. by Clayton Hamilton. Bos: Little, Brown, 1925. 4 vols.

1167 JONES, Henry Arthur. *The Renascence of the English Drama: Essays, Lectures, and Fragments, Related to the Modern English Stage, Written and Delivered in the Years 1883–1894*. Lon: Macmillan, 1895.

1168 JONES, Henry Arthur. *The Foundations of a National Drama: A Collection of Lectures, Essays and Speeches, Delivered and Written in the Years 1896–1912*. New ed. Freeport, NY: Books for Libs., 1967 [c.1913].

1169 JONES, Henry Arthur. "Henry Arthur Jones, Dramatist: Self-Revealed; A Conversation on the Art of Writing Plays with Archibald Henderson." *The Nation and the Athenaeum*, 38 (1925), 349–50, 398–99.

1170 BAILEY, J. O. "Science in the Dramas of Jones." In *Booker Memorial Studies*, ed. Hill Shine. Chapel Hill: Univ. of North Carolina Pr., 1950, 154–83.

1171 CORDELL, Richard A. *Henry Arthur Jones and the Modern Drama*. NY: Long & Smith, 1932.*

1172 DICKINSON, Thomas H. *The Contemporary Drama of England*, **148**, 80–94.

1173 HOWE, Percival P. *Dramatic Portraits*, **155**, 53–82.

1174 JONES, Doris A. *Taking the Curtain Call: The Life and Letters of Henry Arthur Jones*. NY: Macmillan, 1930.

1175 NICOLL, Allardyce. *A History of English Drama*, **192**, 161–72.

1176 NORTHEND, Marjorie. "Henry Arthur Jones and the Development of the Modern English Drama." *Rev of Eng St*, 18 (1942), 448–63.*

1177 SELLE, Carl M. "Introduction." *The New Drama*, **198**. (On *The Liars*.)

1178 TAYLOR, John R. *The Rise and Fall of the Well-Made Play*, **170**, 35–51.

1179 WAUCHOPE, George A. "Henry Arthur Jones and the New Social Drama." *SR*, 29 (1921), 146–52.

1180 WEALES, Gerald. *Religion in Modern English Drama*, **172**, 3–11.

Joyce, James
(1882–1941)

1181 JOYCE, James. *Exiles: A Play in Three Acts*, ed. with intro. by Padraic Colum. NY: Viking, 1961. (Includes "Notes by the Author," pp. 113–27.)†

1182 BEEBE, Maurice, Phillip F. HERRING, and A. Walton LITZ. "Criticism of James Joyce: A Selected Checklist." *MFS*, 15 (1969), 105–82. (On *Exiles*, pp. 147–48.)

JAMES JOYCE

1183 ADAMS, Robert M. "Light on Joyce's *Exiles*? A New MS, a Curious Analogue, and Some Speculations." *St in Bibl*, 17 (1964), 83–105.

1184 AITKEN, D. J. F. "Dramatic Archetypes in Joyce's *Exiles*." *MFS*, 4 (1958), 42–52.

1185 BENSTOCK, Bernard. "*Exiles*: 'Paradox Lust' and 'Lost Paladays.' " *ELH*, 36 (1969), 739–56.*

1186 BRANDABUR, Edward. "*Exiles*: A Rough and Tumble Between de Sade and Sacher-Masoch." *A Scrupulous Meanness: A Study of Joyce's Early Work*. Urbana: Univ. of Illinois Pr., 1971, 127–58.

1187 BRIVIC, Sheldon R. "Structure and Meaning in Joyce's *Exiles*." *JJQ*, 6 (1968), 29–52.

1188 CLARK, Earl J. "James Joyce's *Exiles*." *JJQ*, 6 (1968), 69–78.

1189 CUNNINGHAM, Frank R. "Joyce's *Exiles*: A Problem of Dramatic Stasis." *MD*, 12 (1970), 399–407.

1190 FARRELL, James T. "*Exiles* and Ibsen." *Reflections at 50 and Other Essays*. NY: Vanguard, 1954, 66–96; also in his *Selected Essays*, ed. Luna Wolf (NY: McGraw-Hill, 1964), 131–46; also in *James Joyce: Two Decades of Criticism*, ed. Seon Givens (NY: Vanguard, 1948), 95–131.

1191 FERGUSSON, Francis. "A Reading of *Exiles*." In *Exiles, [by] James Joyce*. Norfolk, CT: New Directions, 1945, v–xviii; repr. in his *The Human Image in Dramatic Literature* (Garden City, NY: Doubleday, 1957), 72–84.*

1192 GORMAN, Herbert. *James Joyce: His First Forty Years*. NY: Huebsch, 1924, 101–15.

1193 KENNER, Hugh. "*Exiles*." *Dublin's Joyce*. Bloomington: Indiana UP, 1956, 69–94. (A 1952 *HudR* article.)*

1194 MacNICHOLAS, John. "Joyce contra Wagner." *CoD*, 9 (1975), 29–43. (*Exiles* and Wagner's *Ring*.)

1195 MacNICHOLAS, John. "Joyce's *Exiles*: The Argument for Doubt." *JJQ*, 11 (1973), 33–40.

1196 MAGALANER, Marvin, and Richard M. KAIN. "*Exiles*." *Joyce: The Man, the Work, the Reputation*. NY: New York UP, 1956, 130–45.

1197 MAHER, R. A. "James Joyce's *Exiles*: The Comedy of Discontinuity." *JJQ*, 9 (1972), 461–74.

1198 METZGER, Deena P. "Variations on a Theme: A Study of *Exiles* by James Joyce and *The Great God Brown* by Eugene O'Neill." *MD*, 8 (1965), 174–84.

1199 MOSELEY, Virginia. *Joyce and the Bible*. DeKalb: Univ. of Northern Illinois Pr., 1967, 45–56.

1200 POUND, Ezra. "Mr. James Joyce and the Modern Stage: A Play and Some Considerations." *The Drama* (Chicago), 21 (Feb. 1916), 122–32.

1201 TINDALL, William Y. *A Reader's Guide to James Joyce*. NY: Noonday, 1959, 104–22.†

1202 TYSDAHL, Björn. *James Joyce and Ibsen: A Study in Literary Influence*. NY: Humanities, 1968, 87–102.

1203 WEBER, Roland von. "On and About Joyce's *Exiles*." In *A James Joyce Yearbook*, ed. Maria Jolas. Paris: Transition Pr., 1949, 47–67.

1204 WILLIAMS, Raymond. *Drama from Ibsen to Brecht*, **72**, 141–46.

Lawrence, D[avid] H[erbert] (1855–1930)

1205 LAWRENCE, D. H. *The Complete Plays*. NY: Viking, 1965.

1206 HEPBURN, James G. "D. H. Lawrence's Plays: An Annotated Bibliography." *Book Collector*, 14 (Spring 1965), 78–81.

1207 MARLAND, Michael, ed. *D. H. Lawrence: The Widowing of Mrs. Holroyd & The Daughter-in-Law*. Lon: Heinemann Educ., 1968. (Long intro.)†

1208 O'CASEY, Sean. "A Miner's Dream of Home." *Blasts and Benedictions*, **1279**, 222–25. (1934 review of *A Collier's Friday Night*.)

1209 PANICHAS, George A. "The Biblical Play *David*." *Adventure in Consciousness: The Meaning of D. H. Lawrence's Religious Quest*. The Hague: Mouton, 1964, 136–50. (Also a 1963 *MD* article.)

1210 ROSTON, Murray. *Biblical Drama in England*, **168**, 274–79.

1211 SAGAR, Keith. "D. H. Lawrence: Dramatist." *D. H. Lawrence Rev*, 4 (1971), 154–82.*

1212 SKLAR, Sylvia. *The Plays of D. H. Lawrence*. NY: Harper, 1975.*

1213 SKLAR, Sylvia. "*The Daughter-in-Law* and *My Son's My Son*." *D. H. Lawrence Rev*, 9 (1976), 254–65. (Versions of the same play.)

1214 WATERMAN, Arthur E. "The Plays of D. H. Lawrence." *MD*, 2 (1960), 349–57; repr. in *D. H. Lawrence: A Collection of Critical Essays*, ed. Mark Spilka (Englewood Cliffs, NJ: Prentice-Hall, 1963), 142–50;† see also Harry E. Mahnken, "The Plays of D. H. Lawrence: Addenda," *MD*, 7 (1965), 431–32.

1215 WILLIAMS, Raymond. *Drama from Ibsen to Brecht*, **72**, 257–60. (On *The Widowing of Mrs. Holroyd*.)

Martyn, Edward (1859–1923)

1216 BOYD, Ernest. *The Contemporary Drama of Ireland*, **417**, 12–31.

1217 COURTNEY, Sister Marie-Thérèse. *Edward Martyn and the Irish Theatre*. NY: Vantage, 1956.

1218 ELLIS-FERMOR, Una. "Martyn and Moore." *The Irish Dramatic Movement*, **420**, 117–35.

1219 GWYNN, Denis R. *Edward Martyn and the Irish Revival*. Lon: Cape, 1930.

1220 McFATE, Patricia. "[Moore's] *The Bending of the Bough* and [Martyn's] *The Heather Field*: Two Portraits of the Artists." *Eire*, 8 (Spring 1973), 52–61.

1221 MALONE, Andrew E. *The Irish Drama*, **427**, 61–69, 256–62.

1222 RYAN, Stephen P. "Edward Martyn's Last Play." *Stu*, 47 (1958), 192–99.

1223 SADDLEMYER, Ann. " 'All Art Is a Collaboration'? George Moore and Edward Martyn." In **2313**, 203–22.

1224 SETTERQUIST, Jan. "*The Heather Field*." *Edda*, 61 (1961), 82–96.

1225 SETTERQUIST, Jan. *Ibsen and the Beginnings of Anglo-Irish Drama. Vol. 2: Edward Martyn*. NY: Oriole Eds., 1973 [c.1960].

1226 WEYGANDT, Cornelius. *Irish Plays and Playwrights*, **432**, 74–95.

Masefield, John
(1878–1967)

1227 MASEFIELD, John. *Prose Plays*. NY: Macmillan, 1925.

1228 MASEFIELD, John. *Verse Plays*. NY: Macmillan, 1925.

1229 MASEFIELD, John. "Play-Writing." *Recent Prose*. NY: Macmillan, 1933, 105–41.

1230 CUNLIFFE, John W. *Modern English Playwrights*, **146**, 180–87.

1231 ELLEHAUGE, Martin O. M. *Striking Figures Among Modern English Dramatists*, **215**, 100–116.

1232 HAMILTON, W. H. "The Plays." *John Masefield: A Critical Study*. Lon: Allen & Unwin, 1922, 63–81.

1233 SPANOS, William V. *The Christian Tradition in Modern British Verse Drama*, **268**, 137–45.

1234 WEALES, Gerald. *Religion in Modern English Drama*, **172**, 134–40.

Maugham, W[illiam] Somerset
(1874–1965)

1235 MAUGHAM, W. Somerset. *The Collected Plays*. Lon: Heinemann, 1931. 3 vols. (With an intro. by Maugham in each vol.)

1236 MAUGHAM, W. Somerset. *The Summing Up*. Garden City, NY: Doubleday, 1938. (Sections 30–42 deal with his drama.)†

1237 MIKHAIL, Edward H. "Somerset Maugham and the Theater: A Selected Bibliography." *BB*, 27 (April–June 1970), 42–48.

1238 SANDERS, Charles. *W. Somerset Maugham: An Annotated Bibliography of Writings About Him*. DeKalb: Northern Illinois UP, 1970.*

1239 SANDERS, Charles. "W. Somerset Maugham: A Supplementary Bibliography." *ELT*, 15 (1972), 168–75.

1240 TOOLE STOTT, Raymond. *A Bibliography of the Works of W. Somerset Maugham*. Rev. ed. Lon: Kaye & Ward, 1973.

1241 BARNES, Ronald E. *The Dramatic Comedy of William Somerset Maugham*. The Hague: Mouton, 1968.

1242 BRANDER, L. "The Plays." *Somerset Maugham: A Guide*. NY: Barnes & Noble, 1963, 37–64.

1243 BROOKS, Cleanth, John T. PURSER, and Robert Penn WARREN. "Discussion [of *The Circle*]." *An Approach to Literature*. 3rd ed. NY: Appleton, 1952, 690–93.

1244 CORDELL, Richard A. "The Theatre of Somerset Maugham." *Somerset*

WILLIAM SOMERSET MAUGHAM

Maugham: A Biographical and Critical Study. Bloomington: Indiana UP, 1961, 194–212.

1245 CURTIS, Anthony. "Mainly Heroines." *The Pattern of Maugham: A Critical Portrait.* Lon: Hamilton, 1974, 114–38.

1246 DOTTIN, Paul. *Le Théâtre de W. Somerset Maugham.* Paris: Perrin, 1937.

1247 ERVINE, St. John. "Maugham the Playwright." In **1253**, 142–62. (A 1935 essay.)

1248 FIELDEN, John S. "The Ibsenite Maugham." *MD*, 4 (1961), 138–51.

1249 FIELDEN, John S. " 'Mrs. Beamish' and *The Circle.*" *Boston Univ St in Eng*, 2 (Summer 1956), 113–23.

1250 FIELDEN, John S. "Somerset Maugham on the Purpose of Drama." *ETJ*, 10 (1958), 218–22.

1251 GRUBER, Christian P. "Somerset Maugham's *Perfect Gentleman*, 1912–13." *Theatre Notebook*, 26 (1972), 151–58. (Adaptation of a Molière play.)

1252 JONAS, Klaus W., ed. *The Maugham Enigma: An Anthology.* NY: Citadel, 1954. (32 reviews, addresses, and appreciations; on plays, 101–13.)

1253 JONAS, Klaus W., ed. *The World of Somerset Maugham: An Anthology.* Lon: Owen, 1959.

1254 KRONENBERGER, Louis. *The Thread of Laughter*, **160**, 289–98.

1255 MacCARTHY, Desmond. "Somerset Maugham." *Theatre.* Lon: MacGibbon & Kee, 1954, 119–39. (Reviews of five plays.)

1256 MANDER, Raymond, and Joe MITCHENSON. *Theatrical Companion to Maugham: A Pictorial Record of the First Performances of the Plays of W. Somerset Maugham.* Lon: Rockliff, 1955. (Synopses, cast lists, some reviews of productions.)

1257 MARLOW, Louis. "Somerset Maugham." In *Writers of To-Day, 2*, ed. Denys V. Baker. Lon: Sidgwick & Jackson, 1948, 37–52.

1258 MONTAGUE, Clifford M. "William Somerset Maugham—Dramatist." *PoL*, 47 (1941), 40–55.

1259 NAIK, M. K. *W. Somerset Maugham.* Norman: Univ. of Oklahoma Pr., 1966. (Chronological study of Maugham's works.)

1260 PARKER, R. B. "*The Circle* of Somerset Maugham." In **1821**, 36–50.

1261 POLLOCK, John. "Somerset Maugham and His Work." *Q Rev*, 304 (1966), 367–78.

1262 SPENCER, Theodore. "Somerset Maugham." *Eng J*, 29 (1940), 523–42.

1263 TAYLOR, John R. *The Rise and Fall of the Well-Made Play*, **170**, 92–109.

1264 TREWIN, John C. "W. Somerset Maugham: An Appreciation of His Work in the Theatre." In **1256**, 1–16.

1265 WILLIAMS, Orlo. "Realistic Prose Drama: Mr. Somerset Maugham's Last Plays." *National Rev*, 102 (1934), 676–83.

Moore, George
(1852–1933)

1266 MOORE, George. *Hail and Farewell: A Trilogy*. Lon: Heinemann, 1911–14. 3 vols. (Autobiographical.)

1267 MOORE, George. "Our Dramatists and Their Literature." *Impressions and Opinions*. N Y: Brentano's, 1891, 139–61.

1268 ELLIS-FERMOR, Una. "Martyn and Moore." *The Irish Dramatic Movement*, **420**, 117–35.

1269 FARROW, Anthony. "Introduction." *Diarmuid and Grania: A Three Act Tragedy by George Moore and W. B. Yeats*. Chicago: De Paul UP, 1974, 1–15.

1270 McFATE, Patricia. "[Moore's] *The Bending of the Bough* and [Martyn's] *The Heather Field:* Two Portraits of the Artists." *Eire*, 8 (Spring 1973), 52–61.

1271 MICHIE, Donald M. "A Man of Genius and a Man of Talent." *TSLL*, 6 (1964), 148–54. (Collaboration with Yeats on *Diarmuid and Grania*.)

1272 NEWLIN, Paul A. "The Artful Failure of George Moore's Plays." *Eire*, 8 (Spring 1973), 62–84.

1273 SADDLEMYER, Ann. " 'All Art Is a Collaboration'? George Moore and Edward Martyn." In **2313**, 203–22.

1274 SCHODET, Mireille. "The Theme of Diarmuid and Grainne." In **412**, 213–21.

1275 WEYGANDT, Cornelius. *Irish Plays and Playwrights*, **432**, 99–113.

O'Casey, Sean
(1880–1964)

1276 O'CASEY, Sean. *Collected Plays*. Lon: Macmillan, 1949–51. 4 vols. (Does not include *The Bishop's Bonfire* or *The Drums of Father Ned*.)

1277 O'CASEY, Sean. *The Sean O'Casey Reader: Plays, Autobiographies, Opinions*, ed. Brooks Atkinson. NY: St. Martin's, 1968. (1,000-page anthology, including O'Casey's opinions on Beckett, Pinter and Artaud.)

1278 O'CASEY, Sean. *Letters*, ed. David Krause. NY: Macmillan, 1975–. (Vol. 1: 1910–41.)

1279 O'CASEY, Sean. "O'Casey on O'Casey." *Blasts and Benedictions: Articles and Stories*, ed. Ronald Ayling. Lon: Macmillan, 1967, 85–149. (Essays, 1926–63, including several on his plays.)*

1280 O'CASEY, Sean. "*The Drums of Father Ned*: O'Casey and the Archbishop." In **462**, 134–51. (Letters on a proposed production of the play.)

1281 O'CASEY, Sean. *The Green Crow*. NY: Braziller, 1956. (Essays.)

1282 O'CASEY, Sean. *Under a Colored Cap: Articles Merry and Mournful, with Comments and a Song*. Lon: Macmillan, 1963. (Includes a few literary essays, one on *Purple Dust*.)

1283 O'CASEY, Sean. *Mirror in My House: The Autobiographies of Sean O'Casey*. NY: Macmillan, 1956. 2 vols. (Contains the six separately publ. vols.: *I Knock at the Door*; *Pictures in the Hallway*; *Drums Under the Windows*; *Inishfallen, Fare Thee Well*; *Rose and Crown*; and *Sunset and Evening Star*.)†

1284 O'CASEY, Sean. *The Sting and the Twinkle: Conversations with Sean O'Casey*, ed. Edward H. Mikhail and John O'Riordan. Lon: Macmillan, 1974.

1285 AYLING, Ronald, and Michael J. DURKAN. *Sean O'Casey: A Bibliography*. Lon: Macmillan, 1978 or 1979.

1286 MIKHAIL, Edward H. *Sean O'Casey: A Bibliography of Criticism*. Seattle: Univ. of Washington Pr., 1972.*

1287 MIKHAIL, Edward H. "Sean O'Casey Studies: An Annual Bibliography." *SOR*, 3– (Fall 1976–).

1288 ARMSTRONG, William A. "History, Autobiography, and *The Shadow of a Gunman.*" *MD*, 2 (1960), 417–24.

1289 ARMSTRONG, William A. "The Integrity of *Juno and the Paycock.*" *MD*, 17 (1974), 1–9.

1290 ARMSTRONG, William A. "The Irish Point of View: The Plays of Sean O'Casey. . . ." In **90**, 79–93.

1291 ARMSTRONG, William A. *Sean O'Casey*. Lon: Longmans for the British Council, 1967. (Pamphlet.)†

1292 ARMSTRONG, William A. "Sean O'Casey, W. B. Yeats and the Dance of Life." In **1300**, 131–42.

1293 ARMSTRONG, William A. "The Sources and Themes of *The Plough and the Stars.*" *MD*, 4 (1961), 234–42.

1294 AYLING, Ronald. "Character Control and 'Alienation' in *The Plough and the Stars.*" *JJQ*, 8 (1970), 29–47.

1295 AYLING, Ronald. *Continuity and Innovation in Sean O'Casey's Drama*. Salzburg: Univ. Salzburg, 1976.

1296 AYLING, Ronald. "Ideas and Ideology in *The Plough and the Stars.*" *SOR*, 2 (1976), 115–36.

1297 AYLING, Ronald. "*Juno and the Paycock*: A Textual Study." *Modernist St*, 2 (1976), 15–26.

1298 AYLING, Ronald. " 'Nannie's Night Out.' " *MD*, 5 (1962), 154–63.

1298A AYLING, Ronald. "Patterns of Language and Ritual in Sean O'Casey's Drama." *Anglo-Irish St*, 2 (1976), 25–44.

1299 AYLING, Ronald. "Popular Tradition and Individual Talent in Sean O'Casey's Dublin Trilogy." *JML*, 2 (1972), 491–504.

1300 AYLING, Ronald, ed. *Sean O'Casey: Modern Judgements*. Lon: Macmillan, 1969.* †

1301 AYLING, Ronald. " 'To Bring Harmony': Recurrent Patterns in O'Casey's Drama." *Eire*, 10 (Autumn 1975), 62–78.

1302 BALASHOV, Peter. "O'Casey." *The Soviet History of English Literature*. Moscow: 1958, 627–46.

1303 BARZUN, Jacques. "O'Casey at Your Bedside." *TDR*, 2 (Feb. 1958), 57–61; repr. in **1300**, 120–25.

1304 BENSTOCK, Bernard. "A Covey of Clerics in Joyce and O'Casey." *JJQ*, 2 (1964), 18–32.

1305 BENSTOCK, Bernard. "The Mother-Madonna-Matriarch in Sean O'Casey." *SoR*, 6 (1970), 603–23.

1306 BENSTOCK, Bernard. *Paycocks and Others: Sean O'Casey's World*. Dub: Gill & Macmillan, 1976.*

1307 BLITCH, Alice F. "O'Casey's Shakespeare." *MD*, 15 (1972), 283–90. (In *Juno*.)

1308 COAKLEY, James, and Marvin FELHEIM. "Thalia in Dublin: Some Suggestions About the Relationships Between O'Casey and Classical Comedy." *CoD*, 4 (1970–71), 265–71.

1309 COSTON, Herbert H. "Sean O'Casey: Prelude to Playwriting." *TDR*, 5 (Sept. 1960), 102–12; repr. in **103**, 125–36, and in **1300**, 47–59.*

1310 COWASJEE, Saros. *O'Casey*. Edinburgh: Oliver & Boyd, 1966. (120-page overview.)†

1311 COWASJEE, Saros. *Sean O'Casey: The Man Behind the Plays*. NY: St. Martin's, 1964.*

1312 DANIEL, Walter C. "The False Paradise Pattern in Sean O'Casey's *Cock-a-Doodle Dandy*." *CLA J*, 13 (1969), 137–43.

1313 DANIEL, Walter C. "Patterns of Greek Comedy in O'Casey's *Purple Dust*." *BNYPL*, 66 (1962), 603–12.

1314 Da RIN, Doris. *Sean O'Casey*. NY: Ungar, 1977. (Introductory.)

1315 DeBAUN, Vincent C. "Sean O'Casey and the Road to Expressionism." *MD*, 4 (1961), 254–59. (On *Plough*.)

1316 DOBREE, Bonamy. "Sean O'Casey and the Irish Drama." In **1300**, 92–105. (1934 lecture.)

1317 DURBACH, Errol. "Peacocks and Mothers: Theme and Dramatic Metaphor in O'Casey's *Juno and the Paycock*." *MD*, 15 (1972), 15–25.

1318 DURKAN, Emile J. "Merriment and Celebration in Sean O'Casey's Plays." *SOR*, 2 (1975), 12–21.

1319 ESSLINGER, Pat. "Sean O'Casey and the Lockout of 1913. *Materia Poetica* of the Two Red Plays." *MD*, 6 (1963), 53–63.

1320 FALLON, Gabriel. *Sean O'Casey: The Man I Knew*. Lon: Routledge, 1965.

1321 FINDLATER, Richard. *The Unholy Trade*, **253**, 170–84.

1322 FRAYNE, John P. *Sean O'Casey*. NY: Columbia UP, 1976. (Pamphlet.)

1323 FREEDMAN, Morris. "The Modern Tragicomedy of Wilde and O'Casey." *The Moral Impulse: Modern Drama from Ibsen to the Present*. Carbondale: Southern Illinois UP, 1967, 63–73. (A 1964 *CE* article.)

1324 GASSNER, John. "Genius Without Fetters." In *Selected Plays of Sean O'Casey*, ed. John Gassner. NY: Braziller, 1954, v-xxi.

1325 GASSNER, John. "The Prodigality of Sean O'Casey." *The Theatre in Our Times*, **105**, 240–48; repr. in **1300**, 110–19.

1326 GOLDSTONE, Herbert. *In Search of Community: The Achievement of Sean O'Casey*. Cork: Mercier Pr., 1972.†

1327 HETHMON, Robert. "Great Hatred, Little Room." *TDR*, 5 (June 1961), 51–55. (On *Kathleen Listens In*.)

1328 HOGAN, Robert. *The Experiments of Sean O'Casey*. NY: St. Martin's, 1960.*

1329 HOGAN, Robert, ed. *Feathers from the Green Crow: Sean O'Casey, 1905–1925*. Columbia: Univ. of Missouri Pr., 1962. (Valuable intro. and notes.)

1330 HOGAN, Robert. "The Haunted Inkbottle: A Preliminary Study of Rhetorical Devices in the Late Plays of Sean O'Casey." *JJQ*, 8 (1970), 76–95.

1331 HOGAN, Robert. "In Sean O'Casey's Golden Days." In **1300**, 162–76, and in **1336**; earlier versions in *DM*, 5 (1966), 80–93, and in his *After the Irish Renaissance*, **443**, 235–52.

1332 JORDAN, John. "Illusion and Actuality in the Later O'Casey." In **1300**, 1434–61.

1333 JORDAN, John. "The Irish Theatre: Retrospect and Premonition." In **100**, 165–83.

1334 KAUFMAN, Michael W. "O'Casey's Structural Design in *Juno and the Paycock*." *QJS*, 58 (1972), 191–98.

1335 KAUFMAN, Michael W. "The Position of *The Plough and the Stars* in O'Casey's Dublin Trilogy." *JJQ*, 8 (1970), 48–63.

1336 KILROY, Thomas, ed. *Sean O'Casey: A Collection of Critical Essays*. Englewood Cliffs, NJ: Prentice-Hall, 1975. (Commentary, most of it reprinted; includes short pieces by Arden and Beckett.)*

1337 KNIGHT, G. Wilson. "Ever a Fighter: On Sean O'Casey's *The Drums of Father Ned*." *The Christian Renaissance*. NY: Norton, 1962, 341–47; repr. in **1300**, 177–82, and in **1336**.

1338 KNIGHT, G. Wilson. *The Golden Labyrinth*, **159**, 373–80.

1339 KOSOK, Heinz. *Sean O'Casey: Das dramatische Werk*. Berlin: Schmidt, 1972.

1340 KRAUSE, David. "The Principle of Comic Disintegration." *JJQ*, 8 (1970), 3–12.

1341 KRAUSE, David. *Sean O'Casey: The Man and His Work*. Enl. ed. NY: Macmillan, 1974.* †

1342 KRAUSE, David. "Sean O'Casey and the Higher Nationalism: The Desecration of Ireland's Household Gods." In **409**, 114–33.

1343 LEWIS, Allan. *The Contemporary Theatre*, **63**, 169–91. (Stresses *Red Roses for Me*.)

1344 LEZON, Jeanne. "The Easter Rising Seen from the Tenements." In **412**, 75–95.

1345 LINDSAY, Jack. "*The Plough and the Stars* Reconsidered." *SOR*, 2 (1976), 187–95.

1346 LINDSAY, Jack. "Sean O'Casey as a Socialist Artist." In **1300**, 192–203.

1347 McHUGH, Roger. "The Legacy of Sean O'Casey." *TQ*, 8 (Spring 1965), 123–37; repr. in **1336**.

1348 McLAUGHLIN, John. "Political Allegory in O'Casey's *Purple Dust*." *MD*, 13 (1970), 47–53.

1349 MALONE, Andrew E. *The Irish Drama*, **427**, 209–19.

1350 MALONE, Maureen. *The Plays of Sean O'Casey*. Carbondale: Southern Illinois UP, 1969.

1351 MARGULIES, Martin B. *The Early Life of Sean O'Casey*. Dub: Dolmen, 1970.

1352 MATHELIN, Bernard. "From the Shadow of War to the Broken Tassie." In **413**, 97–105.

1353 MURPHY, R. Patrick. "Sean O'Casey and the Avant-Garde." *CLQ*, 11 (1975), 235–48. (See also his essay in *JJQ*, 8 [1970], 96 -110.)

1354 O'CASEY, Eileen. *Sean*, ed. John C. Trewin. Lon: Macmillan, 1971.

1355 PARKER, R. B. "Bernard Shaw and Sean O'Casey." In **1835**, 3–29; also in *QQ*, 73 (1966), 13–34.

1356 PIXLEY, Edward E. *"The Plough and the Stars*—The Destructive Consequences of Human Folly." *ETJ*, 23 (1971), 75–82.

1357 REITER, Seymour. *World Theater*, **708**, 203–8. (On *Plough*.)

1358 RITCHIE, Harry M. "The Influence of Melodrama on the Early Plays of Sean O'Casey." *MD*, 5 (1962), 164–73.

1359 ROLLINS, Ronald G. *Verisimilitude and Vision in Selected Plays of Sean O'Casey*. University: Univ. of Alabama Pr., 1978 or 1979.*

1360 ROY, Emil. *British Drama Since Shaw*, **233**, 68–82.

1361 SCHRANK, Bernice. "Dialectical Configurations in *Juno and the Paycock*." *TCL*, 21 (1975), 438–56.

1362 *Sean O'Casey Review*, 1– (Fall 1974–). (Issued twice a year.)

1363 SMITH, Bobby L. "From Athlete to Statue: Satire in Sean O'Casey's *The Silver Tassie*." *ArQ*, 27 (1971), 347–61.

1364 SMITH, Bobby L. "O'Casey's Satiric Vision." *JJQ*, 8 (1970), 13–28.

1365 SMITH, Bobby L. "Satire in O'Casey's *Cock-a-Doodle Dandy*." *Ren*, 19 (1967), 64–73.

1366 SMITH, Bobby L. "Satire in *The Plough and the Stars: A Tragedy in Four Acts*." *Ball State Univ Forum*, 10 (Summer 1969), 3–11.

1367 SNOWDEN, J. A. "Dialect in the Plays of Sean O'Casey." *MD*, 14 (1972), 387–91.

1368 SNOWDEN, J. A. "Sean O'Casey and Naturalism." *E&S*, 24 (1971), 56–68.

1369 SPINNER, Kaspar. *Die alte Dame sagt Nein!* **1165**, 50–157.

1370 STARKIE, Walter. "Sean O'Casey." In **413**, 149–76.

1371 STOCK, A. G. "The Heroic Image: *Red Roses for Me*." In **1300**, 126–30.

1372 STYAN, J. L. *The Elements of Drama*, **71**, 190–95. (On *Plough*.)

1373 TEMPLETON, Joan. "Sean O'Casey and Expressionism." *MD*, 14 (1971), 47–62.

1374 THOMPSON, William I. "The Naturalistic Image: O'Casey." *The Imagination of an Insurrection: Dublin, Easter 1916; A Study of an Ideological Movement*. NY: Oxford UP, 1967, 202–27. (On *Plough*.)

1375 TODD, R. Mary. "The Two Published Versions of Sean O'Casey's *Within the Gates*." *MD*, 10 (1968), 346–55.

1376 WOODBRIDGE, Homer E. "Sean O'Casey." *SAQ*, 40 (1941), 50–59.

1377 WORTH, Katharine J. "O'Casey's Dramatic Symbolism." *MD*, 4 (1961), 260–67; repr. in **1300**, 183–91.

Orton, Joe (1933–1967)

1378 ORTON, Joe. *The Complete Plays*, introduced by John Lahr. Lon: Eyre Methuen, 1976.†

1379 ORTON, Joe. "Joe Orton, Interviewed by Giles Gordon." *TrR*, No. 24 (1967), 93–100; repr. in **114**, 116–24.

1380 FRASER, Keath. "Joe Orton: His Brief Career." *MD*, 14 (1972), 413–19.

1381 LAHR, John. "Joe Orton: Artist of the Outrageous." *Astonish Me*, 111, 83–101.

1381A SMITH, Leslie. "Democratic Lunacy: The Comedies of Joe Orton." *Adam International Rev*, 40, Nos. 394-96 (1976), 73-92.

1382 STRANG, Ronald W. "*What the Butler Saw*." In 173, 86–93.

1383 TAYLOR, John R. *The Second Wave*, 319, 125–40.

1384 WORTH, Katharine J. *Revolutions in Modern English Drama*, 174, 148–56. (Stresses *What the Butler Saw*.)

Osborne, John
(1929–)

1385 OSBORNE, John. "They Call It Cricket." In *Declaration*, ed. Tom Maschler. NY: Dutton, 1958, 45–66; partly repr. in 99, 140–44.

1386 OSBORNE, John. [Interview.] In 121, 90–109.

1387 OSBORNE, John. [Interview.] In *Olivier,* ed. Logan Gourlay. Lon: Weidenfeld & Nicholson, 1973, 145–56.

1388 NORTHOUSE, Cameron, and Thomas P. WALSH. *John Osborne: A Reference Guide*. Bos: Hall, 1974. (Annotated bibl.)

1389 ALLSOP, Kenneth. *The Angry Decade: A Survey of the Cultural Revolt of the Nineteen-Fifties*. Lon: Owen, 1958, 104–30.

1390 ANDERSON, Michael. *Anger and Detachment*, 276, 21–49.

1391 BANHAM, Martin. *Osborne*. Edinburgh: Oliver & Boyd, 1969. (Basic introduction.)†

1392 BROWN, John R. "John Osborne. Theatrical Belief: *Look Back in Anger, The Entertainer, Luther, Inadmissible Evidence* and Other Plays." *Theatre Language*, 281, 118–57.*

1393 CARNALL, Geoffrey. "Saints and Human Beings: Orwell, Osborne and Gandhi." In 1425, 129–37.

1394 CARTER, Alan. *John Osborne*. 2nd ed. Edinburgh: Oliver & Boyd, 1973.

1395 DEMING, Barbara. "John Osborne's War Against the Philistines." *HudR*, 11 (1958), 411–19.

1396 DENTY, Vera D. "The Psychology of Martin Luther." *CathW*, 194 (1961), 99–105. (By a psychologist.)

1397 DYSON, A. E. "*Look Back in Anger*." *CritQ*, 1 (1959), 318–26; repr. in 280, 47–57.

1398 FABER, M. D. "The Character of Jimmy Porter: An Approach to *Look Back in Anger*." *MD*, 13 (1970), 67–77.

1399 FERRAR, Harold. *John Osborne*. NY: Columbia UP, 1973. (Pamphlet.)†

1400 FINDLATER, Richard. "The Case of P. Slickey." *TC*, 167 (1960), 29–38. (The play as a failure.)

1401 FLINT, Martha, and Charlotte GERRARD. "[Sartre's] *Le Diable et le bon Dieu* and an Angry Young Luther." *J of European St*, 2 (1972), 247–55.

1402 FRASER, G. S. *The Modern Writer and His World*, 254, 227–33.

1403 GERSH, Gabriel. "The Theater of John Osborne." *MD*, 10 (1967), 137–43.

1404 HAHNLOSER-INGOLD, Margrit. *Das englische Theater und Bert. Brecht,* **296**, 129–73.

1405 HAYMAN, Ronald. *John Osborne.* 2nd ed. Lon: Heinemann Educ., 1970. (Basic introduction.)

1406 HUSS, Roy. "John Osborne's Backward Half-Way Look." *MD,* 6 (1963), 20–25.

1407 KARRFALT, David H. "The Social Theme in Osborne's Plays." *MD,* 13 (1970), 78–82.

1408 KENNEDY, Andrew K. *Six Dramatists in Search of a Language,* **158**, 192–212.

1409 KERSHAW, John. "John Osborne: A Modern Romantic" and "*Look Back in Anger*: Language and Character." *The Present Stage.* Lon: Fontana, 1966, 21–41.

1410 LAHR, John. "John Osborne: Poor Johnny One-Note." *Up Against the Fourth Wall,* **112**, 230–45.

1411 LUMLEY, Frederick. "The Invective of John Osborne." *New Trends in 20th Century Drama,* **161**, 221–33.

1412 McCARTHY, Mary. "A New Word." In **1425**, 150–60.

1413 MANDER, John. "John Osborne's *Look Back in Anger.*" *The Writer and Commitment.* Lon: Secker & Warburg, 1961, 179–88.

1414 MAROWITZ, Charles. "The Ascension of John Osborne." *TDR,* 7 (Winter 1962), 175–79; repr. in **280**, 117–21, and in **1425**, 161–65.

1415 NICOLL, Allardyce. "Somewhat in a New Dimension." In **100**, 76–95.

1416 O'BRIEN, Charles H. "Osborne's *Luther* and the Humanistic Tradition." *Ren,* 21 (1969), 59–63.

1417 POST, Robert M. "The Outsider in the Plays of John Osborne." *Southern Speech Assn J,* 39 (Fall 1973), 63–74.

1418 RILLIE, John A. M. "*The Entertainer.*" In **173**, 94–102.

1419 ROGERS, Daniel. " 'Not for Insolence, But Seriously': John Osborne's Adaptation of *La fianza satisfecha.*" *Durham Univ J,* 29 (1968), 146–70. (*A Bond Honoured.*)

1420 ROLLINS, Ronald G. "Carroll and Osborne: Alice and Alison in Wild Wonderlands." *Forum* (Houston), 7 (Summer 1969), 16–20.

1421 RUPP, Gordon. "Luther and Mr. Osborne." *Cambridge Q,* 1 (1965–66), 28–42.

1422 SCOTT-KILVERT, Ian. "The Hero in Search of a Dramatist: The Plays of John Osborne." *Encounter,* 9 (Dec. 1957), 26–30.

1423 SPACKS, Patricia M. "Confrontation and Escape in Two Social Dramas [*A Doll's House* and *Look Back in Anger*]." *MD,* 11 (1968), 61–72.

1424 TAYLOR, John R. *Anger & After,* **318**, 39–66.*

1425 TAYLOR, John R., ed. *Look Back in Anger: A Casebook.* Nashville: Aurora, 1970. (Reviews, studies, and essays by Osborne [59–71].)* †

1426 TRUSSLER, Simon. *The Plays of John Osborne: An Assessment.* Lon: Gollancz, 1969.* †

1427 TSCHUDIN, Marcus. *A Writer's Theatre,* **389**, 183–216. (Court Theatre production of *Luther.*)

1428 WEISE, Wolf-Dietrich. *Die "Neuen englischer Dramatiker" in ihren Verhältnis zu Brecht,* **328**, 111–40.

1429 WEISS, Samuel A. "Osborne's Angry Young Play." *ETJ,* 12 (1960), 285–88.

1430 WELLWARTH, George. "John Osborne: 'Angry Young Man'?" *The Theater of Protest and Paradox,* **329**, 254–69.*

1431 WHITING, John. *"Luther." LonM,* 1 (Oct. 1961), 57–59; repr. in **2095**, 37–44.

1432 WILLIAMS, Raymond. *Drama from Ibsen to Brecht,* **72**, 318–22. (On *Look Back.*)

1433 WORTH, Katharine J. "The Angry Young Man: John Osborne." In **90**, 147–68; repr. in **1425**, 101–16.*

1434 WORTH, Katharine J. *Revolutions in Modern English Drama,* **174**, 67–85.

1435 WORTH, Katharine J. "Shaw and John Osborne." *Shavian,* 2 (Oct. 1964), 29–35.

Pinero, Arthur Wing
(1855–1934)

1436 PINERO, Arthur Wing. *The Social Plays,* ed. Clayton Hamilton. NY: Dutton, 1917–22. 4 vols. (Intro. by Clayton Hamilton, I, 3–33.)

1437 PINERO, Arthur Wing. *The Collected Letters,* ed. J. P. Wearing. Minneapolis: Univ. of Minnesota Pr., 1974.

1438 PINERO, Arthur Wing. "Robert Louis Stevenson as a Dramatist." In *Papers on Playmaking,* ed. Brander Matthews. NY: Hill & Wang, 1957, 43–76. (1903 lecture, with intro. by Clayton Hamilton.)†

1439 ARMSTRONG, Cecil F. *Shakespeare to Shaw.* NY: AMS Pr., 1969 [c.1913], 206–45.

1440 BOAS, Frederick S. "Sir Arthur Pinero: Dramatist and Stage Chronicler." *From Richardson to Pinero.* Lon: Murray, 1936, 250–80.

1441 BURNS, Winifred. "Certain Women Characters of Pinero's Serious Drama." *PoL,* 54 (1948), 195–219.

1442 CUNLIFFE, John W. *Modern English Playwrights,* **146**, 33–47.

1443 DAVIES, Cecil W. "Pinero: The Drama of Reputation." *English,* 14 (1962), 13–17.

1444 DICKINSON, Thomas H. *The Contemporary Drama of England,* **148**, 95–115.

1445 DUNKEL, Wilbur D. *Sir Arthur Pinero: A Critical Biography with Letters.* Chicago: Univ. of Chicago Pr., 1941.

1446 FYFE, Hamilton. *Sir Arthur Pinero's Plays and Players.* Lon: Benn, 1930.

1447 HOWE, Percival P. *Dramatic Portraits,* **155**, 11–52.

1448 LAZENBY, Walter. *Arthur Wing Pinero.* NY: Twayne, 1972.*

1449 LEGGATT, Alexander. "Pinero: From Farce to Social Drama." *MD,* 17 (1974), 329–44.

1450 MINER, Edmund J. "The Limited Naturalism of Arthur Pinero." *MD,* 19 (1976), 147–59.

1451 MINER, Edmund J. "The Novelty of Pinero's Court Farces." *ELT,* 19 (1976), 299–305.

1452 NICOLL, Allardyce. *A History of English Drama,* **192**, 173–82.

1453 SELLE, Carl M. "Introduction." *The New Drama,* **198**.

1454 SHORT, Ernest. "The British Drama Grows Up." *Q Rev,* 295 (1957), 216–28.

1455 TAYLOR, John R. *The Rise and Fall of the Well-Made Play*, 170, 52–80.*

1456 WELLWARTH, George E. "The Career of Sir Arthur Wing Pinero: A Study in Theatrical Taste." *Southern Speech J*, 26 (Fall 1960), 45–58.

Pinter, Harold
(1930–)

1457 PINTER, Harold. *Plays*. Lon: Eyre Methuen, 1976–.

1458 PINTER, Harold, and Mel GUSSOW. "A Conversation [Pause] with Harold Pinter." *NY Times Mag*, 5 Dec. 1971, 42–43, 126–36.

1459 PINTER, Harold, Clive DONNER, and Kenneth CAVANDER. "Filming *The Caretaker*." *TrR*, No. 13 (1963), 17–26; repr. in 114, 211–22.

1460 PINTER, Harold, and Lawrence M. BENSKY. "Harold Pinter: An Interview." *Paris Rev*, 10 (Fall 1966), 13–39; repr. in *Writers at Work: The Paris Review Interviews, Third Series* (NY: Viking, 1967), 347–68, and in 1508, 19–33; largely repr. in 121, 171–88.

1461 PINTER, Harold. "Writing for the Theatre." *Evergreen Rev*, 8 (Aug.-Sept. 1964), 80–82; repr. in 137, 574–80.*

1462 GALE, Steven H. "Harold Pinter: An Annotated Bibliography, 1957–1971." *BB*, 29 (1972), 46–56.

1463 IMHOF, Rüdiger. *Pinter, a Bibliography: His Works and Occasional Writings, with a Comprehensive Checklist of Criticism and Reviews of the London Productions*. Lon: TQ Publications for British Theatre Inst., 1975. (Pamphlet.)

1464 SCHROLL, Herman T. *Harold Pinter: A Study of His Reputation (1958-1969) and a Checklist*. Metuchen, NJ: Scarecrow, 1971.

1465 ALEXANDER, Nigel. "Past, Present and Pinter." *E&S*, 27 (1974), 1–17.

1466 ALLISON, Ralph, and Charles WELLBORN. "Rhapsody in an Anechoic Chamber: Pinter's *Landscape*." *ETJ*, 25 (1973), 215–25.

1467 AMEND, Victor E. "Harold Pinter: Some Credits and Debits." *MD*, 10 (1967), 165–74.

1468 ANDERSON, Michael. *Anger and Detachment*, 276, 88–115.

1469 ARONSON, Steven M. L. "Pinter's 'Family' and Blood Knowledge." In 1527, 67–86.

1470 BAKER, William, and Stephen E. TABACHNICK. *Harold Pinter*. NY: Barnes & Noble, 1973.†

1471 BERKOWITZ, Gerald M. "Pinter's Revision of *The Caretaker*." *JML*, 5 (1976), 109–16.

1472 BERMEL, Albert. "The Monarch as Beggar: *A Slight Ache. . . .*" *Contradictory Characters*, 43, 228–42.

1473 BERNHARD, F. J. "Beyond Realism: The Plays of Harold Pinter." *MD*, 8 (1965), 185–91.

1474 BOULTON, James T. "Harold Pinter: *The Caretaker* and Other Plays." *MD*, 6 (1963), 131–40; repr. in 1508, 93–104.

1475 BRODY, Alan. "The Gift of Realism: Hitchcock and Pinter." *JML*, 3 (1973), 149–72. (Stresses *The Birthday Party*.)

1476 BROWN, John R. "Dialogue in Pinter and Others." *CritQ*, 7 (1965), 225–43; repr. in 280, 122–44.

1477 BROWN, John R. "Mr. Pinter's Shakespeare." *CritQ*, 5 (1963), 251–65; repr. in **103**, 352–66.

1478 BROWN, John R. *Theatre Language*, **281**, 15–117.*

1479 BRYDEN, Ronald. "Three Men in a Room" and " A Stink of Pinter." *The Unfinished Hero*, **282**, 86–95.

1480 BURGHARDT, Lorraine H. "Game Playing in Three by Pinter." *MD*, 17 (1974), 377–88. (*Dumb Waiter*, *Birthday Party*, and *Tea Party*.)

1481 BURKMAN, Katherine H. *The Dramatic World of Harold Pinter: Its Basis in Ritual*. Columbus: Ohio State UP, 1971.

1482 CARPENTER, Charles A. "The Absurdity of Dread: Pinter's *The Dumb Waiter*." *MD*, 16 (1973), 279–85.

1483 CARPENTER, Charles A. "Quicksand in Pinterland: *The Caretaker*." *ArQ*, 33 (1977), 65-75.

1484 CARPENTER, Charles A. " 'What Have I Seen, the Scum or the Essence?' Symbolic Fallout in Pinter's *Birthday Party*." *MD*, 17 (1974), 389–402.

1485 COE, Richard M. "Logic, Paradox, and Pinter's *Homecoming*." *ETJ*, 27 (1975), 489–97.

1486 COHN, Ruby. "Latter Day Pinter." *DrS*, 3 (1964), 367–77. (Four short plays.)

1487 COHN, Ruby. "The World of Harold Pinter." *TDR*, 6 (1962), 55–68; repr. in **1508**, 78–92.

1488 COOK, David, and Harold F. BROOKS. "A Room with Three Views: Harold Pinter's *The Caretaker*." *Komos*, 1 (June 1967), 62–69.

1489 CROYDEN, Margaret. "Pinter's Hideous Comedy [*The Homecoming*]." In **1527**, 45–56.

1490 DAWICK, John D. " 'Punctuation' and Patterning in *The Homecoming*." *MD*, 14 (1971), 37–46.

1491 DICK, Kay. "Mr. Pinter and the Fearful Matter." *TQ*, 4 (Autumn 1961), 257–65.

1492 DONOVAN, J. "The Plays of Harold Pinter (1957–61): Victims and Victimization." *Recherches Anglaises et Américaines*, No. 5 (1972), 35–46.

1493 DUKORE, Bernard F. "The Pinter Collection." *ETJ*, 26 (1974), 81–85. (On *The Collection*.)

1494 DUKORE, Bernard F. *Where Laughter Stops: Pinter's Tragicomedy*. Columbia: Univ. of Missouri Pr., 1976.* †

1495 DUKORE, Bernard F. "A Woman's Place." *QJS*, 52 (1966), 237–41; rev. version in **1527**, 109–16.

1496 DURBACH, Errol. " 'The Caretaker': Text and Subtext." *Eng St in Africa*, 18 (1975), 23–29.

1497 EIGO, James. "Pinter's *Landscape*." *MD*, 16 (1973), 179–83.

1498 ESSLIN, Martin. "Alienation in Brecht, Beckett, and Pinter." *Perspectives on Contemporary Lit*, 1 (1975), 3–21.

1499 ESSLIN, Martin. "Godot and His Children: The Theatre of Samuel Beckett and Harold Pinter." In **90**, 128–46; repr. in **280**, 58–70.

1500 ESSLIN, Martin. *Pinter: A Study of His Plays*. Lon: Eyre Methuen, 1973 [c.1970]. (Originally entitled *The Peopled Wound*.)* †

1501 ESSLIN, Martin. *The Theatre of the Absurd*, **54**, 231–57.

1502 FJELDE, Rolf. "Plotting Pinter's Progress." In **1527**, 87–107.

1503 FREE, William J. "Treatment of Character in Harold Pinter's *The Homecoming*." *South Atlantic Bul*, 34 (Nov. 1969), 1–5.

1504 GABBARD, Lucina P. *The Dream Structure of Pinter's Plays: A Psychoanalytic Approach*. Rutherford, NJ: Fairleigh Dickinson UP, 1976.

1504A GALE, Steven H. *Butter's Going Up: A Critical Analysis of Harold Pinter's Work*. Durham, NC: Duke UP, 1977.

1505 GALLAGHER, Kent G. "Harold Pinter's Dramaturgy." *QJS*, 52 (1966), 242–48. (On *The Caretaker*.)

1506 GANZ, Arthur F. "A Clue to the Pinter Puzzle: The Triple Self in *The Homecoming*." *ETJ*, 21 (1969), 180–87.

1507 GANZ, Arthur F. "Mixing Memory and Desire: Pinter's Vision in *Landscape*, *Silence*, and *Old Times*." In **1508**, 161–78.

1508 GANZ, Arthur F., ed. *Pinter: A Collection of Critical Essays*. Englewood Cliffs, NJ: Prentice-Hall, 1972.* †

1509 GILLEN, Francis. " 'All These Bits and Pieces': Fragmentation and Choice in Pinter's Plays." *MD*, 17 (1974), 477–87. (*The Caretaker* and later plays.)

1510 GILLEN, Francis." ' . . . Apart from the Known and the Unknown': The Unreconciled Worlds of Harold Pinter's Characters." *ArQ*, 26 (1970), 17–24.

1511 GOLDSTONE, Herbert. "Not So Puzzling Pinter: *The Homecoming*." *TA*, 25 (1969), 20–27.

1512 GOODMAN, Florence J. "Pinter's *The Caretaker*: The Lower Depths Descended." *Midwest Q*, 5 (1964), 117–26.

1513 GORDON, Lois G. "Harold Pinter—Past and Present." *KanQ*, 3 (Spring 1971), 89–99. (Stresses the later plays.)

1514 GORDON, Lois G. *Stratagems to Uncover Nakedness: The Dramas of Harold Pinter*. Columbia: Univ. of Missouri Pr., 1969. (Pamphlet.)†

1515 HEILMAN, Robert B. "Demonic Strategies: *The Birthday Party* and *The Firebugs*." In *Sense and Sensibility in Twentieth-Century Writing*, ed. Brom Weber. Carbondale : Southern Illinois UP, 1970, 57-74.

1516 HINCHLIFFE, Arnold P. *Harold Pinter*. FY: Twayne, 1967.

1517 HOEFER, Jacqueline. "Pinter and Whiting: Two Attitudes Towards the Alienated Artist." *MD*, 4 (1962), 402–8. (*Birthday Party*.)

1518 HOLLIS, James R. *Harold Pinter: The Poetics of Silence*. Carbondale: Southern Illinois UP, 1970.

1519 HUGHES, Alan. " 'They Can't Take That Away from Me': Myth and Memory in Pinter's *Old Times*." *MD*, 17 (1974), 467–76.

1520 IMHOF, Rüdiger. "Pinter's *Silence*: The Impossibility of Communication." *MD*, 17 (1974), 449–60.

1521 JIJI, Vera M. "Pinter's Four Dimensional House: *The Homecoming*." *MD*, 17 (1974), 433–42.

1522 JONES, John B. "Stasis as Structure in Pinter's *No Man's Land*." *MD*, 19 (1976), 291–304.

1523 KAUFMAN, Michael W. "Actions that a Man Might Play: Pinter's *The Birthday Party*." *MD*, 16 (1973), 167–78.

1524 KENNEDY, Andrew K. *Six Dramatists in Search of a Language*, **158**, 165–91.

1525 KERR, Walter. *Harold Pinter*. NY: Columbia UP, 1967. (Pamphlet.)†

1526 KILLINGER, John. *World in Collapse*, **60**, 38–45.

1527 LAHR, John, ed. *A Casebook on Harold Pinter's The Homecoming*. NY: Grove, 1971.* †

1528 LAHR, John. "The Language of Silence." *Up Against the Fourth Wall*, 112, 50–77. (On late Pinter and Beckett.)

1529 LAHR, John. "Pinter and Chekhov: The Bond of Naturalism." *Astonish Me*, 111, 67–82; repr. in 1508, 60–71.

1530 LAHR, John. "Pinter's Language." In 1527, 123–36.

1531 LAHR, John. "Pinter the Spaceman." *Up Against the Fourth Wall*, 112, 175–94; repr. in 1527, 175–93. (Stresses *The Homecoming* and *Landscape*.)

1532 LAMONT, Rosette. "Pinter's *The Homecoming*: The Contest of the Gods." *Far-Western Forum*, 1 (1974), 47–73.

1533 LEECH, Clifford. "Two Romantics: Arnold Wesker and Harold Pinter." In 100, 11–31.

1534 LESSER, Simon O. "Reflections on Pinter's *The Birthday Party*." *ConL*, 13 (1972), 34–43.

1535 MARTINEAU, Stephen. "Pinter's *Old Times*: The Memory Game." *MD*, 16 (1973), 287–97.

1536 MAST, Gerald. "Pinter's *Homecoming*." *DrS*, 6 (1968), 266–77.

1537 MESSENGER, Ann P. "Blindness and the Problem of Identity in Pinter's Plays." *NS*, 21 (1972), 481–90.

1538 MILBERG, Ruth. "1+ 1 = 1: Dialogue and Character Splitting in Harold Pinter." *NS*, 23 (1974), 225–33.

1539 MORGAN, Ricki. "What Max and Teddy Come Home to in *The Homecoming*." *ETJ*, 25 (1973), 490–99.

1540 MORRIS, Kelley. "*The Homecoming*." *TDR*, 11 (Winter 1966), 185–91.

1541 MORRISON, Kristin. "Pinter and the New Irony." *QJS*, 55 (1969), 388–93. (Stresses *The Room* and *The Homecoming*.)

1542 MURPHY, Robert P. "Non-Verbal Communication and the Overlooked Action in Pinter's *The Caretaker*." *QJS*, 58 (1972), 41–47.

1543 NELSON, Hugh. "*The Homecoming*: Kith and Kin." In 280, 145–63.

1544 OSHEROW, Anita R. "Mother and Whore: The Role of Woman in *The Homecoming*." *MD*, 17 (1974), 423–32.

1545 PESTA, John. "Pinter's Usurpers." *DrS*, 6 (1967), 54–65; repr. in 1508, 123–35.

1546 POWLICK, Leonard. "A Phenomenological Approach to Harold Pinter's *A Slight Ache*." *QJS*, 60 (1974), 25–32.

1547 QUIGLEY, Austin E. "*The Dwarfs*: A Study in Linguistic Dwarfism." *MD*, 17 (1974), 413–22.

1548 QUIGLEY, Austin E. *The Pinter Problem*. Princeton, NJ: Princeton UP, 1975. (Long linguistic analyses of *Room*, *Caretaker*, *Homecoming*, and *Landscape*.)*

1548A ROBERTS, Patrick. "Pinter: The Roots of the Relationship." *The Psychology of Tragic Drama*. Lon: Routledge & K. Paul, 1975, 69–101.

1549 SALMON, Eric. "Harold Pinter's Ear." *MD*, 17 (1974), 363–75. (On his use of language.)

1550 SCHECHNER, Richard. "Puzzling Pinter." *TDR*, 11 (Winter 1966), 176–84.*

1551 SCHIFF, Ellen F. "Pancakes and Soap Suds: A Study of Childishness in Pinter's Plays." *MD*, 16 (1973), 91–101.

1552 SKLOOT, Robert. "Putting out the Light: Staging the Theme of Pinter's *Old Times*." *QJS*, 61 (1975), 265–70.

1553 SMITH, Frederick N. "Uncertainty in Pinter: 'The Dwarfs.' " *TA*, 26 (1970), 81–96.

1554 STATES, Bert O. "Pinter's *Homecoming*: The Shock of Nonrecognition." *HudR*, 21 (1968), 474–86; repr. in **1508**, 147–60.

1555 STORCH, R. F. "Harold Pinter's Happy Families." *MR*, 8 (1967), 703–12; repr. in **1508**, 136–46.

1556 STYAN, J. L. *The Dark Comedy*, **70**, 244–60.

1557 SYKES, Alrene. *Harold Pinter*. NY: Humanities, 1970.

1558 TAYLOR, John R. "A Room and Some Views: Harold Pinter." *Anger & After*, **318**, 323–59.*

1559 TETZELI VON ROSADOR, Kurt. "Pinter's Dramatic Method: *Kullus*, *The Examination*, *The Basement*." *MD*, 14 (1971), 195–204.

1560 THORNTON, Peter C. "Blindness and the Confrontation with Death: Three Plays by Harold Pinter." *NS*, 17 (1968), 213–23. (*Room*, *Birthday Party*, *Slight Ache*.)

1561 TRUSSLER, Simon. *The Plays of Harold Pinter: An Assessment*. Lon: Gollancz, 1973.*

1562 WALKER, Augusta. "Messages from Pinter." *MD*, 10 (1967), 1–10.

1563 WALKER, Augusta. "Why the Lady Does It [in *The Homecoming*]." In **1527**, 117–21.

1564 WARDLE, Irving. "The Territorial Struggle [in *The Homecoming*]." In **1527**, 37–44.

1565 WARNER, John M. "The Epistemological Quest in Pinter's *The Homecoming*." *ConL*, 11 (1970), 340–53.

1566 WELLWARTH, George. "Harold Pinter: The Comedy of Allusiveness." *The Theater of Protest and Paradox*, **329**, 224–42.

1567 WRAY, Phoebe. "Pinter's Dialogue: The Play on Words." *MD*, 13 (1971), 418–22.

Priestley, J[ohn] B[oynton] (1894–1975)

1568 PRIESTLEY, J. B. *Plays*. Lon: Heinemann, 1948–50. 3 vols. (With brief intros. by Priestley.)

1569 PRIESTLEY, J. B. *The Art of the Dramatist: A Lecture Together with Appendices and Discursive Notes*. Lon: Heinemann, 1957.†

1570 PRIESTLEY, J. B. *Margin Released: A Writer's Reminiscences and Reflections*. NY: Harper, 1962.

1571 PRIESTLEY, J. B. *Theatre Outlook*. Lon: Nicholson & Watson, 1947.

1572 COOPER, Susan. "Theatre." *J. B. Priestley: Portrait of an Author*. Lon: Heinemann, 1970, 83–155.

1573 EVANS, Gareth L. *J. B. Priestley, the Dramatist*. Lon: Heinemann, 1964.*

1574 FINDLATER, Richard. "The Two Countesses," **101**.

1575 FINDLATER, Richard. *The Unholy Trade*, **253**, 184–92.

1576 HUGHES, David. "A Leading Playwright of the Thirties" and "A Post-War Dramatist." *J. B. Priestley: An Informal Study of His Work*. Lon: Hart-Davis, 1958, 125–61, 191–207.

1577 ROGERS, Ivor A. "The Time Plays of J. B. Priestley." *Extrapolation*, 10 (Dec. 1968), 9–16.

1577A ROTH, Walter. *"An Inspector Calls."* In *Insight II: Analyses of Modern British Literature,* ed. John V. Hagopian and Martin Dolch. Frankfurt: Hirschgraben, 1970, 294-302.

1578 SCHLÖSSER, Anselm. "A Critical Survey of Some of Priestley's Plays." *ZAA,* 10 (1962), 131–42.

1579 SKLOOT, Robert. "The Time Plays of J. B. Priestley." *QJS*, 56 (1970), 426–31.

1580 SMITH, Grover. "Time Alive: J. W. Dunne and J. B. Priestley." *SAQ*, 56 (1957), 224–33. (Dunne's theories and Priestley's works.)

Robertson, T[homas] W[illiam] (1829 – 1871)

1581 ROBERTSON, T. W. *Principal Dramatic Works, with a Memoir by His Son* [T. W. S. Robertson]. Lon: French, 1889. 2 vols.

1582 ARMSTRONG, Cecil F. *Shakespeare to Shaw*, **1439**, 168–205.

1583 CARLSON, Marvin. "Montigny, Laube, Robertson: The Early Realists." *ETJ*, 24 (1972), 227–36.

1584 DURBACH, Errol. "Remembering Tom Robertson (1829–1871)." *ETJ*, 24 (1972), 284–88.

1585 NICOLL, Allardyce. "The Reform of Robertson." *A History of English Drama*, **192**, 120–31.

1586 PEMBERTON, Thomas E. *The Life and Writings of T. W. Robertson*. Lon: Bentley, 1893.

1587 PINERO, Arthur Wing. "The Theatre in the 'Seventies," **193**.

1588 SAVIN, Maynard. *Thomas William Robertson: His Plays and His Stagecraft*. Providence, RI: Brown UP, 1950.*

1589 TAYLOR, John R. *The Rise and Fall of the Well-Made Play*, **170**, 19–31.

1590 WATSON, Ernest B. "The Robertsonian Comedy." *Sheridan to Robertson: A Study of the Nineteenth-Century London Stage*. Cambridge, MA: Harvard UP, 1926, 380–425.

Robinson, Lennox (1886 – 1958)

1591 ROBINSON, Lennox. *Plays*. Lon: Macmillan, 1928. (Six plays.)

1592 ROBINSON, Lennox. *Curtain Up: An Autobiography*. Lon: Joseph, 1942.

1593 MALONE, Andrew E. *The Irish Drama*, **427**, 175–85.

1594 O'CONOR, Norreys. "A Dramatist of Changing Ireland." *SR*, 30 (1922), 277–85.

1595 O'NEILL, Michael J. *Lennox Robinson*. NY: Twayne, 1964.*

1596 SPINNER, Kaspar. *Die alte Dame sagt Nein! Drei irische Dramatiker*, **1165**, 6–49.

1597 STARKIE, Walter. "Lennox Robinson: 1886–1958." *TA*, 16 (1959), 7–19.

1598 WEYGANDT, Cornelius. *Irish Plays and Playwrights*, **432**, 222–32.

Shaffer, Peter
(1926–)

1599 BARNISH, Valerie L. *Notes on Peter Shaffer's "The Royal Hunt of the Sun."* Lon: Methuen, 1975. (Pamphlet.)†

1600 GLENN, Jules. "Anthony and Peter Shaffer's Plays: The Influence of Twinship on Creativity." *American Imago*, 31 (1974), 270–92.

1601 LEWIS, Allan. *The Contemporary Theatre*, **63**, 326–29.

1602 PENNEL, Charles A. "The Plays of Peter Shaffer: Experiment in Convention." *KanQ*, 3 (Spring 1971), 100–109.

1603 SIMON, John. "Hippodrama at the Psychodrome." *HudR*, 28 (1975), 97–106. (On *Equus*.)

1604 STACY, James R. "The Sun and the Horse: Peter Shaffer's Search for Worship." *ETJ*, 28 (1976), 325–37.

1605 TAYLOR, John R. *Peter Shaffer*. Harlow: Longman for the British Council, 1974. (Pamphlet.)†

1606 VANDENBROUCKE, Russell. "*Equus*: Modern Myth in the Making." *Drama & Theatre*, 12 (1975), 129–33.

Shaw, G[eorge] Bernard
(1856 – 1950)

1607 SHAW, G. Bernard. [Standard Edition of the Works.] Lon: Constable, 1930–50. 36 vols.

1608 SHAW, G. Bernard. *The Bodley Head Bernard Shaw: Collected Plays with Their Prefaces*, ed. Dan H. Laurence. Lon: Reinhardt, 1970–74. 7 vols. (The definitive edition.)*

1609 SHAW, G. Bernard. *Collected Letters*, ed. Dan H. Laurence. Vol. 1, 1874–97; Vol. 2, 1898–1910. Lon: Reinhardt, 1965, 1972. (Superbly edited first vols. of a highly selective edition of Shaw's correspondence.)*

1610 SHAW, G. Bernard. *Major Critical Essays*. Lon: Constable, 1932. (*The Quintessence of Ibsenism*, *The Sanity of Art*, *The Perfect Wagnerite*.)*

1611 SHAW, G. Bernard. *Shaw: An Autobiography, Selected from His Writings*, ed. Stanley Weintraub. NY: Weybright & Talley, 1969–70. 2 vols.

1612 SHAW, G. Bernard. *Shaw on Religion*, ed. Warren S. Smith. NY: Dodd, Mead, 1967.† (See also *Platform and Pulpit*, ed. Dan H. Laurence. NY: Hill & Wang, 1961.)

1613 SHAW, G. Bernard. *Shaw on Shakespeare: An Anthology of Bernard Shaw's Writings on the Plays and Production of Shakespeare*, ed. Edwin Wilson. NY: Dutton, 1961.†

1614 SHAW, G. Bernard. *Shaw on Theatre*, ed. E. J. West. NY: Hill & Wang, 1958.* †

1615 SHAW, G. Bernard, and Paul GREEN. "The Mystical Bernard Shaw [Interview]." In *Dramatic Heritage*, by Paul Green. NY: French, 1953, 112–31.

1616 SHAW, G. Bernard, and Archibald HENDERSON. "George Bernard Shaw Self-Revealed." *FortR*, 125 (1926), 433–42, 610–18. (Conversation concocted from Shaw's replies to a questionnaire.)

1617 SHAW, G. Bernard, and Archibald HENDERSON. *Table-Talk of G.B.S.: Conversations on Things in General . . . [with] Archibald Henderson.* NY: Harper, 1925. (Concocted from questionnaires.)

1618 BEVAN, E. Dean. *A Concordance to the Plays and Prefaces of Bernard Shaw.* Detroit: Gale, 1971. 10 vols. (Keyed to the Constable ed.)

1619 "A Continuing Checklist of Shaviana." *Shaw Bul* (later *ShR*), 1–(each triannual issue, 1951–). (Annotated bibl., greatly expanded in 1958.)*

1620 FARLEY, Earl, and Marvin CARLSON. "George Bernard Shaw: A Selected Bibliography (1945–1955)." *MD*, 2 (1959), 188–202, 295–325.

1621 HARTNOLL, Phyllis. *Who's Who in Shaw.* Lon: Elm Tree Books, 1975.

1622 KEOUGH, Lawrence C. "George Bernard Shaw, 1946–1955: A Selected Bibliography." *BB*, 22 (1959), 224–26; 23 (1960), 20–24, 36–41.

1623 KOZELKA, Paul*A Glossary to the Plays of Bernard Shaw*. NY: Teachers College, Columbia Univ., 1959.†

1624 PHILLIPS, Jill. *George Bernard Shaw: A Review of the Literature.* NY: Gordon Pr., 1977. (First vol. reviews books only.)

1624A WEINTRAUB, Stanley. "Bernard Shaw." In *Anglo-Irish Literature: A Review of Research,* **12A.** 167–215.

1625 ADAMS, Elsie B. *Bernard Shaw and the Aesthetes.* Columbus: Ohio State UP, 1971.

1626 ADAMS, Elsie B. "Shaw's *Caesar and Cleopatra*: Decadence Barely Averted." *ShR*, 18 (1975), 79–82.

1627 ADLER, Jacob H. "Ibsen, Shaw, and *Candida*." *JEGP*, 59 (1960), 50–58; repr. in **1851**, 258–67.

1628 ALBERT, Sidney P. " 'In More Ways Than One': *Major Barbara*'s Debt to Gilbert Murray." *ETJ*, 20 (1968), 123–40.

1629 ALBERT, Sidney P. "More Shaw Advice to the Players of *Major Barbara*." *Theatre Survey*, 11 (1970), 66–85.

1630 ALBERT, Sidney P. "The Price of Salvation: Moral Economics in *Major Barbara*." *MD*, 14 (1971), 307–23.

1631 ANDERSON, Maxwell. *Off Broadway: Essays About the Theater.* NY: Sloane, 1947, 12–17.

1632 AUSTIN, Don. "Comedy Through Tragedy: Dramatic Structure in 'Saint Joan.' " *ShR*, 8 (1965), 52–62.

1633 BARGAINNIER, Earl F. "Mr. Gilbert and Mr. Shaw." *TA*, 31 (1975), 43–54.

1634 BARNET, Sylvan. "Bernard Shaw on Tragedy." *PMLA*, 71 (1956), 888–99.

1635 BARR, Alan. *Victorian Stage Pulpiteer: Bernard Shaw's Crusade.* Athens: Univ. of Georgia Pr., 1973.

1636 BARZUN, Jacques. "From Shaw to Rousseau." *The Energies of Art.* NY: Harper, 1956, 245–80.

1637 BENTLEY, Eric. *Bernard Shaw: A Reconsideration.* NY: Norton, 1976. (Landmark study first publ. 1947.)* †

1638 BENTLEY, Eric. "Ibsen, Shaw, Brecht: Three Stages." *Theatre of War: Comments on 32 Occasions.* NY: Viking, 1972, 183–211;† repr. from *The Rarer Action*, ed. Alan Cheuse and Richard Koffler (New Brunswick, NJ: Rutgers UP, 1970), 3–23.

1639 BENTLEY, Eric. "The Making of a Dramatist (1892–1903)." *TDR*, 5 (Sept. 1960), 3–21; repr. in **93**, 290–312, in **1728**, 57–75, and in his *Theatre of War*, **1638**, 3–21.*

1640 BENTLEY, Eric. *The Playwright as Thinker*, **42**, 107–26, 132–40.

1641 BERMEL, Albert. "Jest and Superjest." *ShR*, 18 (1975), 57–69. (On *Man and Superman*.)

1642 BERMEL, Albert. "The Virgin as Heretic." *Contradictory Characters*, **43**, 185–206. (On *Saint Joan*.)

1643 BERST, Charles A. *Bernard Shaw and the Art of Drama.* Urbana: Univ. of Illinois Pr., 1973.*

1644 BERST, Charles A. "The Craft of *Candida*." *College Lit*, 1 (1974), 157–73.

1645 BORGES, Jorge L. "For Bernard Shaw." *Other Inquisitions, 1937–1952*, tr. Ruth L. C. Simms. NY: Washington Square Pr., 1966, 172–75.†

1646 BOXILL, Roger. "The Plays." *Shaw and the Doctors.* NY: Basic Books, 1969, 97–143.

1647 BRECHT, Bertolt. "Ovation for Shaw." *Brecht on Theatre*, ed. and tr. John Willett. NY: Grove, 1964, 10–13; also in *MD*, 2 (1959), 184–87.

1648 BRIDGWATER, Patrick. *Nietzsche in Anglosaxony: A Study of Nietzsche's Impact on English and American Literature.* Leicester: Leicester UP, 1972, Chapter 5.

1649 BRIDIE, James. "Shaw as Dramatist (Including a Surrealist Life of G.B.S.)." In **1890**, 77–91.

1650 BRUSTEIN, Robert. *The Theatre of Revolt*, **45**, 183–227.*

1651 BULLOUGH, Geoffrey. "Literary Relations of Shaw's Mrs. Warren." *PQ*, 41 (1962), 339–58.

1652 CARPENTER, Charles A. *Bernard Shaw & the Art of Destroying Ideals: The Early Plays.* Madison: Univ. of Wisconsin Pr., 1969.*

1653 CARPENTER, Charles A. "Sex Play Shaw's Way: *Man and Superman*." *ShR*, 18 (1975), 70–74.

1654 CARPENTER, Charles A. "Shaw's Cross Section of Anti-Shavian Opinion [in *Fanny's First Play*]." *ShR*, 7 (1964), 78–86.

1655 CHERRY, D. R. "The Fabianism of Shaw." *QQ*, 69 (1962), 83–93.

1656 CHESTERTON, G. K. *George Bernard Shaw.* Enl. ed. Lon: Bodley Head, 1935. (Brilliant, erratic study first publ. 1909.)

1657 CLURMAN, Harold. "Director's Notes for *Heartbreak House*." *On Directing*. NY: Macmillan, 1972, 229–39; repr. from *TDR*, 5 (March 1961), 58–67.

1658 COHN, Ruby. "Shaw *versus* Shakes." *Modern Shakespeare Offshoots*, **48**, 321–39.

1659 COLEMAN, D. C. "Fun and Games: Two Pictures of *Heartbreak House*." *DrS*, 5 (1966–67), 223–36.

1660 CORRIGAN, Robert W. "The Collapse of the Shavian Cosmos: A Study of Theme and Dramatic Form." *The Theatre in Search of a Fix*, **485**, 161–74. (Stresses *Heartbreak House*.)

1661 COUCHMAN, Gordon W. "Bernard Shaw and the Gospel of Efficiency." *ShR*, 16 (1973), 11–20.

1662 COUCHMAN, Gordon W. *This Our Caesar: A Study of Bernard Shaw's Caesar and Cleopatra*. The Hague: Mouton, 1973.

1663 COXE, Louis O. *"You Never Can Tell*: G. B. Shaw Reviewed." *Western Humanities Rev*, 9 (1955), 313–25.

1664 CRANE, Gladys. "Shaw's Comic Techniques in *Man and Superman*." *ETJ*, 23 (1971), 13–21.

1665 CRANE, Gladys. "Shaw's *Misalliance*: The Comic Journey from Rebellious Daughter to Conventional Womanhood." *ETJ*, 25 (1973), 480–89.

1666 CRANE, Milton. *"Pygmalion*: Bernard Shaw's Dramatic Theory and Practice." *PMLA*, 66 (1951), 879–85.

1667 CRAWFORD, Fred D. "Shaw Among the Houyhnhnms." *ShR*, 19 (1976), 102–19. (On Parts IV–V of *Methuselah*.)

1668 CROMPTON, Louis. *Shaw the Dramatist*. Lincoln: Univ. of Nebraska Pr., 1969. (Background studies of major plays.)*

1669 DAWICK, John D. "Stagecraft and Structure in Shaw's Disquisitory Drama." *MD*, 14 (1971), 276–87. (*Getting Married, Misalliance*, and *Heartbreak House*.)

1670 DEANE, Barbara. "Shaw and Gnosticism." *ShR*, 16 (1973), 104–22.

1671 DERVIN, Daniel. *Bernard Shaw: A Psychological Study*. Lewisburg, PA: Bucknell UP, 1975.

1672 DeSELINCOURT, Aubrey. *Six Great Playwrights*. Lon: Hamilton, 1960, 161–90.

1673 DICKSON, Ronald J. "The Diabolonian Character in Shaw." *UKCR*, 26 (1959), 145–51.

1674 DIETRICH, Richard F. "Shaw and the Passionate Mind." *ShR*, 4 (May 1961), 2–11.

1675 DOLIS, John J. "Bernard Shaw's *Saint Joan*: Language Is Not Enough." *Massachusetts St in Eng*, 4 (Autumn 1974), 17–25.

1676 DOWNER, Alan S. "Shaw's First Play." In **1821**, 3–24. (On both *Widowers' Houses* and *Getting Married*.)

1677 DRIVER, Tom F. *Romantic Quest and Modern Query*, **50**, 249–82.

1678 DUERKSON, Roland A. "Shelley and Shaw." *PMLA*, 78 (1963), 114–27.

1679 DUERKSON, Roland A. "Shelleyan Witchcraft: The Unbinding of Brassbound." *ShR*, 15 (1972), 21–25.

1680 DUKORE, Bernard F. *Bernard Shaw, Playwright: Aspects of Shavian Drama*. Columbia: Univ. of Missouri Pr., 1973.*

1681 EASTMAN, Fred. *Christ in the Drama*, **51**, 42–60. (Stresses *Androcles* and *Saint Joan*.)

1682 ELLEHAUGE, Martin O. M. *The Position of Bernard Shaw in European Drama and Philosophy*. NY: Haskell House, 1966 [c.1931].

1683 ELLIOTT, Robert C. "Shaw's Captain Bluntschli: A Latter-Day Falstaff." *Modern Language Notes*, 67 (1952), 461–64.

1684 ERVINE, St. John. *Bernard Shaw: His Life, Work and Friends*. NY: Morrow, 1956. (Readable biography.)

1685 EVANS, T. F., ed. *Shaw: The Critical Heritage*. Lon: Routledge & K. Paul, 1976. (Selected early commentaries.)

1686 FERGUSSON, Francis. "The Theatricality of Shaw and Pirandello." *The Idea of a Theater*, **905**, 190–98. (Stresses *Major Barbara* and *Heartbreak House*.)

1687 FIELDEN, John. "Shaw's *Saint Joan* as Tragedy." *TCL*, 3 (1957), 59–67; repr. in **1880**, 185–96.

1688 FORTER, Elizabeth T. "Introduction." *Major Barbara*, ed. E. T. Forter. NY: Appleton, 1971, vii–xxx.†

1689 FRANK, Joseph. "Exile and the Kingdom: The Incipient Absurdity of Milton and Shaw." *Mosaic*, 9 (1975), 111–21. (Stresses *Heartbreak House*.)

1690 FRANK, Joseph. "*Major Barbara*—Shaw's 'Divine Comedy.' " *PMLA*, 71 (1956), 61–74; repr. in **1893**, 28–41.

1691 FRANKEL, Charles. "Efficient Power and Inefficient Virtue (Bernard Shaw: *Major Barbara*)." In *Great Moral Dilemmas in Literature, Past and Present*, ed. Robert M. MacIver. NY: Harper, 1956, 15–23.

1692 GANZ, Arthur. "The Ascent to Heaven: A Shavian Pattern (Early Plays, 1894–1898)." *MD*, 14 (1971), 253–63.

1693 GASSNER, John. "Bernard Shaw and the Making of the Modern Mind." *Dramatic Soundings*, **104**, 631–42; repr. from *CE*, 23 (1962), 517–25; repr. in **103**, 64–75.

1694 GASSNER, John. "Shaw on Ibsen and the Drama of Ideas." *Dramatic Soundings*, **104**, 87–105; repr. from *Ideas in the Drama*, ed. John Gassner (NY: Columbia UP, 1964), 71–100.

1695 GASSNER, John. *The Theatre in Our Times*, **105**, 134–69, 208–11, 267–81. (Includes parts on *Saint Joan*, *Man and Superman*, and *Misalliance*.)

1696 GATCH, Katherine H. "The Last Plays of Bernard Shaw: Dialectic and Despair." In **122**, 126–47.

1697 GATCH, Katherine H. " 'The Real Sorrow of Great Men': Mr. Bernard Shaw's Sense of Tragedy." *CE*, 8 (1947), 230–40.

1698 GELBER, Norman. "The 'Misalliance' Theme in 'Major Barbara.' " *ShR*, 15 (1972), 65–70.

1699 GEROULD, Daniel C. "George Bernard Shaw's Criticism of Ibsen." *CL*, 15 (1963), 130–45.

1700 GIBBS, A. M. "Comedy and Philosophy in *Man and Superman*." *MD*, 19 (1976), 161–75.

1701 GIBBS, A. M. *Shaw*. Edinburgh: Oliver & Boyd, 1969. (Excellent concise overview.)* †

1702 GILMARTIN, Andrina. "Mr. Shaw's Many Mothers." *ShR*, 8 (1965), 93–103.

1703 GORDON, David J. "Two Anti-Puritan Puritans: Bernard Shaw and D. H. Lawrence." *YR*, 56 (1966), 76–90.

1704 GRECCO, Stephen. "Vivie Warren's Profession: A New Look at *Mrs. Warren's Profession*." *ShR*, 10 (1967), 93–99.

1705 GRIBBEN, John L. "Shaw's Saint Joan: A Tragic Heroine." *Thought*, 40 (1965), 549–66.

1706 HAMILTON, R. "The Philosophy of Bernard Shaw: A Study of *Back to Methuselah*." *Lon Q and Holborn Rev*, 170 (1945), 333–41.

1707 HAMON, Augustin F. *The Twentieth Century Molière: Bernard Shaw*, tr. Eden and Cedar Paul. Lon: Allen & Unwin, 1915.

1708 HANKIN, St. John. "Mr. Bernard Shaw as Critic." *The Dramatic Works*, **1148**, III, 149–70.

1709 HENDERSON, Archibald. *George Bernard Shaw: Man of the Century*. NY: Appleton, 1956. (Well-documented but erratic authorized biography.)

1710 HENN, T. R. *The Harvest of Tragedy*. Lon: Methuen, 1956, 189–96. (Stresses *Saint Joan*.)

1711 HOBSBAWM, E. J. "Bernard Shaw's Socialism." *Science & Society*, 11 (1947), 305–26.

1712 HOLBERG, Stanley M. "The Economic Rogue in the Plays of Bernard Shaw." *Univ of Buffalo St*, 21 (1953), 29–119.

1713 HOLT, Charles L. " 'Candida': The Music of Ideas." *ShR*, 9 (1966), 2–14.

1714 HOLT, Charles L. "Mozart, Shaw and 'Man and Superman.' " *ShR*, 9 (1966), 102–16.

1715 HOPWOOD, Alison L. "*Too True to Be Good*: Prologue to Shaw's Later Plays." *ShR*, 11 (1968), 109–18.

1716 HORNBY, Richard. "The Symbolic Action of *Heartbreak House*." *DrS*, 7 (1968–69), 5–24.

1717 HOY, Cyrus. "Shaw's Tragicomic Irony: From *Man and Superman* to *Heartbreak House*." *VQR*, 47 (1971), 56–78.

1718 HUIZINGA, Johan. "Bernard Shaw's Saint." *Men and Ideas*, tr. James S. Holmes and Hans van Marle. NY: Meridian, 1959, 207–39; repr. in **1880**, 54–85.

1719 HULSE, James W. "Shaw: Socialist Maverick" and "Shaw: Beyond Socialism." In *Revolutionists in London: A Study of Five Unorthodox Socialists*. Oxford: Clarendon, 1970, 111–37, 192–228.

1720 HUMMERT, Paul A. *Bernard Shaw's Marxian Romance*. Lincoln: Univ. of Nebraska Pr., 1973.

1721 IRVINE, William. *The Universe of G.B.S.* NY: McGraw-Hill, 1949.*

1722 JOAD, C. E. M. "Shaw's Philosophy." In **1735**, 184–205; also in **1890**, 57–76. (Stresses *Back to Methuselah*.)

1723 JOHNSON, Betty F. "Shelley's 'Cenci' and 'Mrs. Warren's Profession.' " *ShR*, 15 (1972), 26–34.

1724 JONES, A. R. "George Bernard Shaw." In **100**, 57–75.

1725 JORDAN, John. "Shaw's *Heartbreak House*." *Threshold*, 1 (1957), 50–56.

1726 JORDAN, Robert J. "Theme and Character in *Major Barbara*." *TSLL*, 12 (1970), 471–80.

1727 KAUFMAN, Michael W. "The Dissonance of Dialectic: Shaw's *Heartbreak House*." *ShR*, 13 (1970), 2–9.

1728 KAUFMANN, R. J., ed. *G. B. Shaw: A Collection of Critical Essays*. Englewood Cliffs, NJ: Prentice-Hall, 1965.†

1729 KAUL, A. N. "George Bernard Shaw: From Anti-Romance to Pure Fantasy." *The Action of English Comedy*. New Haven, CT: Yale UP, 1970, 284–327.

1730 KAYE, Julian B. *Bernard Shaw and the Nineteenth-Century Tradition*. Norman: Univ. of Oklahoma Pr., 1958. (The historical context of his ideas.)

1731 KENNEDY, Andrew K. *Six Dramatists in Search of a Language*, **158**, 38–86.

1732 KING, Carlyle. "G.B.S. on Literature: The Author as Critic." *QQ*, 66 (1959), 135–45.

1733 KING, Walter N. "The Rhetoric of *Candida*." *MD*, 2 (1959), 71–83; repr. in **1851**, 243–58.

1734 KNIGHT, G. Wilson. *The Golden Labyrinth*, **159**, 342–54.

1735 KRONENBERGER, Louis, ed. *George Bernard Shaw: A Critical Survey*. Cleveland: World, 1953.

1736 KRONENBERGER, Louis. *The Thread of Laughter*, **160**, 227–78.

1737 KRUTCH, Joseph W. *"Modernism" in Modern Drama*, **61**, 48–64.

1738 LARSON, Gale K., ed. *Caesar and Cleopatra*. Indianapolis, IN: Bobbs-Merrill, 1974. (Full intro., notes, and bibl.)†

1739 LARSON, Gale K. " 'Caesar and Cleopatra': The Making of a History Play." *ShR*, 14 (1971), 73–89.

1740 LAWRENCE, Kenneth. "Bernard Shaw: The Career of the Life Force." *MD*, 15 (1972), 130–46.

1741 LEARY, Daniel J. "About Nothing in Shaw's *The Simpleton of the Unexpected Isles*." *ETJ*, 24 (1973), 139–48.

1742 LEARY, Daniel J., and Richard FOSTER. "Adam and Eve: Evolving Archetypes in *Back to Methuselah*." *ShR*, 4 (May 1961), 12–23, 25.

1743 LEARY, Daniel J. "Dialectical Action in *Major Barbara*." *ShR*, 12 (1969), 46–58.

1744 LEARY, Daniel J. "The Evolutionary Dialectic of Shaw and Teilhard: A Perennial Philosophy." *ShR*, 9 (1966), 15–34.

1745 LEARY, Daniel J. "The Moral Dialectic in *Caesar and Cleopatra*." *ShR*, 5 (1962), 42–53.

1746 LEARY, Daniel J. "Shaw's Blakean Vision: A Dialectic Approach to *Heartbreak House*." *MD*, 15 (1972), 89–103.

1747 LEARY, Daniel J. "Shaw's Use of Stylized Characters and Speech in *Man and Superman*." *MD*, 5 (1963), 477–90.

1748 LEECH, Clifford. "Shaw and Shakespeare." In **1821**, 84–105. (The "dramas of debate" and the "dark comedies.")

1749 LORICHS, Sonja. *The Unwomanly Woman in Bernard Shaw's Drama and Her Social and Political Background*. Stockholm: Almqvist & Wiksell, 1973.

1750 LUTZ, Jerry. *Pitchman's Melody: Shaw About "Shakespear."* Lewisburg, PA: Bucknell UP, 1974.

1751 MacCARTHY, Desmond. *The Court Theatre, 1904–1907*, **222**.

1752 MacCARTHY, Desmond. *Shaw: The Plays*. Newton Abbot: David & Charles, 1973 [c.1951]. (Also issued under the title *Shaw's Plays in Review*.)

1753 McCOLLOM, William G. "Shaw's Comedy and *Major Barbara*." *The Divine Average: A View of Comedy*. Cleveland: Pr. of Case Western Reserve Univ., 1971, 198–212.

1754 McDOWELL, Frederick P. W. "Another Look at Bernard Shaw." *DrS*, 1 (1961), 34–53.

1755 McDOWELL, Frederick P. W. "Crisis and Unreason: Shaw's *On the Rocks*." *ETJ*, 13 (1961), 192–200.

1756 McDOWELL, Frederick P. W. " 'The Eternal Against the Expedient': Structure and Theme in Shaw's *The Apple Cart*." *MD*, 2 (1959), 99–113.

1757 McDOWELL, Frederick P. W. "Heaven, Hell, and Turn-of-the-Century London: Reflections upon Shaw's *Man and Superman*." *DrS*, 2 (1963), 245–68.*

1758 McDOWELL, Frederick P. W. "The 'Pentecostal Flame' and the 'Lower Centers': *Too True to Be Good*." *ShR*, 2 (Sept. 1959), 27–38.

1759 McDOWELL, Frederick P. W. "Politics, Comedy, Character, and Dialectic: The Shavian World of *John Bull's Other Island*." *PMLA*, 82 (1967), 542–53.

1760 McDOWELL, Frederick P. W. "Spiritual and Political Reality: Shaw's *Simpleton of the Unexpected Isles*." *MD*, 3 (1960), 196–210.

1761 McDOWELL, Frederick P. W. "Technique, Symbol, and Theme in *Heartbreak House*." *PMLA*, 68 (1953), 335–56.*

1762 McDOWELL, Frederick P. W. "The World, God, and World Bettering:

Shaw's *Buoyant Billions." Boston Univ St in Eng*, 3 (1957), 167–76.

1763 McKEE, Irving. "Bernard Shaw's Beginnings on the London Stage." *PMLA*, 74 (1959), 470–81.

1764 MACKSOUD, S. John, and Ross ALTMAN. "Voices in Opposition: A Burkeian Rhetoric of *Saint Joan*." *QJS*, 57 (1971), 140–46.

1765 MANDER, Raymond, and Joe MITCHENSON. *Theatrical Companion to Shaw: A Pictorial Record of the First Performances of the Plays of George Bernard Shaw*. NY: Pitman, 1955. (Synopses and other valuable data for each play.)

1766 MANN, Thomas. "G.B.S.—Mankind's Friend." *YR*, 40 (1951), 412–20; repr. in **1735**, 250–57.

1767 MARTZ, Louis L. "The Saint as Tragic Hero: *Saint Joan* and *Murder in the Cathedral*," **939**; repr. in **1880**, 144–65.

1768 MATLAW, Myron. "The Denouement of *Pygmalion*." *MD*, 1 (1958), 29–34; also in *Shavian*, 1, No. 12 (1958), 14–19.

1769 MAYER, David. "The Case for Harlequin: A Footnote on Shaw's Dramatic Method." *MD*, 3 (1960), 52–59.

1770 MAYNE, Fred. *The Wit and Satire of Bernard Shaw*. NY: St. Martin's, 1967. (Focuses on the style of his dialogue.)

1771 MEISEL, Martin. "Shaw and Revolution: The Politics of the Plays." In **1821**, 106–34.

1772 MEISEL, Martin. *Shaw and the Nineteenth-Century Theater*. Princeton, NJ: Princeton UP, 1963.* †

1773 MENDELSOHN, Michael J. "The Heartbreak Houses of Shaw and Chekhov." *ShR*, 6 (1963), 89–95.

1774 MERRITT, James D. "Shaw and the Pre-Raphaelites." In **1821**, 70–83.

1775 MILLS, Carl H. "*Man and Superman* and the Don Juan Legend." *CL*, 19 (1967), 216–25.

1776 MILLS, Carl H. "Shaw's Superman: A Re-Examination." *ShR*, 13 (1970), 48–58.

1777 MILLS, Carl H. "Shaw's Theory of Creative Evolution." *ShR*, 16 (1973), 123–32.

1778 MILLS, John A. *Language and Laughter: Comic Diction in the Plays of Bernard Shaw*. Tucson: Univ. of Arizona Pr., 1969.†

1779 MIZENER, Arthur. "Poetic Drama and the Well-Made Play." *Eng Institute Essays, 1949* (1950), 45–54. (On *Heartbreak House* and *Saint Joan*.)

1780 MORGAN, Margery M. *The Shavian Playground: An Exploration of the Art of George Bernard Shaw*. Lon: Methuen, 1972.* †

1781 MORSEBERGER, Robert E. "The Winning of Barbara Undershaft: Conversion by the Cannon Factory, or 'Wot prawce selvytion nah?' " *Cos*, 9 (1973), 71–77.

1782 NATHAN, Rhoda B. "Bernard Shaw and the Inner Light." *ShR*, 14 (1971), 107–19.

1783 NELSON, Raymond S. "*Back to Methuselah*: Shaw's Modern Bible." *Cos*, 5 (1972), 117–23.

1784 NELSON, Raymond S. "Blanco Posnet—Adversary of God." *MD*, 13 (1970), 1–9.

1785 NELSON, Raymond S. "*Mrs. Warren's Profession* and English Prostitution." *JML*, 2 (1971–72), 357–66.

1786 NELSON, Raymond S. "The Quest for Justice in *Captain Brassbound's Conversion*." *Iowa Eng Bul Yearbook*, 21 (Fall 1971), 3–9.

1787 NELSON, Raymond S. "Responses to Poverty in *Major Barbara*." *ArQ*, 27 (1971), 335–46.

1788 NELSON, Raymond S. "Shaw's Heaven, Hell, and Redemption." *Cos*, 6 (1972), 99–108. (On *Man and Superman*.)

1789 NELSON, Raymond S. "Wisdom and Power in *Androcles and the Lion*." *Yearbook of Eng St*, 2 (1972), 192–204.

1790 NETHERCOT, Arthur H. "Bernard Shaw, Ladies and Gentlemen." *MD*, 2 (1959), 84–98. (Shaw on the subject.)

1791 NETHERCOT, Arthur H. *Men and Supermen: The Shavian Portrait Gallery*. 2nd ed. NY: Blom, 1966.*

1792 NETHERCOT, Arthur H. "Who *Was* Eugene Marchbanks?" *ShR*, 15 (1972), 2–20.

1793 NETHERCOT, Arthur H. "Zeppelins Over Heartbreak House." *ShR*, 9 (1966), 46–51.

1794 NICKSON, Richard. "The Art of Shavian Political Drama." *MD*, 14 (1971), 324–30.

1795 NICOLL, Allardyce. *A History of English Drama*, **192**, 193–204.

1796 NORWOOD, Gilbert. "Euripides and Shaw: A Comparison." *Euripides and Shaw, with Other Essays*. Bos: Luce, 1921, 1–48.

1797 O'CASEY, Sean. "Shaw's Corner." *Sunset and Evening Star*. NY: Macmillan, 1954, 210–51. (Recollections.)

1798 O'CASEY, Sean. "A Whisper About Bernard Shaw" and "Bernard Shaw: An Appreciation of a Fighting Idealist." *The Green Crow*, **1281**, 197–211.

1799 O'DONNELL, Norbert F. "The Conflict of Wills in Shaw's Tragicomedy." *MD*, 4 (1962), 413–25; repr. in **1728**, 76–87.

1800 O'DONNELL, Norbert F. "Doctor Ridgeon's Deceptive Dilemma." *ShR*, 2 (Jan. 1959), 1–5.

1801 O'DONNELL, Norbert F. "Ibsen and Shaw: The Tragic and the Tragi-Comic." *TA*, 15 (1957–58), 15–27.

1802 O'DONNELL, Norbert F. "On the 'Unpleasantness' of 'Pygmalion.' " *Shaw Bul*, 1, No. 8 (1955), 7–10.

1803 OHMANN, Richard M. *Shaw: The Style and the Man*. Middletown: Wesleyan UP, 1962. (Style in the non-dramatic works.)*

1804 OLSON, Elder. *The Theory of Comedy*. Bloomington: Indiana UP, 1968, 114–24.†

1805 PARK, Bruce R. "A Mote in the Critic's Eye: Bernard Shaw and Comedy." *Texas St in Eng*, 37 (1958), 195–210; repr. in **1728**, 42–56.

1806 PARKER, R. B. "Bernard Shaw and Sean O'Casey." *QQ*, 73 (1966), 13–34; repr. in **1835**, 3–29.

1807 PARKER, William. "Broadbent and Doyle, Two Shavian Archetypes." In **413**, 39–49.

1808 PEACOCK, Ronald. *The Poet in the Theatre*, **67**, 86–93.

1809 PEARSON, Hesketh. *Bernard Shaw: His Life and Personality*. NY: Atheneum, 1963. (Readable biography.)†

1810 PERRY, Henry T. E. *Masters of Dramatic Comedy and Their Social Themes*. Cambridge, MA: Harvard UP, 1939, 359–408.

1811 PILECKI, Gerard A. *Shaw's Geneva: A Critical Study of the Evolution of the Text in Relation to Shaw's Political Thought and Dramatic Practice*. The Hague: Mouton, 1965.

1812 PIRANDELLO, Luigi. "Bernard Shaw's *Saint Joan*." In·**1880**, 23–28.

1813 QUINN, Michael. "Form and Intention: A Negative View of *Arms and the Man*." *CritQ*, 5 (1963), 148–54.

1814 RAKNEM, Ingvald. *Joan of Arc in History, Legend and Literature*. Oslo: Universitetsforlaget, 1971, 180–203.

1815 RATTRAY, Robert F. *Bernard Shaw: A Chronicle*. Rev. ed. NY: Roy, 1951. (Year-by-year record.)

1816 REARDON, Joan. "*Caesar and Cleopatra* and the Commedia dell' Arte." *ShR*, 14 (1971), 120–36.

1817 REED, Robert R. "Boss Mangan, Peer Gynt and *Heartbreak House*." *ShR*, 2 (Jan. 1959), 6–12.

1818 REINERT, Otto. "Old History and New: Anachronism in *Caesar and Cleopatra*." *MD*, 3 (1960), 37–41.

1819 RODENBECK, John von B. "Bernard Shaw's Revolt Against Rationalism." *Victorian St*, 15 (1972), 409–37.

1820 ROPPEN, Georg. *Evolution and Poetic Belief*. Oslo: Oslo UP, 1956, 352–402. (His "evolutionary utopia" in concept and drama.)

1821 ROSENBLOOD, Norman, ed. *Shaw: Seven Critical Essays*. Toronto: Univ. of Toronto Pr., 1971.

1822 ROSSELLI, J. "The Right Joan and the Wrong One." *TC*, 157 (1955), 374–83.

1823 ROSSET, B. C. *Shaw of Dublin: The Formative Years*. Univ. Park: Pennsylvania State UP, 1964.

1824 ROY, Emil. *British Drama Since Shaw*, **233**, 1–20.

1825 RUSSELL, Bertrand. "George Bernard Shaw." *VQR*, 27 (1951), 1–7.

1826 SALMON, Eric. "Shaw and the Passion of the Mind." *MD*, 16 (1973), 239–50. (Stresses *Man and Superman*.)

1827 SCHLAUCH, Margaret. "Symbolic Figures and the Symbolic Technique of George Bernard Shaw." *Science & Society*, 21 (1957), 210–21.

1828 SCHOEPS, Karl-Heinz. "Epic Structures in the Plays of Bernard Shaw and Bertolt Brecht." In *Essays on Brecht*, ed. Siegfried Mews and Herbert Knust. Chapel Hill: Univ. of North Carolina Pr., 1974, 28–43.

1829 SEARLE, William. *The Saint & the Skeptics: Joan of Arc in the Work of Mark Twain, Anatole France, and Bernard Shaw*. Detroit: Wayne State UP, 1976, 97–138.

1830 SHARP, Sister M. C. "The Theme of Masks in *Geneva*: An Example of Shaw's Later Technique." *ShR*, 5 (1962), 82–91.

1831 SHARP, William L. "*Getting Married*: New Dramaturgy in Comedy." *ETJ*, 11 (1959), 103–9.

1832 SHARP, William L. "*Misalliance*: An Evaluation." *ETJ*, 8 (1956), 9–16.

1833 SHATTUCK, Charles H. "Bernard Shaw's 'Bad Quarto.' " *JEGP*, 54 (1955), 651–63. (First ed. of *Widowers' Houses*.)

1834 *Shaw Review*, 1– (1951–). (Valuable triannual journal edited by Stanley Weintraub; formerly entitled *Shaw Bulletin*.)

1835 *Shaw Seminar Papers–65*, ed. Norman Rosenblood. Toronto: Copp Clark, 1966.

GEORGE BERNARD SHAW

1836 SIDNELL, Michael J. *"Misalliance*: Sex, Socialism and the Collectivist Poet." *MD*, 17 (1974), 125–39.

1837 SILVERMAN, Albert H. "Bernard Shaw's Political Extravaganzas." *DrS*, 5 (1966–67), 213–22.

1838 SILVERMAN, Albert H. "Bernard Shaw's Shakespeare Criticism." *PMLA*, 72 (1957), 722–36.

1839 SIMON, Louis. *Shaw on Education*. NY: Columbia UP, 1958.

1840 SMITH, J. Percy. "A Shavian Tragedy: *The Doctor's Dilemma*." In *The Image of the Work: Essays in Criticism*, by B. H. Lehman et al. Berkeley: Univ. of California Pr., 1955, 189–207.

1841 SMITH, J. Percy. *The Unrepentant Pilgrim: A Study of the Development of Bernard Shaw*. Bos: Houghton, 1965.

1842 SMITH, Warren S., ed. *Bernard Shaw's Plays: Major Barbara, Heartbreak House, Saint Joan, Too True to Be Good, with Backgrounds and Criticism*. NY: Norton, 1971.†

1843 SMITH, Warren S. "Future Shock and Discouragement: *The Tragedy of an Elderly Gentleman*." *ShR*, 18 (1975), 22–27.

1844 SMITH, Warren S. *The London Heretics, 1870–1914*. NY: Dodd, Mead, 1968, 270–79.

1845 SOLOMON, Stanley J. *"Saint Joan* as Epic Tragedy." *MD*, 6 (1964), 437–49.

1846 SOLOMON, Stanley J. "Theme and Structure in *Getting Married*." *ShR*, 5 (1962), 92–96.

1847 SPECKHARD, Robert R. "Shaw and Aristophanes: How the Comedy of Ideas Works." *ShR*, 8 (1965), 82–92.

1848 SPECKHARD, Robert R. "Shaw and Aristophanes: Symbolic Marriage and the Magical Doctor/Cook in Shavian Comedy." *ShR*, 9 (1966), 56–65.

1849 SPENKER, Lenyth. "The Dramatic Criteria of George Bernard Shaw." *Speech Monographs*, 17 (1950), 24–36.

1850 SPINK, Judith B. "The Image of the Artist in the Plays of Bernard Shaw." *ShR*, 6 (1963), 82–88.

1851 STANTON, Stephen S., ed. *A Casebook on Candida*. NY: Crowell, 1962. (Includes Shaw comments on *Candida*, 87–94, 165–70.)†

1852 STANTON, Stephen S. "Shaw's Debt to Scribe." *PMLA*, 76 (1961), 575–85. (Stresses *Candida*.)

1853 STEWART, J. I. M. *Eight Modern Writers*. Oxford: Clarendon, 1963, 122–83.

1854 STOCKHOLDER, Fred E. "A Schopenhauerian Reading of *Heartbreak House*." *ShR*, 19 (1976), 22–43.

1855 STOCKHOLDER, Fred E. "Shaw's Drawing-Room Hell: A Reading of *Man and Superman*." *ShR*, 11 (1968), 42–51.

1856 STONE, Susan C. "Biblical Myth Shavianized." *MD*, 18 (1975), 153–63. (In *Methuselah* and *Simpleton*.)

1857 STONE, Susan C. " 'Geneva': Paean to the Dictators?" *ShR*, 16 (1973), 21–29.

1858 STOPPEL, Hans. "Shaw and Sainthood." *Eng St*, 36 (April 1955), 49–63; repr. in **1880**, 166–84.

1859 STYAN, J. L. *The Elements of Drama, 71*, 87–92, 99–103, 146–48, 170–74. (Analyses of *Pygmalion*, *Arms and the Man*, *The Apple Cart*, and *Saint Joan*.)

1860 STYAN, J. L. "The Shavian Touch." *The Dark Comedy, 70*, 124–30.

1861 SWABEY, Marie T. C. *Comic Laughter: A Philosophical Essay.* New Haven, CT: Yale UP, 1961, 171–78. (On *Major Barbara.*)

1862 TETZELI VON ROSADOR, Kurt. "The Natural History of *Major Barbara.*" *MD*, 17 (1974), 141-53.

1863 THOMPSON, Alan R. *The Dry Mock: A Study of Irony in Drama.* Berkeley: Univ. of California Pr., 1948, 103-27.

1864 TURCO, Alfred. *Shaw's Moral Vision: The Self and Salvation.* Ithaca, NY: Cornell UP, 1976.

1865 TURCO, Alfred. "Sir Colenso's White Lie." *ShR*, 13 (1970), 14–25.

1866 URE, Peter. "Master and Pupil in Bernard Shaw." *EIC*, 19 (1969), 118–39; repr. in his *Yeats and Anglo-Irish Literature,* **2328**, 261–80.

1867 USSHER, Arland. *Three Great Irishmen: Shaw, Yeats, Joyce.* NY: New American Lib., 1957, 11–49.†

1868 VALENCY, Maurice J. *The Cart and the Trumpet: The Plays of George Bernard Shaw.* NY: Oxford UP, 1973.*

1869 WALL, Vincent. *Bernard Shaw, Pygmalion to Many Players.* Ann Arbor: Univ. of Michigan Pr., 1973.

1870 WASSERMAN, Marlie P. "Vivie Warren: A Psychological Study." *ShR*, 15 (1972), 71–75.

1871 WATSON, Barbara B. "The New Woman and the New Comedy." *ShR*, 17 (1974), 2–16.

1872 WATSON, Barbara B. "Sainthood for Millionaires: *Major Barbara.*" *MD*, 11 (1968), 227–44.

1873 WATSON, Barbara B. *A Shavian Guide to the Intelligent Woman.* Lon: Chatto & Windus, 1964.

1874 WEALES, Gerald. *Religion in Modern English Drama,* **172**, 54–79.

1874A WEINTRAUB, Rodelle, ed. *Fabian Feminist: Bernard Shaw and Woman.* Univ. Park: Pennsylvania State UP, 1977. (25 essays.)

1875 WEINTRAUB, Stanley. "The Avant-Garde Shaw." In **1835**, 33–52.

1876 WEINTRAUB, Stanley. "Exploiting Art: The Pictures in Bernard Shaw's Plays." *MD*, 18 (1975), 215–38.

1877 WEINTRAUB, Stanley. "Four Fathers for Barbara." In *Directions in Literary Criticism,* ed. Stanley Weintraub and Philip Young. Univ. Park: Pennsylvania State UP, 1973, 201–10.

1878 WEINTRAUB, Stanley. "*Heartbreak House*: Shaw's *Lear.*" *MD*, 15 (1972), 255–65; previous version in **1879**, 333–43.

1879 WEINTRAUB, Stanley. *Journey to Heartbreak: The Crucible Years of Bernard Shaw, 1914–1918.* NY: Weybright & Talley, 1971.*

1880 WEINTRAUB, Stanley, ed. *Saint Joan Fifty Years After, 1923/24–1973/74.* Baton Rouge: Louisiana State UP, 1973. (Essays on the play, several newly translated.)

1881 WEINTRAUB, Stanley. "Shaw's Mommsenite Caesar." In *Anglo-German and American-German Crosscurrents,* ed. Philip A. Shelley and Arthur O. Lewis. Chapel Hill: Univ. of North Carolina Pr., 1962, II, 257–72.

1882 WEISSMAN, Philip. *Creativity in the Theater: A Psychoanalytic Study.* NY: Basic Books, 1965, 146–70. (On *Pygmalion.*)

1883 WEST, Alick. *George Bernard Shaw: "A Good Man Fallen Among Fabians."* NY: International, 1950. (Interesting Marxist view.)

1884 WEST, E. J. " 'Arma Virumque' Shaw Did Not Sing." *Colorado Q*, 1 (1953), 267–80.

1885 WEST, E. J. "*Saint Joan*: A Modern Classic Reconsidered." *QJS*, 40 (1954), 249–59; repr. in **1880**, 125–40.

1886 WHITMAN, Robert F. "The Dialectic Structure in Shaw's Plays." In **1835**, 65–84.

1887 WHITTEMORE, Reed. "Shaw's Abstract Clarity." *TDR*, 2 (Nov. 1957), 46–57. (Stresses *Major Barbara*.)

1888 WILKENFELD, Roger B. "Perpetual Motion in *Heartbreak House*." *TSLL*, 13 (1971), 321–35.

1889 WILSON, Edmund. "Bernard Shaw at Eighty." *The Triple Thinkers*. Rev. ed. NY: Oxford UP, 1948, 180–96.

1890 WINSTEN, Stephen, ed. *G.B.S. 90: Aspects of Bernard Shaw's Life and Work*. Lon: Hutchinson, 1946. (Brief essays on many aspects of Shaw.)

1891 WISENTHAL, J. L. *The Marriage of Contraries: Bernard Shaw's Middle Plays*. Cambridge, MA: Harvard UP, 1974.*

1892 WOODBRIDGE, Homer E. *George Bernard Shaw, Creative Artist*. Carbondale: Southern Illinois UP, 1963.†

1893 ZIMBARDO, Rose A., ed. *Twentieth Century Interpretations of Major Barbara: A Collection of Critical Essays*. Englewood Cliffs, NJ: Prentice-Hall, 1970.†

Simpson, N[orman] F[rederick] (1919–)

1894 SIMPSON, N. F. "Making Nonsense of Nonsense." *TrR*, No. 21 (1966), 5–13. (Enigmatic "interview" probably written by Simpson.)

1895 ESSLIN, Martin. *The Theatre of the Absurd*, **54**, 258–65.

1896 FOTHERGILL, C. Z. "Echoes of *A Resounding Tinkle*: N. F. Simpson Reconsidered." *MD*, 16 (1973), 299–306.

1897 SWANSON, Michele A. "*One Way Pendulum*: A New Dimension in Farce." *DrS*, 2 (1963), 322–32.

1898 TAYLOR, John R. *Anger & After*, **318**, 66–73.

1899 TSCHUDIN, Marcus. *A Writer's Theatre*, **389**, 133–57. (Court Theatre production of *One Way Pendulum*.)

1900 WELLWARTH, George. "N. F. Simpson: Parallel to Logic." *The Theater of Protest and Paradox*, **329**, 243–52.

1901 WORTH, Katharine J. "Avant Garde at the Royal Court Theatre: John Arden and N. F. Simpson." In **90**, 214–23.

Stoppard, Tom
(1937–)

1902 STOPPARD, Tom. "Ambushes for the Audience: Towards a High Comedy of Ideas." *ThQ*, 4 (May–July 1974), 3–17. (Interview.)*

1903 STOPPARD, Tom [Interview with Giles Gordon.] In **114**, 77–87.

1904 BABULA, William. "The Play-Life Metaphor in Shakespeare and Stoppard." *MD*, 15 (1972), 279–81.

1905 BERLIN, Normand. "*Rosencrantz and Guildenstern Are Dead*: Theater of Criticism." *MD*, 16 (1973), 269–77.

1906 BIGSBY, C. W. E. *Tom Stoppard*. Harlow: Longman for the British Council, 1976. (Pamphlet.)†

1907 CALLEN, Anthony. "Stoppard's Godot: Some French Influences on Post-War English Drama." *NTM*, 10 (Winter 1969–70), 22–30.

1908 COHN, Ruby. *Modern Shakespeare Offshoots*, **48**, 211–18.

1909 FARISH, Gillan. "Into the Looking-Glass Bowl: An Instant of Grateful Terror." *Univ of Windsor Rev*, 10 (1975), 14–29. (Stresses *Rosencrantz*.)

1910 GIANAKARIS, C. J. "Absurdism Altered: *Rosencrantz & Guildenstern Are Dead*." *DrS*, 7 (1968–69), 52–58.

1911 KEYSSAR-FRANKE, Helene. "The Strategy of *Rosencrantz and Guildenstern Are Dead*." *ETJ*, 27 (1975), 85–97.

1912 LEE, R. H. "The Circle and Its Tangent." *Theoria: A J of St in the Arts, Humanities and Social Sciences*, 33 (1969), 37–43; see also the response by C. O. Gardner, *Theoria*, 34 (1970), 83–84. (On *Rosencrantz*.)

1913 LEVENSON, Jill. "Views from a Revolving Door: Tom Stoppard's Canon to Date." *QQ*, 78 (1971), 431–42.

1914 SALTER, Charles H. "*Rosencrantz and Guildenstern Are Dead*." In **173**, 144–50.

1915 TAYLOR, John R. *The Second Wave*, **319**, 94–107.

1916 WHITAKER, Thomas R. "Notes on Playing the Player." *CentR*, 16 (1972), 1–22. (Part on *Rosencrantz*.)

Storey, David
(1933–)

1917 STOREY, David, and Ronald HAYMAN. "David Storey." *Playback*, **108**, 7–21. (Essay-interview.)

1918 BYGRAVE, Mike. "David Storey: Novelist or Playwright?" *ThQ*, 1 (April–June 1971), 31–36.

1919 FREE, William J. "The Ironic Anger of David Storey." *MD*, 16 (1973), 307–16.

1920 KALSON, Albert E. "Insanity and the Rational Man in the Plays of David Storey." *MD*, 19 (1976), 111–28.

1921 TAYLOR, John R. *The Second Wave*, **319**, 141–54.

1922 WORTH, Katharine J. *Revolutions in Modern English Drama*, **174**, 26–30, 38–40.

Synge, John Millington (1871–1909)

1923 SYNGE, John M. *Collected Works*. Vols. 3–4: *Plays*, ed. Ann Saddlemyer. Lon: Oxford UP, 1968. (Full textual apparatus, plus Synge's worksheets and notes.)

1924 SYNGE, John M. *The Plays and Poems*, ed. T. R. Henn. Lon: Methuen, 1963. (Long intros. and notes.)†

1925 SYNGE, John M., and Max MEYERFELD. "Letters of John Millington Synge." *YR*, 13 (1924), 690–709.

1926 SYNGE, John M. *Letters to Molly: John Millington Synge to Maire O'Neill, 1906–1909*, ed. Ann Saddlemyer. Cambridge, MA: Harvard UP, 1971.

1927 SYNGE, John M. *The Autobiography of J. M. Synge, Constructed from the Manuscripts*, ed. Alan Price. Dub: Dolmen, 1965.

1928 BLISS, Alan J. "A Synge Glossary." In **1938**, 297–315.

1929 LEVITT, Paul M. *J.M. Synge: A Bibliography of Published Criticism*. Dub: Irish UP, 1974.

1930 MIKHAIL, Edward H. *J.M. Synge: A Bibliography of Criticism*. Totowa, N. J.: Rowman & Littlefield, 1974.

1931 ALEXANDER, Jean. "Synge's Play of Choice: *The Shadow of the Glen*." In **1938**, 21–32.

1932 BAUMAN, Richard. "John Millington Synge and Irish Folklore." *SFQ*, 27 (1963), 267–79.

1933 BENNETT, Charles A. "The Plays of John M. Synge." *YR*, 1 (1912), 192–205.

1934 BESSAI, Diane E. "Little Hound in Mayo: Synge's Playboy and the Comic Tradition in Irish Literature." *DR*, 48 (1968), 372–83.

1935 BLISS, Alan J. "The Language of Synge." In **1974**, 35–62.

1936 BOURGEOIS, Maurice. *John Millington Synge and the Irish Theatre*. Lon: Constable, 1913. (The fullest and best early study.)

1937 BOYD, Ernest. *The Contemporary Drama of Ireland*, **417**, 88–109.

1938 BUSHRUI, Suheil B., ed. *A Centenary Tribute to John Millington Synge, 1871–1909: Sunshine and the Moon's Delight*. NY: Barnes & Noble, 1972.*

1939 CLARK, David R., ed. *Riders to the Sea*. Columbus: Merrill, 1970. (Text and critical essays.)†

1940 CLARK, David R. "Synge's 'Perpetual "Last Day" ': Remarks on *Riders to the Sea*." In **1938**, 41–52.

1941 COLLINS, R. L. "The Distinction of *Riders to the Sea*." *UKCR*, 13 (1947), 278–84.

1942 COMBS, William W. "J. M. Synge's *Riders to the Sea*: A Reading and Some Generalizations." *Papers of the Michigan Academy of Science, Arts and Letters*, 50 (1965), 599–607.

1943 CORKERY, Daniel. *Synge and Anglo-Irish Literature*. Dub: Cork UP, 1931.

1944 COXHEAD, Elizabeth. *J. M. Synge and Lady Gregory*. Lon: Longmans, 1962. (Pamphlet.)†

1945 CURRIE, Ryder H., and Martin BRYAN. "*Riders to the Sea*: Reappraised." *TQ*, 11 (Winter 1968), 139–46.

1946 DEANE, Seamus. "Synge's Poetic Use of Language." *Mosaic*, 5 (Fall 1971), 27–36; repr. in **1974**, 127–44.

1947 DONOGHUE, Denis. "Synge: *Riders to the Sea*; A Study." *Univ Rev*, 1 (1955), 52–58.

1948 DONOGHUE, Denis. " 'Too Immoral for Dublin': Synge's 'The Tinker's Wedding.' " *Irish Writing*, 30 (March 1955), 56–62.

1949 DURBACH, Errol. "Synge's Tragic Vision of the Old Mother and the Sea." *MD*, 14 (1972), 363–72.

1950 ECKLEY, Grace. "Truth at the Bottom of a Well: Synge's *The Well of the Saints*." *MD*, 16 (1973), 193–98.

1951 EDWARDS, Bernard W. "The Vision of J. M. Synge: A Study of *The Playboy of the Western World*." *ELT*, 17 (1974), 8–18.

1952 ELLIS-FERMOR, Una. *The Irish Dramatic Movement*, **420**, 163–86.*

1953 EMPSON, William. *Seven Types of Ambiguity*. 3rd ed. NY: Meridian, 1955, 46–51. (On *Deirdre*.)†

1954 FACKLER, Herbert V. "J. M. Synge's *Deirdre of the Sorrows*: Beauty Only." *MD*, 11 (1969), 404–9.

1955 FARRIS, Jon R. "The Nature of the Tragic Experience in *Deirdre of the Sorrows*." *MD*, 14 (1971), 243–51.

1955A FAULK, C. S. "John Millington Synge and the Rebirth of Comedy." *Southern Humanities Rev*, 8 (1974), 431-48.

1956 FAUSSET, Hugh I'A. "Synge and Tragedy." *FortR*, 115 (1924), 258–73.

1957 FERRIS, William R. "Folklore and Folklife in the Works of John M. Synge." *NY Folklore Q*, 27 (1971), 339–56.

1958 FLOOD, Jeanne A. "Thematic Variation in Synge's Early Peasant Plays." *Eire*, 7 (Fall 1972), 72–81.

1959 FOSTER, Leslie D. "Heroic Strivings in *The Playboy of the Western World*." *Eire*, 8 (Spring 1973), 85–94.

1960 FREE, William J. "Structural Dynamics in *Riders to the Sea*." *CLQ*, 11 (1975), 162-68.

1961 GASKELL, Ronald. *Drama and Reality*, **57**, 99–105. (On *Riders*.)

1962 GASSNER, John. "John Millington Synge: Synthesis in Folk Drama." *The Theatre in Our Times*, **105**, 217–24; also 537–43.

1963 GERSTENBERGER, Donna. *John Millington Synge*. NY: Twayne, 1964.*

1964 GREENE, David H., and Edward M. STEPHENS. *J. M. Synge, 1871–1909*. NY: Macmillan, 1959. (Excellent critical biography, actually written by Greene alone.)* †

1965 GREENE, David H. "J. M. Synge: A Centenary Appraisal." *Eire*, 6 (Winter 1971), 71–86.

1966 GREENE, David H. "The *Playboy* and Irish Nationalism." *JEGP*, 46 (1947), 199–204.

1967 GREENE, David H. "*The Shadow of the Glen* and the Widow of Ephesus." *PMLA*, 62 (1947), 233–38. (Source study.)

1968 GREENE, David H. "Synge and the Celtic Revival." *MD*, 4 (1961), 292–99.

1969 GREENE, David H. "Synge's Unfinished Deirdre." *PMLA*, 63 (1948), 1314–21.

1970 GREENE, David H. "*The Tinker's Wedding*, a Revaluation." *PMLA*, 62 (1947), 824–27.

1971 GREGORY, Lady. "Synge." *Eng Rev*, 13 (1913), 556–66.

1972 GRENE, Nicholas. *Synge: A Critical Study of the Plays*. Totowa, NJ: Rowman & Littlefield, 1976.

1973 GUTIERREZ, Donald. "Coming of Age in Mayo: Synge's *Playboy of the Western World* as a Rite of Passage." *Hartford St in Lit*, 6 (1974), 159–66.

1974 HARMON, Maurice, ed. *J. M. Synge Centenary Papers, 1971*. Dub: Dolmen, 1972.*

1975 HART, William. "Synge's Ideas on Life and Art: Design and Theory in *The Playboy of the Western World*." *YeS*, No. 2 (1972), 35–51.

1976 HENN, T. R. "*Riders to the Sea*: A Note." In **1938**, 33–40.

1977 HENN, T. R. "Yeats and Synge." *The Lonely Tower*, **2241**, 72–87.

1978 HOGAN, Robert. "Synge's Influence in Modern Irish Drama." In **1938**, 231–44.

1979 HOWARTH, Herbert. *The Irish Writers*, **1142**, 212–44.*

1980 HOWE, Percival P. *J. M. Synge: A Critical Study*. Lon: Secker, 1912.

1981 JOHNSTON, Denis. *John Millington Synge*. NY: Columbia UP, 1965. (Pamphlet.)†

1982 KILROY, James F. "The Playboy as Poet." *PMLA*, 83 (1968), 439–42.

1983 KILROY, James F. *The 'Playboy' Riots*. Dub: Dolmen, 1971.

1984 KILROY, Thomas. "Synge and Modernism." In **1974**, 167–79.

1985 KRAUSE, David. " 'The Rageous Ossean': Patron-Hero of Synge and O'Casey." *MD*, 3 (1961), 268–91.

1986 KRONENBERGER, Louis. *The Thread of Laughter*, **160**, 279–88.

1987 LEBLANC, Gerard. "Ironic Reversal as Theme and Technique in Synge's Shorter Comedies." In **412**, 51–63.

1988 LEECH, Clifford. "John Synge and the Drama of His Time." *MD*, 16 (1973), 223–37.

1989 LEVITT, Paul M. "The Whole Analysis: *Riders to the Sea*." *A Structural Approach to the Analysis of Drama*. The Hague: Mouton, 1971, 84–116.

1990 LEYBURN, Ellen D. "The Theme of Loneliness in thePlays of Synge." *MD*, 1 (1958), 84–90.

1991 LUCAS, Frank L. *The Drama of Chekhov, Synge, Yeats, and Pirandello*. Lon: Cassell, 1963, 167–237.

1992 MacLEAN, Hugh H. "The Hero as Playboy." *UKCR*, 21 (1954), 9–19.

1993 McMAHON, Seán. "The Road to Glenmalure." *Eire*, 7 (Spring 1972), 142–51. (*In the Shadow of the Glen*.)

1994 MARTIN, Augustine. "*The Playboy of the Western World*: Christy Mahon and the Apotheosis of Loneliness." In **1938**, 61–74.

1995 MASEFIELD, John. "John M. Synge." *Recent Prose*, **1229**, 163–87.

1996 MERCIER, Vivian. "*The Tinker's Wedding*." In **1938**, 75–90.

1997 MIKHAIL, Edward H. "Two Aspects of Synge's *Playboy*." *CLQ*, 9 (1971), 322–30. (Stresses parallel to *Peer Gynt*.)

1998 MOORE, John R. "*Deirdre* and the Sorrows of Mortality." In **1938**, 91–106.

1999 MUNRO, John. "J. M. Synge and the Drama of the Late Nineteenth Century." In **1938**, 219–30.

2000 MURPHY, Brenda. "Stoicism, Asceticism, and Ecstasy: Synge's *Deirdre of the Sorrows." MD,* 17 (1974), 155-63.

2001 MURPHY, Daniel J. "The Reception of Synge's *Playboy* in Ireland and America: 1907–1912." *BNYPL*, 64 (1960), 515–33.

2002 O'CASEY, Sean. "John Millington Synge." *Blasts and Benedictions*, **1279**, 35–41.

2003 O'CONNOR, Frank. "Synge." In **413**, 31–52.

2004 OREL, Harold. "Synge's Concept of the Tramp." *Eire*, 7 (Summer 1972), 55–61.

2005 OREL, Harold. "Synge's Last Play: 'And a Story Will Be Told For Ever.' " *MD*, 4 (1961), 306–13.

2006 ORR, Robert H. "The Surprise Ending: One Aspect of J. M. Synge's Dramatic Technique." *ELT*, 15 (1972), 105–15.

2007 PEACOCK, Ronald. *The Poet in the Theatre*, **67**, 105–16.

2008 PEARCE, Howard D. "Synge's Playboy as Mock-Christ." *MD*, 8 (1965), 303–10; repr. in **2037**, 87–97.

2009 PODHORETZ, Norman. "Synge's *Playboy*: Morality and the Hero." *EIC,* 3 (1953), 337–44; repr. in **2037**, 68–74.

2010 PRICE, Alan. *Synge and Anglo-Irish Drama*. Lon: Methuen, 1961.*

2011 QUINN, Owen. "No Garland for John Synge." *Envoy*, 3 (Oct. 1950), 44–51.

2012 RAJAN, Balachandra. "Yeats, Synge and the Tragic Understanding." *YeS*, No. 2 (1972), 66–79.

2013 REYNOLDS, Lorna. "Collective Intellect: Yeats, Synge and Nietzsche." *E&S*, 26 (1973), 83–98.

2014 REYNOLDS, Lorna. "The Rhythms of Synge's Dramatic Prose." *YeS*, No. 2 (1972), 52–65.

2015 RILLIE, John A. M. "John Millington Synge." In **173**, 150–65. (Analyses of *Playboy* and *Riders*.)

2016 ROY, Emil. *British Drama Since Shaw*, **233**, 54–67.

2017 SADDLEMYER, Ann. "*Deirdre of the Sorrows*: Literature First . . . Drama Afterwards." In **1974**, 88–107.

2018 SALMON, Eric. "J. M. Synge's *Playboy*: A Necessary Reassessment." *MD*, 13 (1970), 111–28.

2019 SANDERLIN, R. Reed. "Synge's *Playboy* and the Ironic Hero." *Southern Q*, 6 (1968), 289–301.

2020 SETTERQUIST, Jan. *Ibsen and the Beginnings of Anglo-Irish Drama. Vol. 1: John Millington Synge*. NY: Oriole Eds., 1973 [c. 1951].

2021 SIDNELL, M. J. "Synge's Playboy and the Champion of Ulster." *DR*, 45 (1965), 51–59. (Mythic background of the play.)

2022 SKELTON, Robin. *J. M. Synge*. Lewisburg, PA: Bucknell UP, 1972. (89-page overview.)†

2023 SKELTON, Robin, ed. *Riders to the Sea*. Lon: Oxford UP, 1969. (Edited from the Harvard manuscripts.)

2024 SKELTON, Robin. *The Writings of J. M. Synge*. Lon: Thames & Hudson, 1971.*

2025 SMITH; Harry W. "Synge's *Playboy* and the Proximity of Violence." *QJS*, 55 (1969), 381–87.

2026 SPACKS, Patricia M. "The Making of the Playboy." *MD*, 4 (1961), 314–23; repr. in **2037**, 75–87.

2027 SPENDER, Stephen. "Books and the War—VII." *Penguin New Writing*, No. 18, ed. John Lehmann. NY: Penguin, 1941, 120–34. (On Synge's language.)

2028 STEPHENS, Edward M. *My Uncle John: Edward Stephens's Life of J. M. Synge*, ed. Andrew Carpenter. Lon: Oxford UP, 1974.

2029 STRONG, Leonard A. G. *Personal Remarks*. NY: Liveright, 1953, 46–60. (Stresses *Playboy*.)

2030 STYAN, J. L. *The Elements of Drama*, **71**, 57–63, 126–29, 257–60. (On *Playboy* and *Deirdre*.)

2031 SÚILLEABHÁIN, Seán O. "Synge's Use of Irish Folklore." In **1974**, 18–34.

2032 SULLIVAN, Mary R. "Synge, Sophocles, and the Un-making of Myth." *MD*, 12 (1969), 242–53. (On *Playboy*.)

2033 SULTAN, Stanley. "The Gospel According to Synge." *PLL*, 4 (1968), 428–41. (On *Playboy*.)

2034 TUAMA, Seán Ó. "Synge and the Idea of a National Literature." In **1974**, 1–17.

2035 VAN LAAN, Thomas F. "Form as Agent in Synge's *Riders to the Sea*." *DrS*, 3 (1964), 352–66.

2036 WEYGANDT, Cornelius. *Irish Plays and Playwrights*, **432**, 160–97.

2037 WHITAKER, Thomas R., ed. *Twentieth Century Interpretations of The Playboy of the Western World: A Collection of Critical Essays*. Englewood Cliffs, NJ: Prentice-Hall, 1969.* †

2038 WILLIAMS, Raymond. *Drama from Ibsen to Brecht*, **72**, 129–40.

2039 YEATS, W. B. "The Controversy over *The Playboy of the Western World*" and "On Taking *The Playboy* to London." *Explorations*, **2179**, 225–30.

2040 YEATS, W. B. "The Death of Synge." *Dramatis Personae*, **433**, 125–54.

2041 YEATS, W. B. "J. M. Synge and the Ireland of His Time." *Essays and Introductions*, **2178**, 311–42.*

2042 YEATS, W. B. "Preface to the First Edition of *The Well of the Saints*." *Essays and Introductions*, **2178**, 298–305.

Thomas, Dylan
(1914–1953)

2043 THOMAS, Dylan. *Under Milk Wood: A Play for Voices*. NY: New Directions, 1953.

2044 ACKERMAN, John. *Dylan Thomas: His Life and Work*. Lon: Oxford UP, 1964, 170–83.

2045 BRINNIN, John M. *Dylan Thomas in America: An Intimate Journal*. Bos: Little, Brown, 1955. (Detailed background of *Under Milk Wood*.)

2046 CLEVERDON, Douglas. *The Growth of Milk Wood, with the Textual Variants of Under Milk Wood*. NY: New Directions, 1969.

2047 DAVIS, Cynthia. "The Voices of '*Under Milk Wood*.' " *Criticism*, 17 (1975), 74–89.

2048 HOLBROOK, David. "Laughing Delightedly at Hate: *Under Milk Wood*." *Dylan Thomas: The Code of Night*. Lon: Athlone Pr., 1972, 221–44.

2049 HOLBROOK, David. " 'A Place of Love': *Under Milk Wood*." *Dylan Thomas and Poetic Dissociation*. Carbondale: Southern Illinois UP, 1964, 135–72; repr. in *Dylan Thomas: A Collection of Critical Essays*, ed. C. B. Cox. Englewood Cliffs, NJ: Prentice-Hall, 1966, 99–116.

2050 JENKINS, David C. "Dylan Thomas' *Under Milk Wood*: The American Element." *Trace*, 51 (1964), 325–38.

2051 MOYNIHAN, William T. *The Craft and Art of Dylan Thomas*. Ithaca, NY: Cornell UP, 1966, 282–89.

2052 REA, J. "A Topographical Guide to *Under Milk Wood*." *CE*, 25 (1964), 535–42.

2053 WELLS, Henry W. "Voice and Verse in Dylan Thomas' Play." *CE*, 15 (1954), 438–44.

2054 WILLIAMS, Raymond. "Dylan Thomas's Play for Voices." *Drama from Ibsen to Brecht*, **72**, 238–47; from *CritQ*, 1 (1959), 18–26; repr. in *Dylan Thomas*, ed. Cox, **2049**, 89–98.

Wesker, Arnold
(1932–)

2055 WESKER, Arnold. *The Plays of Arnold Wesker*. NY: Harper & Row, 1976–.

2056 WESKER, Arnold. *Fears of Fragmentation*. Lon: Cape, 1970. (Lectures, stressing the progress of Centre 42.)

2057 WESKER, Arnold. *Six Sundays in January*. Lon: Cape, 1971. (Essays largely unrelated to theatre.)

2058 WESKER, Arnold. "Let Battle Commence!" *Encore*, 5 (Nov.–Dec. 1958), 18–24; repr. in **308**, 96–103, and in **137**, 566–73.

2059 WESKER, Arnold. [Interview.] In **121**, 269–90.

2060 WESKER, Arnold. "Arnold Wesker." [Interview with Giles Gordon.] *TrR*, No. 21 (1966), 15–25; repr. in **114**, 137–48. (Focuses on *The Four Seasons*.)

2061 WESKER, Arnold. "Arnold Wesker and John Dexter Talking to Ronald Hayman." *TrR*, No. 48 (1973–74), 89–99.

2062 WESKER, Arnold, and Abraham ROTHBERG. "Waiting for Wesker." *Antioch Rev*, 24 (1964–65), 492–505.

2063 WESKER, Arnold, and Rainer TAËNI. "Interview with Arnold Wesker." *NS*, 20 (1971), 410–18.

2064 WESKER, Arnold, and Simon TRUSSLER. "His Very Own and Golden City." *TDR*, 11 (Winter 1966), 192–202; repr. in **309**, 78–95.

2065 ANDERETH, Max. "Sartre and Wesker: Committed Playwrights." *Comment*, 5 (July–Aug. 1964), 18–28.

2066 ANDERSON, Michael. "Arnold Wesker: The Last Humanist?" *NTM*, 8 (Summer 1968), 10–27.

2067 BROWN, John R. "Arnold Wesker. Theatrical Demonstration: *Roots*, *The Kitchen* and *Chips with Everything*." *Theatre Language*, **281**, 158–89.*

2068 COPPIETERS, Frank. "Arnold Wesker's Centre Fortytwo: A Cultural Revolution Betrayed." *ThQ*, 5 (Summer 1975), 37–54.

2069 FINDLATER, Richard. "Plays and Politics." *TC*, 168 (1960), 235–42. (On the trilogy.)

2070 GARFORTH, John. "Arnold Wesker's Mission." In **308**, 223–30.

2071 GOODMAN, Henry. "Arnold Wesker." *DrS*, 1 (1961), 215–22.

2072 HAYMAN, Ronald. *Arnold Wesker*. 2nd ed. Lon: Heinemann Educational, 1974. (Includes two interviews.)

2073 KERSHAW, John. "*Roots*: Arnold Wesker, the Determined Missionary." *The Present Stage*. Lon: Fontana, 1966, 43–53.

2074 KITCHIN, Laurence. "Drama with a Message: Arnold Wesker." In **90**, 169–85; repr. in **280**, 71–82. (Some stress on *The Kitchen*.)

2075 KLEINBERG, Robert. "Seriocomedy in *The Wesker Trilogy*." *ETJ*, 21 (1969), 36–40.

2076 KLOTZ, Günther. *Individuum und Gesellschaft im englischen Drama der Gegenwart: Arnold Wesker und Harold Pinter*. Berlin: Akademie, 1972.

2077 LATHAM, Jacqueline. "*Roots*: A Reassessment." *MD*, 8 (1965), 192–97.

2078 LEECH, Clifford. "Two Romantics: Arnold Wesker and Harold Pinter." In **100**, 11–31.

2079 LEEMING, Glenda, and Simon TRUSSLER. *The Plays of Arnold Wesker: An Assessment*. Lon: Gollancz, 1971.*

2080 LEROY, Bernard. "Two Committed Playwrights: Wesker and O'Casey." In **413**, 107–17.

2081 MANDER, John. "Arnold Wesker's *Roots*." *The Writer and Commitment*. Lon: Secker & Warburg, 1961, 194–211.

2082 MANNHEIMER, Monica. "Ordering Chaos: The Genesis of Arnold Wesker's *The Friends*." *Eng St*, 56 (1975), 34–44.

2083 O'CONNOR, Garry, ed. "Arnold Wesker's 'The Friends.' " *ThQ*, 1 (April–June 1971), 78–92. (A "production casebook" with notes by Wesker and others.)

2084 PAGE, Malcolm. "Whatever Happened to Arnold Wesker? His Recent Plays." *MD*, 11 (1968), 317–25.

2085 RIBALOW, Harold U. *Arnold Wesker*. NY: Twayne, 1965.

2086 ROTHBERG, Abraham. "East End, West End: Arnold Wesker." *Southwest Rev*, 52 (1967), 368–78.

2087 TAYLOR, John R. *Anger & After*, **318**, 147–70.*

2088 TSCHUDIN, Marcus. *A Writer's Theatre*, **389**, 159–82. (Court Theatre production of *The Kitchen*.)

2089 WEIAND, Hermann J. "The Chicken Soup Trilogy: *Roots*." In **173**, 167–73.

2090 WEISE, Wolf-Dietrich. *Die "Neuen englischen Dramatiker" in ihrem Verhältnis zu Brecht*, **328**, 79–110.

2091 WELLWARTH, George. "Arnold Wesker: 'Awake and Sing' in Whitechapel." *The Theater of Protest and Paradox*, **329**, 271–82.

2092 WOODROFE, K. S. "Mr. Wesker's *Kitchen*." *Hibbert J*, 62 (1964), 148–51.

Whiting, John
(1917–1963)

2093 WHITING, John. *The Collected Plays*, ed. Ronald Hayman. Lon: Heinemann, 1969. 2 vols.

2094 WHITING, John. *The Art of the Dramatist*, ed. Ronald Hayman. Lon: Lon. Mag. Eds., 1970. (Essays and reviews.)†

2095 WHITING, John. *John Whiting on Theatre*. Lon: Ross, 1966.†

2096 CAIRNS, Adrian. "The Significance of John Whiting's Plays." *ITA*, 1 (1956), 148–52.

2097 FRY, Christopher. "The Plays of John Whiting." *Essays by Divers Hands*, 34 (1966), 36–54. (Stresses *Saint's Day*.)*

2098 HAYMAN, Ronald. *John Whiting*. Lon: Heinemann, 1969.†

2099 HOEFER, Jacqueline. "Pinter and Whiting: Two Attitudes Towards the Alienated Artist." *MD*, 4 (1962), 402–8. (On *Saint's Day*.)

2100 HURRELL, John D. "John Whiting and the Theme of Self-Destruction." *MD*, 8 (1965), 134–41. (Stresses *Saint's Day*.)

2101 LYONS, Charles R. "The Futile Encounter in the Plays of John Whiting." *MD*, 11 (1968), 283–98.

2102 MANGHAM, Ian L. "Plays of a Private Man." *NTM*, 6, No. 2 (1965), 21–25.

2103 O'CONNOR, Garry. "The Obsession of John Whiting." *Encore*, 11 (July–Aug. 1964), 26–36.

2104 ROBINSON, Gabriele S. "Beyond the Waste Land: An Interpretation of John Whiting's *Saint's Day*." *MD*, 14 (1972), 463–77.

2105 ROBINSON, Gabriele S. "A Private Mythology: The Manuscripts and Plays of John Whiting." *MD*, 14 (1971), 23–36.

2106 ROBINSON, Gabriele S. "The Shavian Affinities of John Whiting." *ShR*, 17 (1974), 86–98.

2107 SALMON, Eric. *John Whiting*. NY: Twayne, 1975.

2108 SALMON, Eric. "John Whiting's Unpublished Novel." *LonM*, 12 (Feb.–March 1973), 44–69.

2109 TREWIN, John C. "Two Morality Playwrights: Robert Bolt and John Whiting." In **90**, 105–19. (Stresses *Saint's Day*.)

2110 TRUSSLER, Simon. *The Plays of John Whiting: An Assessment*. Lon: Gollancz, 1972.*

2111 WILLIAMS, Raymond. *Drama from Ibsen to Brecht*, **72**, 316–18. (On *Marching Song*.)

2112 WOOD, E. R. "Introduction." *Saint's Day*. Lon: Heinemann Educational, 1963, v–xxxii.

Wilde, Oscar
(1854–1900)

2113 WILDE, Oscar. *Complete Works*. New ed., with intro. by Vyvyan Holland. Lon: Collins, 1966. (Prints all the plays.)

2114 WILDE, Oscar. *The Original Four-Act Version of The Importance of Being Earnest*, with intro. by Vyvyan Holland. Lon: Methuen, 1957.

2115 WILDE, Oscar. *The Artist as Critic: Critical Writings*, ed. Richard Ellmann. NY: Random, 1969.

2116 WILDE, Oscar. *Letters*, ed. Rupert Hart-Davis. NY: Harcourt, 1962.

2117 MASON, Stuart. *Bibliography of Oscar Wilde*. New ed. Lon: Rota, 1967.

2118 BECKSON, Karl, ed. *Oscar Wilde: The Critical Heritage*. Lon: Routledge, 1970. (Reprints significant early reviews of the plays.)*

2119 BENTLEY, Eric. *The Playwright as Thinker*, **42**, 140–45. (On *Earnest*.)

2120 BROOKS, Cleanth, and Robert B. HEILMAN. *Understanding Drama*. NY: Holt, 1945, 43–45, 54–56, 63–66, 73–81. (On *Lady Windermere's Fan*.)

2121 CROFT-COOKE, Rupert. *The Unrecorded Life of Oscar Wilde*. NY: McKay, 1972.

2122 DONOHUE, Joseph W. "The First Production of *The Importance of Being Earnest*: A Proposal for a Reconstructive Study." In *Essays on Nineteenth Century British Theatre*, ed. Kenneth Richards and Peter Thomson. Lon: Methuen, 1971, 125–43.

2123 ELLMANN, Richard, ed. *Oscar Wilde: A Collection of Critical Essays*. Englewood Cliffs, NJ: Prentice-Hall, 1969.†

2124 ELLMANN, Richard. "Overtures to Wilde's *Salomé*." *Yearbook of Comparative and General Lit*, 17 (1968), 17–28; also in *TriQuarterly*, 15 (1969), 45–64; repr. in **2123**, 73–91.

2125 ELLMANN, Richard. "Romantic Pantomime in Oscar Wilde." *Partisan Rev*, 30 (1963), 342–55. (A general revaluation.)

2126 ERVINE, St. John. *Oscar Wilde: A Present Time Appraisal*. Lon: Allen & Unwin, 1951.

2127 FOSTER, Richard. "Wilde as Parodist: A Second Look at *The Importance of Being Earnest*." *CE*, 18 (1956), 18–23.

2128 FREEDMAN, Morris. "The Modern Tragicomedy of Wilde and O'Casey," **1323**.

2129 FUSSELL, B. H. "The Masks of Oscar Wilde." *SR*, 80 (1972), 124–39.

2130 GANZ, Arthur. "The Divided Self in the Society Comedies of Oscar Wilde." *MD*, 3 (1960), 16–23; repr. in *British Victorian Literature: Recent Revaluations*, ed. Shiv K. Kumar (NY: New York UP, 1969), 481–90.

2131 GANZ, Arthur. "The Meaning of *The Importance of Being Earnest*." *MD*, 6 (1963), 42–52.

2132 GREGOR, Ian. "Comedy and Oscar Wilde." *SR*, 74 (1966), 501–21.*

2133 HANKIN, St. John. "The Collected Plays of Oscar Wilde." *The Dramatic Works*, **1148**, III, 181–201; repr. in **2123**, 61–72.

2134 JOOST, Nicholas, and Franklin E. COURT. *"Salomé*, the Moon, and Oscar Wilde's Aesthetics: A Reading of the Play." *PLL*, 8, Suppl. (1972), 96–111.

2135 JORDAN, Robert J. "Satire and Fantasy in Wilde's 'The Importance of Being Earnest.' " *Ariel*, 1 (July 1970), 101–9.

2136 JULLIAN, Philippe. *Oscar Wilde*, tr. Violet Wyndham. NY: Viking, 1969.

2137 KRONENBERGER, Louis. *The Thread of Laughter*, **160**, 209–25.

2138 MARCUS, Jane. "Salomé: The Jewish Princess Was a New Woman." *BNYPL*, 78 (1974), 95–113.

2139 MATLOCK, Kate. "The Plays of Oscar Wilde." *JIL*, 4 (May 1975), 95–106.

2140 MIKHAIL, Edward H. "The Four-Act Version of *The Importance of Being Earnest*." *MD*, 11 (1968), 263–66.

2141 MIKHAIL, Edward H. "The French Influences on Oscar Wilde's Comedies." *Revue de Littérature Comparée*, 42 (1968), 220–33.

2142 MIKHAIL, Edward H. "Self-Revelation in *An Ideal Husband*." *MD*, 11 (1968), 180–86.

2143 MORGAN, Charles. *The Writer and His World: Lectures and Essays*. Lon: Macmillan, 1961, 106–10.

2144 MUDRICK, Marvin. "Restoration Comedy and Later." In **122**, 120–25. (On *Earnest*.)

2145 NASSAAR, Christopher S. *Into the Demon Universe: A Literary Exploration of Oscar Wilde*. New Haven: Yale UP, 1974, 80–146.*

2146 NETHERCOT, Arthur H. "Oscar Wilde and the Devil's Advocate." *PMLA*, 59 (1944), 833–50; see also his further note, "Oscar Wilde on His Subdividing Himself," *PMLA*, 60 (1945), 616–17.

2147 NETHERCOT, Arthur H. "Prunes and Miss Prism." *MD*, 6 (1963), 112–16.

2148 OLSON, Elder. *The Theory of Comedy*, **1804**, 107–14. (On *Earnest*.)

2149 PARKER, David. "Oscar Wilde's Great Farce: *The Importance of Being Earnest*." *MLQ*, 35 (1974), 173–86.

2150 PARTRIDGE, E. B. "The Importance of Not Being Earnest." *Bucknell Rev*, 9 (1960), 143–58.

2151 PAUL, Charles B., and Robert D. PEPPER. "The Importance of Reading Alfred: Oscar Wilde's Debt to Alfred de Musset." *BNYPL*, 75 (1971), 506–42. (*Earnest* as a "masterful adaptation" of a Musset play.)

2152 PEARSON, Hesketh. *Oscar Wilde: His Life and Wit*. NY: Grosset & Dunlap, 1946.†

2153 PECKHAM, Morse. "What Did Lady Windermere Learn?" *CE*, 18 (1956), 11–14.

2154 POAGUE, L. A. "*The Importance of Being Earnest*: The Texture of Wilde's Irony." *MD*, 16 (1973), 251–57.

2155 POPKIN, Henry, ed. *The Importance of Being Earnest: An Authoritative Text Edition*. NY: Avon, 1965. (Full intro. and comments by Shaw, Beerbohm, Hankin, and Agate.)†

2156 REINERT, Otto. "Satiric Strategy in *The Importance of Being Earnest*." *CE*, 18 (1956), 14–18.

2157 RODITI, Edouard. *Oscar Wilde*. Norfolk, CT: New Directions, 1947, 125–44.*

2158 ROY, Emil. *British Drama Since Shaw*, **233**, 21–35.

2159 SAN JUAN, Epifanio. "Structure and Style in the Poetic Drama" and "The Action of the Comedies." *The Art of Oscar Wilde*. Princeton, NJ: Princeton UP, 1967, 105–204.*

2160 SPININGER, Dennis J. "Profiles and Principles: The Sense of the Absurd in *The Importance of Being Earnest.*" *PLL*, 12 (1976), 49–72.

2160A STONE, Geoffrey. "Serious Bunburyism: The Logic of 'The Importance of Being Earnest.' " *EIC*, 26 (1976), 28-41.

2161 STYAN, J. L. *The Elements of Drama*, **71**, 20–24, 142–46. (On *Earnest*.)

2162 SULLIVAN, Kevin. *Oscar Wilde*. NY: Columbia UP, 1972. (Pamphlet.)

2163 TOLIVER, Harold E. "Wilde and the Importance of 'Sincere and Studied Triviality.' " *MD*, 5 (1963), 389–99.

2164 WARE, James M. "Algernon's Appetite: Oscar Wilde's Hero as Restoration Dandy." *ELT*, 13 (1970), 17–26.

2165 WOODCOCK, George. *The Paradox of Oscar Wilde*. NY: Macmillan, 1949, 161–66.

Williams, Charles
(1886–1945)

2166 WILLIAMS, Charles. *Collected Plays*, with intro. by John Heath-Stubbs. Lon: Oxford UP, 1963.

2167 WILLIAMS, Charles. "Religious Drama." *The Image of the City, and Other Essays*, ed. Anne Ridler. Lon: Oxford UP, 1958, 55–59.

2168 GLENN, Lois. *Charles W. S. Williams: A Checklist*. Kent, OH: Kent State UP, 1975.

2169 AUDEN, W. H. "The Martyr as Dramatic Hero." *Secondary Worlds: Essays*. NY: Random, 1968, 15–45. (On *Cranmer*.)

2170 HADFIELD, Alice M. *An Introduction to Charles Williams*. Lon: Hale, 1959. (Largely biographical.)

2171 MOORMAN, Charles. "Zion and Gomorrah: Charles Williams." *The Precincts of Felicity: The Augustinian City of the Oxford Christians*. Gainesville: Univ. of Florida Pr., 1966, 30–64.

2172 RIDLER, Anne. "Introduction." *Seed of Adam, and Other Plays*. Lon: Oxford UP, 1948, i–x.

2173 SHIDELER, Mary M. *The Theology of Romantic Love: A Study in the Writings of Charles Williams*. Grand Rapids: Eerdmans, 1966 [c.1962].

2174 SPANOS, William V. *The Christian Tradition in Modern British Verse Drama*, **268**, 40–45, 68–80, 104–24, 155–80, 295–304.*

2175 WEALES, Gerald. *Religion in Modern English Drama*, **172**, 142–64.

Yeats, William Butler
(1865–1939)

2176 YEATS, W. B. *The Variorum Edition of the Plays*, ed. Russell K. and Catharine C. Alspach. NY: Macmillan, 1966.*

2177 YEATS, W. B. *Autobiographies*. [*Reveries over Childhood and Youth; The Trembling of the Veil; Dramatis Personae; Estrangement; The Death of Synge; The Beauty of Sweden.*] Lon: Macmillan, 1956.

2178 YEATS, W. B. *Essays and Introductions*. NY: Collier Books, 1968 [c.1961].

WILLIAM BUTLER YEATS

(See esp. "Certain Noble Plays of Japan," "The Tragic Theatre," "A General Introduction for My Work," and "An Introduction for My Plays.")†

2179 YEATS, W. B. *Explorations*, ed. Mrs. W. B. Yeats. Lon: Macmillan, 1962. (Includes "The Irish Dramatic Movement: 1901–1919," intros. to *The Words upon the Window-Pane* and *The Resurrection*, and other material.)†

2180 YEATS, W. B. "From One Theatrical Reformer to Another: W. B. Yeats's Unpublished Letters to Gordon Craig," ed. Christiane Thilliez. In **412**, 275–86.

2181 YEATS, W. B. *Letters*, ed. Allan Wade. NY: Macmillan, 1955.

2182 YEATS, W. B. *Memoirs*, transcribed and ed. by Denis Donoghue. NY: Macmillan, 1973.

2183 YEATS, W. B. "Two Lectures on the Irish Theatre by W. B. Yeats," ed. Robert O'Driscoll. In **409**, 66–88.

2184 CROSS, K. G. W., and R. T. DUNLOP. *A Bibliography of Yeats Criticism, 1887–1965*. Lon: Macmillan, 1971. (Excellent, but soon to be superseded by another work by K. P. S. Jochum.)

2185 DOMVILLE, Eric. *A Concordance to the Plays of W. B. Yeats*. Ithaca, NY: Cornell UP, 1972. 2 vols.

2186 JEFFARES, A. Norman, and A. S. KNOWLAND. *A Commentary on the Collected Plays of W. B. Yeats*. Stanford, CA: Stanford UP, 1975. (Scholarly reference guide to each play.)*

2187 JOCHUM, Klaus P. S. *W. B. Yeats's Plays: An Annotated Checklist of Criticism*. Saarbrücken: Anglistisches Institut der Univ. des Saarlandes, 1966. (Soon to be superseded.)†

2188 WADE, Allan. *A Bibliography of the Writings of W. B. Yeats*. 3rd ed., rev. and ed. Russell K. Alspach. Lon: Hart-Davis, 1968.

2189 ALLT, Peter. "Yeats, Religion, and History." *SR*, 60 (1952), 624–58. (Stresses *Calvary* and *Resurrection*.)

2190 ARCHIBALD, Douglas N. "*The Words upon the Window-Pane* and Yeats's Encounter with Jonathan Swift." In **2275**, 176–214.

2191 BAIRD, Sister Mary J. "A Play on the Death of God: The Irony of Yeats's *The Resurrection*." *MD*, 10 (1967), 79–86.

2192 BAKSI, Pronoti. "The Noh and the Yeatsian Synthesis." *Rev of Eng Lit*, 6 (July 1964), 34–43.

2193 BECKER, William. "The Mask Mocked: Or, Farce and the Dialectic of Self (Notes on Yeats's *The Player Queen*)." *SR*, 61 (1953), 82–108.

2194 BENTLEY, Eric. "Yeats's Plays." *In Search of Theater*, **91**, 315-26; repr. from *KR*, 10 (1948), 196–208; repr. in **2236**, 213-23.*

2195 BHOWANI-SETHI, Uma, and Lewis T. CETTA. "The Theme of Reincarnation in Yeats's *Purgatory*." *TA*, 30 (1974), 7–13.

2196 BJERSBY, Birgit. *The Interpretation of the Cuchulain Legend in the Works of W. B. Yeats*. Upsala: Lundequistska, 1950.*

2197 [BJERSBY], Birgit Bramsbäck. "The Musician's Knife in Yeats's *Deirdre*." *Studia Neophilologica*, 41 (1969), 359–66.

2198 BLOCK, Haskell M. "Yeats's *The King's Threshold*: The Poet and Society." *PQ*, 34 (1955), 206–18.

2199 BLOOM, Harold. *Yeats*. NY: Oxford UP, 1970.* †

2200 BOYD, Ernest. *The Contemporary Drama of Ireland*, **417**, 47–87.

WILLIAM BUTLER YEATS

2201 BOYD, Ernest.·"William Butler Yeats: The Plays." *Ireland's Literary Renaissance*. Rev. ed. NY: Knopf, 1922, 145–65.

2202 BRADBROOK, Muriel C. "Yeats and the Revival." *English Dramatic Form*, **142**, 123–42.

2203 BRADFORD, Curtis B. "Plays." *Yeats at Work*. Carbondale: Southern Illinois UP, 1965, 169–304. (Full discussions of *At the Hawk's Well*, *Words upon the Window-Pane*, *Resurrection*, *Full Moon*, and *Purgatory*.)

2203A BRADFORD, Curtis B. *The Writing of The Player Queen: Manuscripts of W. B. Yeats*, ed. with commentary. DeKalb: Northern Illinois UP, 1975.

2204 BROGUNIER, Joseph. "Expiation in Yeats's Late Plays." *DrS*, 5 (1966), 24–38.

2205 BUSHRUI, Suheil B. "*The Hour-Glass*: Yeats's Revisions, 1903–1922." In *W. B. Yeats, 1865–1965*, **2301**, 189–216.

2206 BUSHRUI, Suheil B. "Synge and Yeats." In **1938**, 189–204.

2207 BUSHRUI, Suheil B. *Yeats's Verse-Plays: The Revisions 1900–1910*. Oxford: Clarendon, 1965.

2208 BYARS, John A. "Yeats's Introduction of the Heroic Type." *MD*, 8 (1966), 409–18. (*The King's Threshold* and *On Baile's Strand*.)

2209 CLARK, David R. "Vision and Revision: Yeats's *The Countess Cathleen*." In **2313**, 158–76.

2210 CLARK, David R. *W. B. Yeats and the Theatre of Desolate Reality*. Dub: Dolmen, 1965. (Long analyses of *Deirdre*, *Dreaming of the Bones*, *Words upon the Window-Pane*, and *Purgatory*.)*

2211 CLARK, David R. "Yeats, Theatre, and Nationalism." In **409**, 134–55.

2212 CLARK, David R., and James B. McGUIRE. "Yeats's Versions of Sophocles: Two Typescripts." In **2275**, 215-77.

2213 CLARKE, Austin. "W. B. Yeats and Verse Drama." *Threshold*, No. 19 (1965), 14–29.

2214 COHN, Ruby. "The Plays of Yeats Through Beckett-Coloured Glasses." *Threshold*, No. 19 (1965), 41–47.

2215 COLUM, Padraic. "A Poet's Progress in the Theatre." *DM*, 11 (April–June 1936), 10–23.

2216 DESAI, Rupin W. "Shakespearean Echoes in Yeats's Early Plays" and "Echoes in Yeats's Later Plays." *Yeats's Shakespeare*. Evanston, IL: Northwestern UP, 1971, 157–223.

2217 DONOGHUE, Denis. "Yeats and the Clean Outline." *The Third Voice*, **251**, 32–61.*

2218 DORN, Karen. "Dialogue into Movement: W. B. Yeats's Theatre Collaboration with Gordon Craig." In **2275**, 109–36.

2219 DORN, Karen. "Stage Production and the Greek Theatre Movement: W. B. Yeats's Play *The Resurrection* and His Versions of *King Oedipus* and *Oedipus at Colonus*." *Theatre Research International*, 1 (1976), 182–204.

2220 EGELSON, Janet F. "Christ and Cuchulain: Interrelated Archetypes of Divinity and Heroism in Yeats." *Eire*, 4 (Spring 1969), 76–85.

2221 ELIOT, T. S. "Yeats." *On Poetry and Poets*. NY: Farrar, 1957, 295–308; repr. from *SoR*, 7 (1941–42); repr. in **2236**, 296–307, and in *Yeats: A Collection of Critical Essays*, ed. John Unterecker (Englewood Cliffs, NJ: Prentice-Hall, 1963), 54–63.†

2222 ELLIS-FERMOR, Una. *The Irish Dramatic Movement*, **420**, 59–116.*

2223 ELLMANN, Richard. *Yeats: The Man and the Masks*. Lon: Macmillan, 1948. (Critical biography.)†

2224 FLANAGAN, Thomas. "A Discourse by Swift, a Play by Yeats." *Univ Rev*, 5 (1968), 9–22.

2225 FRIEDMAN, Barton R. *Adventures in the Deeps of the Mind: The Cuchulain Cycle of W. B. Yeats*. Princeton, NJ: Princeton UP, 1977.*

2227 FRIEDMAN, Barton R. "Under a Leprous Moon: Action and Image in *The King's Threshold*." *ArQ*, 26 (1970), 39–53.

2228 GASKELL, Ronald. "*Purgatory*." *MD*, 4 (1962), 397–401.

2229 GASSNER, John. "Yeats: The Limits of Drama." *The Theatre in Our Times*, **105**, 226–33.

2230 GERSTENBERGER, Donna. "W. B. Yeats: 'Everything Sublunary Must Change.' " *The Complex Configuration*, **255**, 10–40.

2231 GORDON, David J. "The Poet and the Theatre." In *W. B. Yeats: Images of a Poet*, ed. D. J. Gordon. Manchester: Manchester UP, 1961, 56–65.

2232 GORSKY, Susan R. "A Ritual Drama: Yeats's Plays for Dancers." *MD*, 17 (1974), 165–78.

2233 GOSE, Elliott B. "The Lyric and the Philosophic in Yeats' *Calvary*." *MD*, 2 (1960), 370–76.

2234 GRAB, Frederic D. "Yeats's *King Oedipus*." *JEGP*, 71 (1972), 336–54.

2235 GREGORY, Horace. "W. B. Yeats and the Mask of Jonathan Swift." *The Shield of Achilles*. NY: Harcourt, 1944, 136–55; repr. from *SoR*, 7 (1941–42), 492–509; repr. in his *Spirit of Time and Place: Collected Essays* (NY: Norton, 1973), 122–35.

2236 HALL, James, and Martin STEINMANN, eds. *The Permanence of Yeats*. NY: Collier Books, 1961.†

2237 HARPER, George M. " 'Intellectual Hatred' and 'Intellectual Nationalism': The Paradox of Passionate Politics." In **409**, 40–65.

2238 HARPER, George M. *The Mingling of Heaven and Earth: Yeats's Theory of Theatre*. Dub: Dolmen, 1975. (Pamphlet.)†

2239 HARPER, George M. "The Reconciliation of Paganism & Christianity in Yeats' *Unicorn from the Stars*." In *All These to Teach*, ed. Robert A. Bryan et al. Gainesville: Univ. of Florida Pr., 1965, 224–36.

2240 HENN, T. R. "*The Green Helmet* and *Responsibilities*." In *An Honoured Guest: New Essays on W. B. Yeats*, ed. Denis Donoghue and J. R. Mulryne. Lon: Arnold, 1965, 34–53.

2241 HENN, T. R. "The Poetry of the Plays." *The Lonely Tower: Studies in the Poetry of W. B. Yeats*. 2nd ed. Lon: Methuen, 1965, 272–96.†

2241A HENN, T. R. "Yeats and the Theatre." In *Studies in the Arts,* ed. Francis Warner. NY: Barnes & Noble, 1968, 62-81.

2242 HINDEN, Michael. "Yeats's Symbolic Farce: *The Player Queen*." *MD*, 14 (1972), 441–48.

2243 HIRSCH, Foster L. "The Hearth and the Journey: The Mingling of Orders in the Drama of Yeats and Eliot." *ArQ*, 27 (1971), 293–307.

2244 HOFFMAN, Daniel. "Cuchulain and the Epic Theme." *Barbarous Knowledge: Myth in the Poetry of Yeats, Graves, and Muir*. NY: Oxford UP, 1967, 84–125.†

2245 HONE, Joseph. *W. B. Yeats, 1865–1939*. 2nd ed. Lon: Macmillan, 1962. (The authorized biography, first publ. 1943.)†

2246 ISHIBASHI, Hiro. "Yeats and the Noh: Types of Japanese Beauty and Their Reflection in Yeats's Plays," ed. Anthony Kerrigan. In *The Dolmen*

Press Yeats Centenary Papers MCMLXV, ed. Liam Miller. Lon: Oxford UP, 1968, 125–96. (Also publ. separately by Dolmen Press, 1966.)

2247 JEFFARES, A. Norman. "Introduction." *W. B. Yeats: Selected Plays*. Lon: Macmillan, 1964, 1–15. (See also his notes, 257–76.)†

2248 JEFFARES, A. Norman. *W. B. Yeats, Man and Poet*. 2nd ed. Lon: Routledge, 1962. (Critical biography.)†

2249 JOCHUM, Klaus P. S. "Yeats's Last Play." *JEGP*, 70 (1971), 220–29. (*The Death of Cuchulain*.)

2250 KAWIN, Bruce F. *Telling It Again and Again: Repetition in Literature and Film*. Ithaca, NY: Cornell UP, 1972, 72–84. (On *Purgatory*.)

2251 KENNELLY, Brendan. "The Heroic Ideal in Yeats's Cuchulain Plays." *Hermathena*, 101 (1965), 13–21.

2252 KERMODE, Frank. "Players and Painted Stage." In *The Integrity of Yeats*, ed. Denis Donoghue. Cork: Mercier Pr., 1964, 47–57.

2253 KERSNOWSKI, Frank L. "Portrayal of the Hero in Yeats' Poetic Drama." *Ren*, 18 (1965), 9–15.

2254 KIM, Myung W. "Dance and Rhythm: Their Meaning in Yeats and Noh." *MD*, 15 (1972), 195–208.

2254A LENSON, David. "Toward Lyric Tragedy: W. B. Yeats." *Achilles' Choice: Examples of Modern Tragedy*. Princeton, NJ: Princeton UP, 1975, 65-97. (Stresses his theories; analyzes *Unicorn*.)

2255 LIGHTFOOT, Marjorie J. "*Purgatory* and *The Family Reunion*: In Pursuit of Prosodic Description." *MD*, 7 (1964), 256–66.

2256 LUCAS, Frank L. *The Drama of Chekhov, Synge, Yeats, and Pirandello*. Lon: Cassell, 1963, 241–355.

2257 McCARTHY, Patrick A. "Talent and Tradition in Yeats' *On Baile's Strand*." *Eire*, 11 (1976), 45–62.

2258 McFATE, Patricia, and William E. DOHERTY. "W. B. Yeats's *Where There Is Nothing*." *IUR*, 2 (1972), 149–63.

2259 McGREEVY, Thomas. "Mr. W. B. Yeats as a Dramatist." *Revue Anglo-Américaine*, 7 (Oct. 1929), 19–36.

2260 MALONE, Andrew E. *The Irish Drama*, **427**, 42–52, 129–46.

2261 MARCUS, Phillip L. "Myth and Meaning in Yeats's *The Death of Cuchulain*." *IUR*, 2 (1972), 133–48. (From his forthcoming book.)

2262 MATHELIN, Pascale. "Irish Myths in the Theatre of W. B. Yeats." In **412**, 163–71.

2263 MELCHIORI, Giorgio. *The Whole Mystery of Art: Pattern into Poetry in the Work of W. B. Yeats*. Lon: Routledge, 1960, 38–72, etc.

2264 MENON, V. K. N. "Plays." *The Development of William Butler Yeats*. 2nd ed. Phila: Dufour, 1960, 74–89.

2265 MERCIER, Vivian. "In Defense of Yeats as a Dramatist." *MD*, 8 (1965), 161–66.

2266 MILLER, Liam. *The Noble Drama of W. B. Yeats*. Dub: Dolmen, 1976.

2267 MILLER, Liam. "W. B. Yeats and Stage Design at the Abbey Theatre." *Malahat Rev*, No. 16 (1970), 50–64.

2268 MINER, Earl. "The Nō and Yeats's Plays." *The Japanese Tradition in Literature*. Princeton, NJ: Princeton UP, 1958, 251–65.

2269 MOORE, Gerald. "The Nō and the Dance Plays of W. B. Yeats." *Japan Q*, 7 (1960), 177–87.

2270 MOORE, John R. *Masks of Love and Death: Yeats as Dramatist*. Ithaca, NY: Cornell UP, 1971.*

2271 MURPHY, Daniel J. "Lady Gregory, Co-author and Sometimes Author of the Plays of W. B. Yeats." In **1145**, 43–52.

2272 NATHAN, Leonard E. *The Tragic Drama of William Butler Yeats: Figures in a Dance*. NY: Columbia UP, 1965.*

2273 NEWTON, Norman. "Yeats as Dramatist: *The Player Queen*." *EIC*, 8 (1958), 269–84.

2274 OATES, Joyce Carol. "Tragic Rites in Yeats's 'A Full Moon in March.' " *The Edge of Impossibility: Tragic Forms in Literature*. NY: Vanguard, 1972, 165–87;† repr. from *Antioch Rev*, 29 (1969–70), 547–60.

2275 O'DRISCOLL, Robert, and Lorna REYNOLDS, eds. *Yeats and the Theatre*. Niagara Falls: Maclean-Hunter Pr., 1975.*

2276 OREL, Harold. "Dramatist." *The Development of William Butler Yeats: 1885–1900*. Lawrence: Univ. of Kansas Publ., 1968, 64–80.

2277 PARKER, J. Stewart. "Yeats' *The Hour-Glass*." *MD*, 10 (1968), 356–63.

2278 PARKIN, Andrew. "Singular Voices: Monologue and Monodrama in the Plays of W. B. Yeats." *MD*, 18 (1975), 141–52.

2279 PARKINSON, Thomas. "The Later Plays of W. B. Yeats." In **93**, 385–93.

2280 PARKINSON, Thomas. "A Poet's Stagecraft: 1899–1911." *W. B. Yeats, Self-Critic: A Study of His Early Verse*. Berkeley: Univ. of California Pr., 1951, 51–78.†

2281 PEACOCK, Ronald. *The Poet in the Theatre*, **67**, 117–28.

2282 PEARCE, Donald R. "Yeats' Last Plays: An Interpretation." *ELH*, 18 (1951), 67–76.

2283 POPKIN, Henry. "Yeats as Dramatist." *TDR*, 3 (March 1959), 73–82.

2284 PRIOR, Moody E. *The Language of Tragedy*, **166**, 326–40.

2285 QAMBER, Akhtar. *Yeats and the Noh, with Two Plays for Dancers by Yeats and Two Noh Plays*. NY: Weatherhill, 1974.

2286 RAJAN, Balachandra. *W. B. Yeats: A Critical Introduction*. 2nd ed. Lon: Hutchinson, 1969, 45–64, 94–106, 156–70.†

2287 RAJAN, Balachandra. "Yeats and the Absurd." *Tri-Quarterly*, No. 4 (1965), 130–37.

2288 RAJAN, Balachandra. "Yeats, Synge and the Tragic Understanding." *YeS*, No. 2 (1972), 66–79.

2289 REID, Forrest. *W. B. Yeats: A Critical Study*. Lon: Secker, 1915, 92–118, 150–98.

2290 REIMAN, Donald H. "Yeats's *Deirdre*." *Eng St*, 42 (1961), 218–32.

2291 REVARD, Stella. "Yeats, Mallarmé, and the Archetypal Feminine." *PLL*, 8, Suppl. (1972), 112–27. (Stresses *Great Clock Tower* and *Full Moon*.)

2292 REXROTH, Kenneth. "The Plays of Yeats." *Bird in the Bush*, **709**, 235–41.

2293 REYNOLDS, Lorna. "Collective Intellect: Yeats, Synge and Nietzsche." *E&S*, 26 (1973), 83–98.

2294 RILLIE, John A.M. "*Purgatory*." In **173**, 175–81.

2295 ROBINSON, Lennox. "The Man and the Dramatist." In *William Butler Yeats: Essays in Tribute*, ed. Stephen Gwynn. Port Wash., NY: Kennikat, 1965 [orig. publ. 1940 as *Scattering Branches*], 55–114.

2296 [ROSE], Marilyn Gaddis. "The Purgatory Metaphor of Yeats and Beckett." *LonM*, 7 (1967), 33–46.

2297 ROSE, Marilyn Gaddis. "Yeats's Use of *Axël*." *CoD*, 4 (1970–71), 253–64. (In *The Countess Cathleen*.)

2298 ROSTON, Murray. *Biblical Drama in England*, **168**, 264–74.

2299 ROY, Emil. *British Drama Since Shaw*, **233**, 36–53.

2300 SADDLEMYER, Ann. " 'The Heroic Discipline of the Looking-Glass': W. B. Yeats's Search for Dramatic Design." In **2313**, 87–103.

2301 SAUL, George B. "Yeats's Dramatic Accomplishment." In *W. B. Yeats, 1865–1965: Centenary Essays on the Art of W. B. Yeats*, ed. D. E. S. Maxwell and S. B. Bushrui. Lon: Nelson, 1965, 137–53.

2302 SCANLON, Sister Aloyse. "The Sustained Metaphor in *The Only Jealousy of Emer*." *MD*, 7 (1964), 273–77.

2303 SCHMITT, Natalie C. "Curing Oneself of the Work of Time: W. B. Yeats's *Purgatory*." *CoD*, 7 (1973–74), 310–33.

2304 SCHMITT, Natalie C. "Dramatic Multitude and Mystical Experience: W. B. Yeats." *ETJ*, 24 (1972), 149–58. (Stresses *Full Moon*.)

2305 SCHMITT, Natalie C. "Ecstasy and Insight in Yeats." *British J of Aesthetics*, 11 (1971), 257–67. (Focuses on his drama.)

2306 SCHROETER, James. "Yeats and the Tragic Tradition." *SoR*, 1 (1965), 835–46.

2307 SEIDEN, Morton I. *William Butler Yeats: The Poet as a Mythmaker, 1865–1939*. East Lansing: Michigan State UP, 1962, 203–32.

2308 SENA, Vinod. "Yeats on the Possibility of an English Poetic Drama." *MD*, 9 (1966), 195–205; see also Rupin W. Desai's comment, *MD*, 11 (1969), 396–99.

2309 SHARONI, Edna G. "*At the Hawk's Well*: Yeats's Unresolved Conflict Between Language and Silence." *CoD*, 7 (1973), 150–73.

2310 SHARP, William L. "W. B. Yeats: A Poet Not in the Theatre." *TDR*, 4 (Dec. 1959), 67–82. (On *Four Plays for Dancers*.)

2311 SIDNELL, Michael J. "Yeats's First Work for the Stage: The Earliest Versions of *The Countess Kathleen*." In *W. B. Yeats, 1865–1965*, **2301**, 167–88.

2312 SIDNELL, Michael J., George P. MAYHEW, and David R. CLARK, eds. *Druid Craft: The Writing of The Shadowy Waters*. Amherst: Univ. of Massachusetts Pr., 1971. (Manuscripts with full commentary.)

2313 SKELTON, Robin, and Ann SADDLEMYER, eds. *The World of W. B. Yeats: Essays in Perspective*. Seattle: Univ. of Washington Pr., 1965.* †

2314 SKENE, Reg. *The Cuchulain Plays of W. B. Yeats: A Study*. Lon: Macmillan, 1974.*

2315 SMITH, Bobby L. "The Dimensions of Quest in *Four Plays for Dancers*." *ArQ*, 22 (1966), 197–208.

2316 STARKIE, Walter. "W. B. Yeats and the Abbey Theatre." *SoR*, 5 (1969), 886–921; also in *Homage to Yeats, 1865–1965*, ed. Walter Starkie and A. Norman Jeffares (Los Angeles: U.C.L.A., Clark Memorial Lib., 1966), 3–39.*

2317 STAUB, August W. "The 'Unpopular Theatre' of W. B. Yeats." *QJS*, 47 (1961), 363–71. (Stresses his theories.)

2318 STEWART, J. I. M. "Yeats." *Eight Modern Writers*. Oxford: Clarendon, 1963, 294–421, esp. 322–38, 391–409.

2319 STOCK, A. G. "The First Plays." *W. B. Yeats: His Poetry and Thought*. Cambridge, Eng.: Univ. Pr., 1961, 25–36. †

2320 STUCKI, Yasuko. "Yeats's Drama and the Nō: A Comparative Study in Dramatic Theories." *MD*, 9 (1966), 101–22.

2321 SUSS, Irving D. "Yeatsian Drama and the Dying Hero." *SAQ*, 54 (1955), 369–80.

2322 TAYLOR, Richard. *The Drama of W. B. Yeats: Irish Myth and the Japanese Nō*. New Haven, CT: Yale UP, 1976.*

2323 THATCHER, David S. "Yeats's Repudiation of *Where There Is Nothing.*" *MD*, 14 (1971), 127–36.

2324 TORCHIANA, Donald T. "Study That House . . . Study That Tree." *W. B. Yeats & Georgian Ireland*. Evanston, IL: Northwestern UP, 1966, 340–65. (On *Purgatory*.)

2325 TSUKIMURA, Reiko. "A Comparison of Yeats's *At the Hawk's Well* and Its Noh Version, *Taka no izumi.*" *Lit East and West*, 11 (1967), 385–97.

2326 UNTERECKER, John. "The Shaping Force in Yeats's Plays." *MD*, 7 (1964), 345–56. (Stresses *Purgatory*.)

2327 URE, Peter. "The Plays." In *An Honoured Guest*, **2240**, 143–64.

2328 URE, Peter. *Yeats and Anglo-Irish Literature: Critical Essays*, ed. C. J. Rawson. Liverpool: Liverpool UP, 1974, 153–224. (Four essays on the plays.)

2329 URE, Peter. "Yeats and the Two Harmonies." *MD*, 7 (1964), 237–55. (Stresses *The Green Helmet*.)

2330 URE, Peter. *Yeats the Playwright: A Commentary on Character and Design in the Major Plays*. NY: Barnes & Noble, 1963.* †

2331 VANDERWERKEN, David L. "*Purgatory*: Yeats's Modern Tragedy." *CLQ*, 5 (1974), 261–69.

2332 VENDLER, Helen H. "Yeats's Changing Metaphors for the Otherworld." *MD*, 7 (1964), 308–21.

2333 VENDLER, Helen H. *Yeats's VISION and the Later Plays*. Cambridge, MA: Harvard UP, 1963.*

2334 VOGT, Kathleen M. "Counter-Components in Yeats's *At the Hawk's Well.*" *MD*, 17 (1974), 319–28.

2335 WARSCHAUSKY, Sidney. "Yeats's Purgatorial Plays." *MD*, 7 (1964), 278–86.

2336 WEBSTER, Brenda A. S. *Yeats: A Psychoanalytic Study*. Stanford, CA: Stanford UP, 1973. (Much discussion of his plays.)

2337 WEYGANDT, Cornelius. *Irish Plays and Playwrights*, **432**, 37–71.

2338 WILLIAMS, Raymond. *Drama from Ibsen to Brecht*, **72**, 115–28.

2339 WILSON, F. A. C. "The Last Plays." *W. B. Yeats and Tradition*. Lon: Gollancz, 1958, 53–195.* †

2340 WILSON, F. A. C. *Yeats's Iconography*. NY: Macmillan, 1960, 27–244.* †

2341 WORTH, Katharine J. "Yeats and the French Drama." *MD*, 8 (1966), 382–91. (Affinities with Beckett.)

2342 ZWERDLING, Alex. *Yeats and the Heroic Ideal*. NY: New York UP, 1965.

INDEX

INDEX

INDEX

INDEX

INDEX

INDEX

INDEX

INDEX

INDEX

INDEX